LEARNING TO FEEL—
FEELING TO LEARN

Humanistic Education for the Whole Man

STUDIES OF THE PERSON

edited by

Carl R. Rogers
William R. Coulson

LEARNING TO FEEL—
FEELING TO LEARN

Humanistic Education for the Whole Man

Harold C. Lyon, Jr.

*Deputy Associate Commissioner of Education
for Libraries and Educational Technology,
U.S. Office of Education*

CHARLES E. MERRILL PUBLISHING COMPANY
A Bell & Howell Company   Columbus, Ohio

The opinions expressed herein do not necessarily reflect the
position or policy of the U.S. Office of Education and no
official endorsement should be inferred.

International Standard Book Number: 0-675-09267-1 casebound
0-675-09232-9 paperback

Library of Congress Catalog Card Number: 74-148507

1 2 3 4 5 6 7 8 9 10/75 74 73 72 71

PRINTED IN THE UNITED STATES OF AMERICA

To the future: my sons, Eric and Gregg
and my brother, Bob

FOREWORD

By CARL R. ROGERS
Center for Studies of the Person

This is a vital book for those responsible for classroom learning at every level. It is a book one cannot help but *use*, tempting everyone to try out some of the practical ways described for humanizing learning. And once one has tried some of the procedures, one returns for more.

It is a very factual, down-to-earth book, giving straight-forward accounts of the results experienced by the author as he tried out novel methods of bringing the whole student into the classroom, with the feeling aspects of himself, the intellectual aspects, and the capacity for self-responsibility. It is also filled with descriptions of procedures tried by others. It will stimulate innovation in all but the most torpid.

But it is not simply a "how-to-do-it" book. There is a profound rationale, a philosophy of life and of education, underlying each of the many suggested innovations. Hal Lyon is a sensitive person who has learned deeply from his experiences in the military, in teaching and educational administration, in personal living and personal crises, and these learnings have come together in a deeply felt series of beliefs about the human being which shines through every page. To me it is strange to find experiences from combat training, from the classroom, and from intensive group experiences, all between two covers—strange but very enlightening. And to those who, like myself, have a prejudice against the military, let me hasten to add that one gains a totally new perspective through becoming acquainted with this gentle but dynamic, idealistic but practical man. He is honest, personal, direct. He doesn't mince matters. He names names and describes specific situations. He "tells it the way it is."

What he is saying is that from teacher training institutions to the primary school, from the superintendent's office to the lowliest teacher's aide, from kindergarten through graduate school, we can, *if we have the desire,* transform our backward educational system into an exciting voyage of discovery for warm, living persons. We can bring feelings into the process of learning, and learning into the process of being a feeling human being.

Dr. Coulson and I are proud to have this book as one of the series, "Studies of the Person." It is not primarily a study of persons, though it is that. It is something different and in many ways better. It will make every reader a student of persons, suggesting ways in which he can discover new facets of richness in persons and in the ways they feel and learn.

PREFACE

When Carl Rogers first communicated with me about the manuscript for this book, he ended his letter with the question: "How did an individual with your West Point and military background ever come to hold the point of view which you now have?"

I am still doing some intense searching for the answer to this question. When a former combat-type army officer writes a book in an attempt to make education more humanistic, the reader deserves an explanation of this apparent paradox.

I am beginning to think that it isn't really such a paradox at all, for the tests of courage and character a professional soldier must endure in a combat situation—tests which bring him in closer touch with values that really matter and reveal his inner self—parallel the risks and trials one must go through to achieve self-growth in encounter groups or therapy. A certain amount of pain must be endured by any individual in achieving self-growth. The pain of such activities as ranger training or combat—regardless of how inhuman the ends may be—can also bring one closer to self-growth and awareness, though this does not necessarily happen. Tests of character and courage all require a willingness to take individual risks. A certain integrity, dignity, or self respect accrues from assuming such risks in the military as well as at a place such as Esalen. An intense experience involving risks sharpens the ability to do or not do what is required. If one moves too far from humanistic ends, the intensity of the means which he must employ to achieve inhuman ends can have a therapeutic effect, bringing him back in a complete circle toward a position of humanism. Of course, there's a vital need to question the ends one is working toward before one worries about making the means more humanistic. Once when I spoke with a friend about training managers in the military and government to be more humanistic or "people-oriented," he responded that he didn't want to make military men more humanistic since their ends are war and he didn't want the means to be more pleasant when they led to such horrible ends. I had to disagree with him because, first of all, contrary to popular belief, the ends of most people in the military are to prevent war; secondly, becoming humanistic in the means can cause one to question the ends toward which one is working.

The potential for humanism which exists, even in those people who outwardly seem least people-oriented, is amazingly close to the surface and, though buried beneath a military veneer, it reveals itself in different ways. Combat releases the expression of a wide range of extreme feelings and emotions—grief, sorrow, exhilaration, comradeship, dependency, courage, fear. These emotions, in another setting, might be labeled phoney, sentimental, or exaggerated by critics in much the same way as are the feelings evoked by encounter groups or sensitivity training.

The fact is that there are some amazingly sensitive men in the military profession in spite of its inhuman end—war. One of my dearest and closest friends, Lon Spurlock, who was killed in combat in Vietnam, was one of the greatest soldiers and human beings I will ever know. He was one of those rare individuals who knew he could accomplish almost anything. He was a courageous, intelligent, emotional, rational, and loyal friend, husband, and scholar, as well as a poet of great sensitivity. His sensitivity, paradoxically honed to a keen edge by combat, is apparent in the following:

To his daughter on her birthday:

> High upon an Asian wind
> Your father flies above
> and wishes you on this your day
> a life of play
> with one true love
> and one real friend.

To his wife:

> My love for you is always with me—in the helicopter, in the swamps, in the ambush—and I feel it especially strong when the bullets zip and crack and hiss and thud nearby. It strengthens me, gives me confidence, and always stands as a reason for pressing on when things look grim. . . .

You are my foundation, my source of strength, my hope, my best friend, my only value, and my only concrete reason for living. On the fringe of existence—and I have been there—everything else disappears.

Helicopters fly
Soldiers shoot
People die
Statesmen talk.

Is it a paradox that Lon Spurlock, a man of great strengths—physical and visceral—lived an intense life as a professional soldier yet was a delicately sensitive man? I think not. Certainly Lon Spurlock was exceptional. However, his intense experiences and those of other military men, including myself, sometime sharpen an inner sensitivity beneath the military veneer.

I spent four years being educated and conditioned at West Point to be a professional soldier—"Wipe that frown off, mister, you don't display emotions around here!" (I even received twenty demerits and twenty hours of confinement for: "Public display of affection at entraining formation, University of Virginia–Army football game" for kissing my date goodby.) The West Point years were followed by Ranger and paratrooper schools, working for General Westmoreland setting up a counter-guerrilla warfare school, commanding a combat-ready Rifle Company in the 101st Airborne Division, a year in East Asia, and a year as aide to the Commanding General of a combat division during which we integrated James Meredith into "Ol Miss," and almost went to Cuba.

During these years, my fellow cadets and officers and I were efficiently conditioned not to display personal emotions or feelings. Of course, there's a reason for this. In the totally encompassing business of combat, the mission is all-important, and commanders must be objective and mission-oriented. Display of personal emotion can undermine the military poise, bearing, and "instantaneous, unquestioned obedience" which is vital during the inhumanity of warfare.

It's strange the way emotions and feelings manifest themselves in other acceptable ways in the military. Rather than revealing the inner, personal feelings just under the surface, soldiers are conditioned to sublimate, to mask their feelings or submerge them. Emotion is allowed venting only toward accepted abstract forms such as patriotism, the flag, courage, or in the tears which used to fill my eyes at stirring military ceremonies or parades.

In the process of allowing emotions about "Duty, Honor and Country"[1] we forbid personal feelings and, hence, deny the importance of the individual human beings for whom this motto exists. In addition to suppressing personal feelings and emotions in the military, I was conditioned to deny my personal desires and natural inclinations in order to earn the rewards given for proper achievement toward the rigidly-structured goals set by the military. The important thing in most of my formative years was to "develop character," and I never really questioned that value. From that place I have traveled across the spectrum to where I now agree pretty much with what the late Fritz Perls, the father of Gestalt Therapy, has to say about character:

> Once you have a *character*, you have developed a rigid system. Your behavior becomes petrified, predictable, and you lose your ability to cope freely with the world with all your resources. You are predetermined just to cope with events in one way, namely, as your character prescribed . . . so it seems a paradox when I say that the richest person, the most productive, creative person, is a person who has *no* character. In our society we *demand* a person to have character, and especially *good* character, because then you are predictable, and you can be pigeon holed. . . .[2]

Now I'm not suggesting that I became a total conformist. On the contrary, among my military contemporaries I was considered a risk-taking maverick in spite of the fact that in the world outside of the military I am probably classified as a moderate liberal. I was particularly fond of Lt. General James M. Gavin's philosophy that:

> Wars are usually infrequent, and the thinking of our younger generation of officers is critically contaminated by the veterans of past wars. Thus, the younger officers frequently find themselves feverishly preparing to fight the last war better.[3]

In an article I published in *Army Magazine* in 1965 entitled "The Courage of Your Convictions" I advanced the point that in the military there is tremendous pressure to wait for the "security of seniority" before you become an independent thinker. But, by the time you become senior (with promotions based almost entirely on time in grade rather than your contribution), you may have become a conditioned

---

[1] The West Point Motto

[2] Frederick S. Perls, *Gestalt Therapy Verbatim* (Lafayette, Calif.: Real People Press, 1969), p. 7

[3] James M. Gavin, Lt. General, *War and Peace in the Space Age* (New York: Harper and Row, Publishers, 1958).

"yes man" who parrots what he expects the boss wants to hear instead of what he really believes. I went on to suggest that though the Army tries to make everyone a well-rounded person, we really don't need more well-rounded people: we have too many. We need more "square" people who won't roll in the first direction they are pushed. I recall the flood of conservative reactions which poured in as letters to the editor of *Army Magazine*, all wondering about the young Army Captain who was preaching revolution.

But as I look back on this and other examples of my behavior, I realize that my sense of urgency to prove myself was my driving force and, at the same time, actually a conformity in itself. My bosses—especially when I was aide to Major General Charles Billingslea, the Commanding General of the Second Infantry Division—were some refreshingly nonconformist officers whose praise and acceptance I was eager to win. I developed in my early years and in this environment an intense compulsion to succeed. I became an overachiever who displayed—rather than my own real feelings of inadequacy, frustration, or anger—a compulsive need to solve every problem which confronted me in an effort to prove my worthiness to others. Rather than *self*-actualizing, I was busy self-*image*-actualizing, and they are quite different things.

The behavior traits I developed are not all bad. In fact, they are the traits usually highly valued by parents, establishments, and teachers. They developed in me some valuable assets and abilities, and they netted me a comfortable measure of success, status, and material satisfaction. Then, through a combination of personal experiences, I became involved in some serious crises which caused my entire superachiever world to come crashing in on me. Somehow, the painful process of surviving that crisis which involved psychotherapy, various therapeutic group experiences, some humanistic education and bosses, a few very loyal and rewarding friends, and a great deal of inner probing and examination, enabled me to grow to realize that it is much more comfortable, relaxing, and fun to be Hal Lyon, a human being with some strengths and some weaknesses, rather than Hal Lyon, a superman who has to accomplish everything.

I think that this is probably true for many of us, and one of the messages of this book is that we shouldn't ignore these emotional or affective peak-experiences in the classroom but should learn to integrate them with the cognitive. In the words of Maslow:

We must learn to treasure the "jags" of the child in school, his fascination, absorptions, his persistent wide-eyed wondering, his

> Dionysian enthusiasm. . . . They can lead to much. Especially they
> can lead to hard work, persistent, absorbed, fruitful, educative.[4]

Venturing into the impasses of my crises has helped lead me toward an
entirely new insight into myself—into life.

I am not suggesting that this is a typical pattern for a West Pointer
or Army officer to develop. I owe a great deal to West Point and to the
military when I served for what seemed to me to be seven highly rewarding years. The point is that even the most seemingly inhuman
profession can produce sensitive human beings. In fact, if the profession involves intense tests or trials of character, my guess is that the
potential for humanness is all the greater. I have gathered increasing
evidence which will be discussed further in Chapter 7 which supports
my belief that the most successful leaders, military or otherwise, are
very human "people-oriented" individuals rather than the autocratic,
punitive type of individuals depicted in the prevailing stereotype of
the military man. It is my view that potential for realizing one's humanness is present in most individuals, regardless of occupation or profession.

Let me share some other things that are happening to me now which
I hope will help make it clear how, through learning to feel and feeling
to learn, a former military man could hold the view I hold and even
have the audacity to write a book about humanistic education.

I feel that the "overachiever" is in many ways the product of a
society that encourages and reinforces getting rewards and approval
from outside sources rather than from within the individual.

I am discovering (present tense, not past) that I became an overachiever to be approved by others. It goes back to wanting to be held
more as a child—a compulsion for approval, acceptance, a natural need
for love that gets titilated but never fully satiated by substituting the
approval that achievement brings for the chronic love need that I and
so many others have.

As infants we freely and instinctively do what we want. The infant
reaches for and pulls his mother's hair. The mother says "no!" She
trains the child to give up what he wants by withholding affection
(slapping his hand or the word "no!"). Finally, the child gives up many
things he wants to do to get the love and approval he craves. In short,
he begins emitting the behavior which will give him love and approval,
sublimating his own desire to do other things. In other words, his

---

[4] Abraham H. Maslow, "Some Educational Implications of the Humanistic
Psychologies. *Harvard Educational Review* 38, no. 4 (Fall, 1968): 689.

behavior flows, not from within, but from what he detects and learns will give him approval. Most people—particularly those that young people would label as "establishment"—never outgrow this second stage. Granted, people can be independent thinkers in a way that seems more than tokenistic, as I fancied myself to be, but basically most of the major directions in their lives are determined by the strength of the doses of approval that they will get from outside sources—parents, friends, teachers, organizations, society.

Carl Rogers says that to achieve what he calls "psychological maturity," we must go back to being like we were as infants—that is, doing what we feel like doing, but getting most of our satisfactions from within instead of being completely dependent on others for approval. Because of the overwhelming pressures this society puts on us to achieve and be rewarded externally, there are only a few ways for the individual to reach this third stage of maturation. One path is through therapy. Another is for him to experience some therapeutic relationships with people—not usually parents or teachers, often intimate friends or lovers—with whom he can be open and honest enough to achieve the self-awareness and growth needed.

There are people around who, somehow, through traumatic infancies, never have been through the second phase of development. They never have had clear signals about what behavior on their part will generate love and acceptance. Hence, they have never become dependent on others for their approval because they have not learned to trust others. These people continue as they did as infants to do what they want, but in an erratic way that is different from those who have gone through what I feel can be an important second stage—the "achiever stage" of development. A person who has developed his talents, stretched his mind and body, faced and passed significant tests of courage and character (even as one must do in achieving self-awareness in therapy), is much more likely to be happy in or out of society than the person who has skipped or bypassed the second "achievement" stage of development. I predict that he is much more likely to develop, for example, a practicable constructive solution to a campus problem than he is to destructively burn the campus down.

I feel that, after 35 years, I am just beginning to leave this "achiever" stage and enter the "psychological maturity" stage. I am in the transition of really beginning to get my major satisfactions from within me instead of from everyone else. I'm not completely there yet. I'm still a bit of the achiever (and that isn't bad), and I will probably always be to an extent, but more and more I find the things I am achieving in are things I really "dig"—things that give me warmth and approval from within, regardless of what comes from outside. It's really a kind of falling in love with myself—not the false, all-too-familiar, kind of "ego trip" thing that is a cover up for feelings of inadequacy, but a real freeing of the self. When you're not dependent on everyone else for approval, it's really a freeing thing! When you do something— give to someone, love someone—it has a new pureness, an untaintedness to it. You're giving or loving because it's genuinely within you, rather than loving or giving because you want something in return or because it is expected of you. What a dependency you have if you need praise or love from everybody! You then make everybody your judge and you do all kinds of things to make yourself lovable. Fritz Perls reinforces this philosophy. He defines maturing as:

> *. . . The transformation from environmental support to self-support* and the aim of therapy is to make the patient *not* depend upon others but to make the patient discover . . . that he can do . . . much more than he thinks he can do.

> The average person of our time, believe it or not, lives only 5% to 15% of his potential at the highest. A person who has even 25% of his potential available is already considered a genius. So 85% of our potential is lost. Sounds tragic, doesn't it? And the reason for this is very simple: we live in cliches . . . patterned behavior . . . playing the same roles over and over again. So if you find out how you prevent yourself from growing, from using your potential, you have a way of . . . making life richer . . . making you more capable of mobilizing yourself. And our potential is based upon a very peculiar attitude: to live [here and now] and review every second afresh.

> The "trouble" with people who are capable of reviewing every second what the situation is like, is that we are not predictable. The role of the good citizen requires that he be predictable, because our hankering for security, for not taking risks . . . is just horrifying. So what do we do? We *adjust*, and in most kinds of therapy you find that adjustment to society is the high goal. If you don't adjust, you are either a criminal, or psychopath, or looney, or beatnik or something like that. Anyhow, you are undesirable and have to be thrown out of the boundary of that society. So where do we find ouselves? We find ourselves on the one hand as individuals who want to actualize themselves; we find ourselves also embedded in a society, in our case in the progressive American society, and this society might make demands different from the individual demands. So there is the basic clash.[5]

---

[5] Perls, op. cit., pp. 29–31

I recently spent a few days with Baba Ram Dass (formerly Richard Alpert, Harvard professor, writer, celloist, pilot, therapist, businessman, and former achiever extraordinaire). Ram Dass, who has spent a year and a half in India (achieving "Holyman" non-status!), is one of the wisest men I have ever met. Ram Dass shared with me the Hindu tradition of "the non-giving of gifts." In the Western world we manage to weave an enormously complicated network of obligations which entrap us as barter goes on back and forth between associates, husbands and wives, and others. In this system, even love becomes currency to be spent or invested, or earned, or withheld. We give something to someone and they owe us something back. Someone has us out to dinner and we must repay them, not necessarily for the joy of being with them, but because we owe them. Our commercialized concept of gift giving at Christmas is a frightening example of this. In the Hindu tradition of "the non-giving of gifts," no obligations are created. If you give, it's because of an inwardly felt desire to give. You give because it feels good rather than giving because you want something in return. If I hold something in my left hand and give it to my right hand, it illustrates the concept of "the non-giving of gifts." Because both hands belong to the same body, there is no obligation created—my left hand doesn't owe my right hand anything, nor does it need approval from my right hand.

As I spoke with Ram Dass I could feel us telescoping closer, then farther apart, and then closer. I mentioned this to him, and he observed that when we got farther apart it was when either or both of us began playing roles—he playing a "Guru" role or I playing a "teacher" or "Deputy Associate Commissioner" role. He pointed out that to the extent we play roles, distance comes between. To the extent we become human beings digging each other, relating, sharing, really communicating, we become closer. What a lesson there is for teachers in this—for parents, for husbands and wives, for everyone! I looked at my two sons that evening, and I took off my "father role" and one by one looked into their eyes as a human being rather than as "father." What startlingly beautiful people they are when viewed in a "roleless" way! I saw them in a new light, and I saw a new light within them. They could feel it and saw me in a much warmer, closer way. It takes effort for those of us not used to this to do it, but it can be a very pure and rewarding experience. I have since done this with others—students, friends, and even my boss in the "establishment" world where I work —and it unlocks the warmth and light that is within every human being—the light that is altogether too often hidden by all the masks we wear, the roles we play, and the crap which has been laid on us by society and ourselves.

Falling in love with yourself does another thing for which I have no explanation. It somehow makes you into a mirror—a mirror that enables those who look into you to see their own beauty. When you look into the light behind the eyes of someone who loves himself, it unlocks in you the ability to see your own beauty in their reflection. My fantasy is somehow to bring this into the classroom. I don't have all the answers as to how, but I feel the concepts I am trying to share in this book move in the right direction. My fantasy is to help provide teachers the power that loving one's self gives—the power to take off their teacher roles and become human beings, sharing in learning experiences with a group of colleagues. This is the power that can unlock in their students self love and the ability to feel and learn which accompanies that love.

H.C.L.

ACKNOWLEDGMENTS

Carol Carter, Marta Hahne, Gabe Heilig, Linda Jackson, Dr. Susan LaFrance, Mr. and Mrs. Robert Mackin, and Dr. David Yarington gave generously, not only their ideas, but their support and themselves as well, as I developed this manuscript. Mrs. Rose Keresky of the University of Massachusetts School of Education gave generously of her time and energy to the preparation of the pages which follow—editing and making suggestions. Miss Marianne Brink spent many hours helping me to organize and reorganize material which appears in the chapters which follow. Miss Julie Estadt's skilled editorial eye and warmth have contributed significantly to this book and my disposition. Warm thanks to Barb and Herb Green, two of the most free humanistic teachers I know, for field testing almost every page of this book in their own lives and in their classrooms. To these people and others who have shown a sincere interest in my ideas and work, I wish to express my gratitude.

CONTENTS

part III
Feeling to Learn

part IV
Training Humanistic Teachers and Managers

Prologue

Facilitating Discovery

I am writing this book in an attempt to share with others what has become one of the most exciting and important discoveries in my life: that learning can be enjoyable when one learns to feel and then goes on to feel to learn. Nonsense? Perhaps, until one experiences what I'm talking about. My biggest fear in writing this book (purely verbal expression by necessity) is that I will lose much of the feeling that I might convey if we sat down together to actually discuss and experience rather than read about the things I am trying to share.

Recognizing that much feeling will be lost in writing rather than in sharing experiences in person, I have chosen to use several descriptions of experiences by others—especially students from whom I think we as teachers have a great deal to learn—or prescriptions or recipes for experiences which you may try with your own students or children. If I can get you to take that step—experiencing and feeling some of these things for yourself—then I know I will have accomplished my purpose. You will be hooked! You won't be able to return to the emptiness of the purely intellectual classroom once you have felt the charged atmosphere and warmth of the humanistic classroom—an environment where feelings are integrated with intellectual content. So in this book I have attempted to concentrate on the first step— getting you to want to try these things yourself and presenting some things you might try, knowing that if you do, you will probably go far beyond this book in developing your own individual techniques. In a way this book is meant to be a launching pad, a catalyst, a stimulator, or a fuse.

Humanistic Education, the integration of cognitive learning with affective learning, is a natural outgrowth of Humanistic or Third Force psychology which has grown in large part as a reaction against the fact that the more academic psychologies (Behavioristic and Freudian) seem inadequate in dealing with the higher nature or humanness of man. We can see the influence of the Behaviorists in most of our schools today as we watch teachers trying to shape students according to the academic goals of the teacher and frequently ignoring the actualization or growth of the individual.

I am not advocating that the classroom become primarily a therapeutic "couch" for children, though there should be some therapeutic things happening. I'm not advancing a set of therapeutic procedures for teachers to use, though dealing with feelings can be therapeutic. I am not advocating that teachers become amateur psychoanalysts or that they replace counselors or school psychologists, though perhaps in a humanistic school, counselors and psychologists might be freer from the rush of overwhelming anxiety problems that prevent them from helping normal children find their own productive and fulfilling place in this world. Most teachers are not professionally or legally qualified to perform the function of psychoanalyst, though some research has shown that perhaps we shouldn't be as timid about this as we have been. The argument has been that therapy should be attempted only by a professional with a Ph.D. or an MD. According to Carl Rogers:

> There is solid evidence that this is a mistaken view. An outstanding example is the work of Rioch[1] showing that selected housewives can be given training in a year's time which enables them to carry on therapy with disturbed individuals—therapy which in its quality is indistinguishable from the work of experienced professionals.[2]

So, in spite of the fact that I am not pushing for teachers to become amateur psychoanalysts, there is ample room and a great need for a bold move by educators and teachers toward the affective realm.

What this book is trying to say is that isolating cognitive learning from affective learning is a mistake—a mistake, the impact of which we are feeling on campuses and in classrooms all over the country. It's a mistake which has created a large number of intellectual "half-men," brilliantly developed, perhaps, on the intellectual end of the continuum, but severely lacking on the feeling or affective end. Most of the activities students enjoy about school are those highly charged with feelings and emotions and which have absolutely nothing to do with the curriculum; in fact they are usually classroom taboos. I'm talking about

---

[1] Margaret J. Rioch, E. Elkes, A. A. Flint, B. S. Usdansky, R. G. Newman, & E. Sibler, "NIMH pilot study in training mental health counselors." *American Journal of Orthopsychiatry* 33, 1963: 678–689.

[2] Carl Rogers, *Freedom to Learn* (Columbus, Ohio: Charles E. Merrill Publishing Company), p. 319.

what we have labeled as extracurricular activities. I'm talking about boy-girl relationships, love-making, protests, social çauses, dances, rock music, cars, and really getting to know someone.

I'm not advocating that we should all gravitate to the affective end of this continuum, shedding all our inhibitions as a few unfortunate businessmen have done after visiting Esalen or Bethel, Maine. They quickly found that their bosses didn't appreciate being honestly and openly called the "sons of bitches" they were felt to be. The better therapists and group leaders at such institutions as Esalen and the National Training Labs at Bethel, Maine, though admitting that the chief drawback to such group experiences is the lack of a mechanism for effective follow-up, are careful to make it clear to participants that the healthiest place for someone to be is somewhere between the two extremes of this continuum. Society is not ready for the purely "affective" human being. There are some of these hyper-open individuals around, and most suffer from the severe frustration that's bound to result from dealing with a world that is largely closed and "up-tight." One of the few courses of action open to these people is to withdraw from society into their own fantasy worlds or communes. The healthy individual in the 1970's hopefully will be somewhere in the middle ground with, perhaps, a few clear and wide open channels with one's husband or wife, or a few close friends. He or she will be able to deal with feelings and intellectual matters.

Nor is this book advocating that teachers become such totally open individuals that their classes are "T-groups." It does advocate an integration of the intellectual atmosphere *with* feelings in the classroom. It is proposing that we begin to accept students, teachers, parents, and friends as being more than intellectual beings. It advocates that we begin to look upon people as whole human beings who have feelings—feelings which directly influence their intellectual growth.

Such a practice can replace our old ideas of teaching with the joy of discovery. Anyone who has watched a class of fifth graders transform a classroom from utter chaos into one buzzing with children discovering things, after having been allowed to evolve their own rules for behavior, has discovered the lesson of "allowing" rather than "making." For instance, a child who feels a need to ask for his own word—a particular gut feeling word of anger, joy, or fear that is gripping him that day—and has it written for him in his own word book, discovers the word instantaneously and most likely never forgets it. To him,

writing and reading become a natural extension of speech as he discovers what he is actually trying to tell. How much more effective it
is to facilitate a child's own discovery of words through integration of
his own feelings than it is to force inane "Dick and Janisms" on him
day after day!

A student who has discovered something significant needs no instruc-
tor-assigned grade as a measure of his accomplishment. He deeply feels
the accomplishment immediately, and that's the best reward possible.

Humanistic education, the integration of cognitive learning and affective experience, is present in many forms. It's really a name for a
practice that a few of those rare human teachers have been practicing
for generations.

A pertinent example of "humanistic education" and the results it can
produce was made vividly clear to me while serving as a consultant to
the White House Task Force on the Education of the Gifted. The
Task Force members toured various institutions of higher education
throughout the country in an attempt to pinpoint what it is that makes
certain gifted individuals realize their high potential while so many
others fall short. This enlightening encounter took place while visiting
the U. S. Military Academy at West Point to see how the military
treats its gifted. The Social Science Department at West Point, under
the leadership of General George A. Lincoln (later Director in the
Nixon Administration Office of Emergency Preparedness), has always
been a hotbed of gifted individuals. At the time of our visit, I believe
they had at least eight Rhodes Scholars on the Social Science Faculty
plus a number of other extremely gifted and distinguished young officers. The Task Force visiting team arranged to meet with a group of
about twelve of these officers, including such notables as Peter Dawkins,
the Rhodes Scholar—All American football player whose picture appeared on the covers of *Life*, *Newsweek*, and *Time* several times before
he reached the age of 25. Harold Gores, one of the Task Force members, put the following question to the group: "To what predominant
factor, if any, do you attribute your exceptional success and achievement?" To me, the fascinating thing was that almost every one of
them had the same answer. In each of their lives some one or two individuals had built an unusual relationship with them, either in their
latter few years of high school or at West Point. In most cases the
individuals had been either teachers or athletic coaches. They had put
social or military status aside and had built a more intimate relationship

than tradition dictated, pushing and encouraging the students as individuals to step out and achieve far more than the students thought they were capable of doing. In other words, a humanistic bond was developed between two people. The fascinating part of it was that about four of these officers named the same one or two instructors without knowing that this was the case. If we could only identify what these special teachers have that others do not and pay attention to this in our teacher training institutions, we might be on the way to a breakthrough. Ironically enough, Colonels Bob Gard and Ab Greenleaf, both of whom had later served as military assistants to the Secretary of Defense, were two of the inspirational instructors mentioned by several of the young officers and were also two very personable officers whom I recalled as being exceptional. In most of the cases described, the push and encouragement to stand on tiptoe had come personally, but in a particular area of endeavor such as academics, debating, or athletics, rather than in general vague encouragement. There are many different kinds of humanistic education stories, but this serves as an example of the far-reaching effects humanistic education can have.

The idea of giving students as many tastes of success as is possible has great application to the classroom, especially in a child's very early years. The teachers who have cared to celebrate a child's tiniest achievements and to encourage his feelings have the power to transform their classrooms into humanistic ones in which children bloom rather than wilt. Robert Rosenthal's research on teacher expectations provides some indication of this.[3]

Although Robert Thorndike has shown that the conclusions reached by Rosenthal's study are inadequately supported by data, there is little doubt that the theory being tested is a correct one.[4] Rosenthal set out to test the hypothesis that, rather than disadvantaged children doing poorly because they came from disadvantaged families, they really do poorly because teachers expect them to do so. He and his colleagues divided rats into two groups at random, giving them to two different groups of people. They instructed both groups to teach their rats to run a maze. However, the first group was told that their rats would learn the maze quickly because they came from good genetic back-

---

[3] Robert Rosenthal and Lenore F. Jacobson, "Teacher Expectations for the Disadvantaged," *The Scientific American*, no. 4 (April, 1968), pp. 19–23.

[4] Robert L. Thorndike, Book Review of Rosenthal and Jacobson's *Pygmalion in the classroom*, *American Educational Research Journal* 8, no. 4 (November, 1968), pp. 708–711.

grounds. The second group was told that their rats would learn very slowly, if at all, because they were of poor genetic background. The first group's rats learned the maze much more quickly and better than those from the group which had low expectations for their rats. They then took the experiment into the classroom. They told the teachers from a school district that they were going to administer a new validated test which would accurately predict which students would progress rapidly during the coming year (the test was actually an I.Q. test in disguise). A few weeks after the testing, they visited each teacher and casually mentioned the names of several children who had scored as "rapid achievers." (The names were actually chosen at random.) At the end of the year, the children mentioned during the visit had surpassed the others significantly in all subjects. The reason? The teachers had expected them to do well, and hence worked with them, believed in them, and encouraged them. A humanistic relationship had been contrived and it worked!

A similar experiment has been conducted with Mexican–American children in Arizona which also adds to the evidence that children will tend to perform better if the teacher expects this of them. Mexican–American children who the teachers identified as special achievers did far better under those conditions than when in control groups.

Les Rollins, former Assistant Dean of Harvard Graduate School of Business, has spent his lifetime identifying young leadership talent and attempting to determine what it is that makes a young person succeed. He feels that the crucial years for setting a pattern of success, mediocrity, or failure come early in life, but that the individual's pattern can be and frequently is set *firmly* in the last few years of high school and the first few years of college. The bigger the taste of success achieved in these years, the greater the chances of later success. A teacher who puts feeling into his or her work has a far greater chance of giving students tastes of success than the impersonal or entirely cognitive teacher who stands officially behind status authority rather than natural authority.

When a torpedo shoots at a submarine, the servo-mechanism in the torpedo cranks in feedback causing the torpedo to change course, locking in on the submarine as its goal. Humans have a similar mechanism in them which can lock in on either success or failure as a goal. The more early "success experiences," the more likely that success becomes an individual's goal. When the "success oriented" individual progresses through life and approaches one of the many obstacles or by-paths leading to failure, he consciously (and often unconsciously) increases his energy and effort to get over the obstacle or by-path and stay on the path to success, his goal. The pessimist, who has made failure his goal, on the other hand, comes to one of these by-paths, takes it, fails, and says, "I failed. I knew I would!" Accordingly, it seems vital for us to allow, to inject, or even to contrive, as many success experiences in our children's and student's lives as we are able. The human teacher who has learned to feel, and hence uses feelings in his teaching, has at his or her disposal so many of the attributes helpful for giving "success experiences" to others.

I hope that the chapters which follow will stimulate you to make your own personal, joyful discovery of what it can mean to deal with students as human beings and to appreciate their feelings which abound within the classroom.

part **I**

The Problem of the Intellectual Half-Man

Introduction to Part I

If we, the faculty, aren't to become wholly irrelevant, we must somehow leapfrog over the progress made by the young. . . . Clearly, we need to follow the example of the young and put more room into the research-oriented university for the parts of the human we have excluded: there must be institutional support for learning to love, for enhancing sensory awareness, for exploring non-rational ways of knowing. . . . These subjects must have a place in the curriculum, and they must be integrated with the present highly rational and analytic course of study. No one can give what he does not have: a faculty of one-dimensional men cannot teach rounding youngsters how to be properly round.

Stuart Miller

Part I of this book defines the problems created by an educational system dominated by one-dimensional teachers and faculty who are concerned almost entirely with the development of the cognitive or intellectual capacities of their students. Ours is an educational system which has conditioned teachers to deny feelings and, hence, has cut them and their students off from the richness of learning which feeling can open.

This part of the book will present the problem of the intellectual half-man whose cognitive side is, perhaps, highly developed, but whose affective capacity is severely stunted. Examples from a contemporary academic setting, Columbia University, will be cited, as well as the work of such people as Paul Goodman, George Williams, John Corson, and Carl Rogers. The idea of the two-sided man—intellectual and feeling—will be developed further in the second chapter with emphasis on the need to integrate cognitive and affective development in producing human development. In this part of the book we will try to identify the causes of why the following statement from Bertrand Russell is applicable to society today: "We are faced with the paradoxical fact that education has become one of the chief obstacles to intelligence and freedom of thought."

1

The Two Sides of Man—
Intellectual and Feeling

The world feels that drudgery, discipline, and conformity are the social virtues par excellence.

Jacques Barzun

Why are drudgery, discipline, and conformity the social and educational "virtues *par excellence*" of our society? Why must learning be presented in a way that makes it such unpleasant work?

The answers to these questions are obviously that education does not have to involve drudgery, discipline, and conformity. Learning does not have to be unpleasant work. Why is it then that many teachers and educators insist upon making it so?

It seems that our system dictates that everything good must be "hardgotten" if one is to reap the rewards—job, security, swimming pool, happiness—that await the educated man. But only after struggling through the all-important educational hoops is all this "happiness" obtained. Indeed, if this morality that "happiness must be earned" is inherent in Western man, then what of his children who live by the "happiness is free" theory? Are these children perverts? Perhaps this is why so many lock-step schools set out to punish them—taking the joy and discovery out of learning, and conditioning them to respond like trained seals. By the clock, from nine until three, all make-believe often ends for this captive audience, while it begins for the teacher-performer whose favorite role is Creator. And create they do: exact replicas of themselves—intellectual beings conditioned not to accept or face their feelings.

The pure joy of playing with one's wiggly toes, of rolling in the crunchy autumn leaves, of playing in the gooey mud, or of just fantasizing, "I'll be this and you can be that" diminishes as the child is programmed for practicality. He soon learns to trade in his spontaneous desires for the affection and approval which abstinence promises. The greatest substitute satisfaction the school has to offer is the Scarlet Letter— the Big A—for correctly digested and regur-

17

gitated material. All too often a child's curiosity is a worthless commodity put down by the teacher who will not answer the "Why?" with anything but the institutionally correct, intellectual answer.

And so the miniature adult grows in mind and body, hardly aware of himself as a unique and feeling individual. The curiosity and sensuality which he once possessed have been repressed. But at last he emerges, his joyless education behind him, ready to find the supposed security and happiness that he so well deserves.

Youths who somehow manage to keep their spontaneity are often treated by teachers as if they have not learned that the cognitive is the preferred mode of behaving and that emotion and feelings are taboo. Because these young people react spontaneously, they are presumed to be irrational or impulsive and, therefore, constitute a threat to the adult society. Our educational practices tend to restrict rather than enlarge the choices children are permitted to make and the alternatives they have for behaving, and this is done in the name of protection for them and society.

Educators have traditionally emphasized the development of the cognitive capacities of their students. The school's or university's prime responsibility has been the fostering of intellectual learning. The nurturing of the affective or emotional side of the student—love, empathy, awareness, and fantasy—either has been neglected or left to the individual, his family, or chance. All too often, chance prevails, and the result becomes a half-man who, like his teachers, has been educated, at best, to function effectively on only the intellectual plane.

Learning can be enjoyable if it is humanized. What's more, learning which retains the human element is much more relevant to life. The intellectual must be coupled with the emotional if behavior is to retain a human quality.

In contrast to what is practiced in our educational system, it is the thesis of this book that, of these two elements in behavior, feelings are more important than the intellectual element. The fact is, the intellect divorced from feelings is empty and meaningless. An education that is to be effective in preparing a child for life must take into account emotional as well as mental development. Schools must recognize that pleasure, spontaneity, and feelings are as vital, if not more vital, than intellectual achievement.

The answer to the question "Why must teachers insist on making learning unpleasant and inhuman?" lies partially in Stuart Miller's quotation at the beginning of this chapter: "No one can give what he does not have: a faculty of one-dimensional men cannot teach rounding youngsters how to be properly round." Teachers and faculty who have been conditioned to avoid feelings have difficulty facing and dealing with feelings in the classroom. Intellectual matters when divorced from feelings are empty to students, who, much more than their elders, are struggling openly and honestly with their feelings. Paul Goodman makes this point very well in his book *Compulsory Mis-Education*:

> . . . let us try to be realistic, as a youngster is. For most people, I think, a candid self-examination will show that their most absorbing, long and satisfactory hours are spent in activities like friendly competitive sports, gambling, looking for love and lovemaking, earnest or argumentative conversation, political action with signs and sit-ins, solitary study and reading, contemplation of nature and cosmos, arts and crafts, music, and religion. Now, none of these requires much money. Indeed, elaborate equipment takes the heart out of them. Friends use one another as resources. God, nature, and creativity are free. The media of the fine arts are cheap stuff. Health, luck, and affection are the only requirements for good sex. Good food requires taking pains more than spending money.
>
> What is the moral for our purposes? Can it be denied that in some respects the drop-outs make a wiser choice than many who go to school, not to get real goods but to get money?[1]

The adult's idea of the most important activity of youth is attending school, itself done for the purpose of getting good grades in preparation for the competition of society (perhaps very accurately labeled as "the rat race"). All other activities of youth—music, driving, dating, friendship, hobbies, need for one's own money and time—are treated by the adults as something maturity or education will help youth outgrow. These activities are where youngsters should be exploring their feelings and identity and formulating concepts and ideals for life. However, if any one of these even hints at interfering with the serious business of school, it is immedi-

---

[1] Paul Goodman, *Compulsory Mis-Education, and the Community of Scholars* (New York: Vintage Books, 1964), p. 30.

ately challenged by the adult world, frequently with sanctions or threats. Yet, many students view the competition on the corporate ladder that their fathers are busy climbing, as a rat race. They see the corporate recruiters hovering around the campus with their offers of impressive salaries as seekers of fresh new rats to run the race. Not wanting to be another rat in the race, they drop out.

Goodman goes on to say that:

> From early childhood, the young are subjected to a lockstep . . . tightly geared to the extra-mural demands. There is little attention to individual pace, rhythm or choice and none whatever to the discovery of identity. . . . The aptitude and achievement testing and the fierce competition for high grades are a race up the ladder to high salaried jobs in the business of the world, including the schooling business. In this race, time is literally money. Middle-class youngsters—or their parents—realistically opt for advanced placement and hasten to volunteer for the National Merit exam. The colleges and universities go along with this spiritual destruction, and indeed devise the tests and the curricula to pass the tests. Thereby, they connive at their own spiritual destruction; yet it is not surprising, for that is where the money and grandeur are.[2]

Seniors from an urban Hartford, Connecticut, high school were asked to write for new freshmen what they might expect in high school. What follows are revealing excerpts from the papers written by two of them:

1. You'll have to adjust to having to stay in school all day.
2. You must be prepared to have lunch in school.
3. You'll go from class to class. You very seldom have the same teacher for two subjects, so they don't know your name.
4. You must be willing to learn, because you'll no longer be a child and it's up to you to become a good student.
5. Good grades are important.
6. There is sometimes a lot of homework for you to do, and it's up to you to do this and get good grades, and you have to do it to be a successful person in life.
7. If you are a good student, you may be able to get a scholarship which will help you to go further on in school.
8. Discipline is for those who are not getting good grades or those who are not being good students.

---

[2] *Ibid.*, p. 123.

9. Ways of being disciplined: You may be kept after school for being late too many times or for being a bad student in class. It is important to be a good student, to be prompt, polite, and kind.
10. They think of lots of things for you to join, such as clubs, after-school activities, arts and crafts, even learning to drive a car.
11. There will be movies to go to, speeches to hear, even a library in the school you can go to.

This was written by anxious children, anxious because if they do not correctly regurgitate what the teacher has said or what they have been forced to read, they will fall behind in the rat race and become dropouts.

As Goodman vividly puts it:

> At a childish level, all this adds up to brainwashing. The components are: a. a uniform world-view
> b. the absence of any viable alternative
> c. confusion about the relevance of one's own experience and feelings
> d. a chronic anxiety, so that one clings to the one world view as the only security.
> This is brainwashing.[3]

Small wonder that, as James Coleman of John Hopkins states, "The average adolescent is really in school, academically, for about ten minutes a day! Not a very efficient enterprise."

This fearful comment on education applies to our universities and colleges as well as to our elementary and secondary schools. Many college students, if accepting the system at all, regard it as a boring necessity, a dull appendage to the really exciting portions of college life—boy-girl relationships, athletics, social functions and causes, political issues, and personal relationships with other students and a handful of rare faculty members.

It is understandable why education is being attacked violently by students who doubt its relevancy to their lives, by black people demanding attention to their needs for pride, identity, and dignity, and by hippies protesting the hypocrisies of an unfeeling adult world. In fact, many of the problems facing our educational insti-

---

[3] *Ibid.*, p. 70.

tutions today can be traced to the intellectual half-man manifest-
ing his reluctance to feel and deal with feelings of his students and
associates.

In January, 1969, I was invited to take part in a conference
hosted by the President of Columbia University entitled "Columbia
—After the Crisis." The conference took place on a weekend in the
comfortable seclusion of Arden House in Harriman, New York.
Among the participants were the trustees of Columbia, the key
administrators and faculty, student leaders, and a group of outside
voyeurs who had been invited for objectivity, I suppose. The Conference was organized into eight or ten small encounter groups led
by Dr. Carl Rogers and a team of trained group leaders who, though
they had nothing to do with the organizing of the conference,
were called in at the last minute in a desperate attempt to open
communications. Each small group was composed of a mixture of
trustees, faculty, administrators, students, and outsiders.

In the author's group, which was led by Carl Rogers, it became
apparent that one of the faculty members, a distinguished physicist,
was gradually moving his chair back from the group circle. Dr.
Rogers remarked to the faculty member that he had the feeling that
he was trying to withdraw from the group. The faculty member
replied that indeed he was. He had *not* come to the conference to
be psychoanalyzed but rather to learn. "Learning," he stated, "takes
place on an intellectual, rational level not on an emotional plane.
Not a wise intellectual statement has been uttered here today," he
declared. "If anyone else would care to engage in an intellectual
discussion, I propose they leave this group and join me in the next
room for some profitable learning."

After this statement, one of the outsiders, the president of a
foundation, remarked that he now understood a little better what
the problem at Columbia was all about. A student responded that
this reluctance of the faculty to deal on any level except the intellectual was at the root of Columbia's difficulties—in fact at the root
of the difficulties all over our campuses today.

It became more and more obvious to the outsiders, including the
author, that the essence of the Columbia student demands was for
faculty members to deal with them humanly, with emotion and
feelings, rather than purely on the intellectual level—a "safe" plane

where most faculty members at the conference struggled to remain and where, of course, their competence was unquestioned.

In a large general session of the conference, the students decided to take the floor and present their side of the problem. In a great display of emotion, the students, with lack of pomp and dignity but with great vividness and articulateness, attempted to communicate their feelings to the trustees, administration, and faculty. Throughout this session the top administration and faculty denied that Columbia had a communication problem—a naive declaration, at best, for any university to claim. Throughout this session, the lack of communication between students, faculty, and administrators was flagrantly obvious to the outside observers. In a burst of emotion and frustration at his inability to communicate, one student, tears streaming down his face, stood before one of the key administrators and shouted, "Take off your title just for a moment and show us that there's a human being underneath! Admit you've made a mistake in your life!" The administrator began to respond dignifiedly, "It is not my policy . . ." whereupon the student shouted, "Fuck your policy!"

An extremely articulate longhaired student wearing a "Jesus Saves" T-shirt stood and remarked that, "The crisis at Columbia all boils down to the dichotomy of 'intellect' versus 'feelings' or to put it another way 'duplicity' versus 'morality'." This statement went over the heads of most of the conferees and, as invariably occurred after such an outburst, a faculty member rose and began to lecture in an intellectual monotone. An outsider, a distinguished psychologist and philosopher, remarked to me that no one seemed to hear the important key point that the student had just made: that faculty members dealing on an emotionally "safe" intellectual level were practicing duplicity in failing to face up to their feelings. They were half-men—the brilliantly developed intellectual-half—but they lacked the capacity to express their feelings directly, and such a practice was seen as duplicity if not immoral. Students, on the other hand, were dealing openly and honestly with their feelings and, consequently, were moral and honest in spite of adult hypocritical views of their morality.

The denial of most faculty at Columbia to nurture and deal with feelings is, in the author's opinion, one of the underlying reasons for the crisis at Columbia and at other institutions. After making such desperate attempts to communicate and still failing, it is understandable how students become alienated.

Throughout this conference I was greatly impressed by the articulateness of the students who, time and time again, rose without preparation or notes to deliver brilliantly organized human messages which integrated both emotional and intellectual content.

What follows is the almost complete text of a letter written after the conference to one of the participants (an administrator at Columbia) by one of the articulate students, Greg Knox, who felt that the Columbia administration was alienated from reality. It highlights vividly the severity of the problems faculty, administrators, and students should be facing together:

> It can only be with little pleasure that I write of my reflections on the weekend we spent together at Arden House, for it was not a pleasant weekend. I saw several students disintegrate in front of me that Saturday night; it was absurd and shameful that we bared our souls before an unworthy company. You are aware, no doubt, that at least one of the students did not recover from that episode and dropped out of Columbia some three miserable weeks afterwards. My own experience at Arden House was similarly painful, for I arrived at the closest understanding to date of what "the opposition" was really like.

> Before I present any reflections, it will perhaps be worthwhile for me to describe my own position in the University political matters. I enjoy a somewhat difficult position, branded by the left as an "administration tool" because I even talk with the ruling powers, yet at the same time branded by them "a threat" with the result that they don't listen anyway. In any case, it is clear in my mind, as a result of the weekend, that there will be very little further conversation with the powers that be—they are incorrigible, for they do not have the will to change—my future will now have to be devoted solely to destroying them. This will be perhaps my final attempt at non-violent communication.

> Clearly, the Saturday night episode was the most obvious horror of the weekend, for it indicated precisely where the difficulty lay, in the relationship between young and old. We were, one might say, worlds apart: one group speaking the language of the soul, the other of the mind. The problem was not just one of

understanding but also one of translation. This, of course, results from a conscious effort on our part, not to mislead you, but to reject your terms. We do this because these terms—and the intellects which spawn them—are a disgrace to humanity, and we will have no part of it. Consequently, if you wish to understand us, it is you who must do the work; not we who express the emotional in terms of the intellect, but you who express the mental in terms of the human. Mentality and intellect no longer count for much, and count for nothing when devoid of humanity. That we are speaking two different languages, then, is one problem; of course, it is merely symptomatic of the greater problem: that we are living two different lives.

Before I continue my reflections, it will perhaps be worthwhile to define two important words: "you" and "we". "You" is certainly not you personally (if it is to be used this way it will be appropriately qualified), but rather designates "the opposition", that is to say, anyone who currently has power, but either refuses, or is unable, to wield it for the improvement—concrete and extensive—of the world in which he or she is active. "We" means anyone who is in "the movement," whether it be its political, social, artistic, etc. aspect, dedicated to using all our resources to make good and human the institutions with which we abide. "We" and "you" are not necessarily chronological differentiations; for example, I would suspect that John D. Rockefeller III is one of "us" . . . And while Youth is probably the greatest single binding element, the distinction is, for the most part, spiritual.

To return to the Saturday night affair, you will remember that at the introductory session on Friday, I said that one of the reasons that I came to the Conference was that I had been increasingly bothered by the realization that it seemed impossible for the two factions ("us" and "you") to work together, and that the Weekend would be as good an opportunity as any to see if this realization was in fact valid. I found Saturday night that it certainly was. I delivered at the beginning of that evening what someone termed an "harangue"; the "harangue" part of it was meant primarily to indicate that we meant business and that the business was urgent— in any case, I think, perhaps with some immodesty, that my words did have some value. Since I do not like to lecture, far preferring discussion, I did not elaborate too much on the points I made, but spoke briefly and waited for questions. The questions never came. While the unquestioning spirit is inappropriate in general, and for the educator in specific, I think it was especially unfortunate at that time and place.

Since this will be, as I have said, probably my last attempt at informing the opposition, may I briefly go over the points I made then? I have no record, but I recall four major themes: 1) that the faculty were, by and large, half-men, and that this caused a certain amount of difficulty in our relating to them; 2) that you could not expect logic from us, as our reasoning and decisions were based more upon intuition (soul) than facts, which were relatively unimportant; 3) that what we wanted now from you in general, and the University in particular, was graceful capitulation; and 4) that as far as the future was concerned, the function of the University should be to serve as a revolutionary base for all kinds of revolutions. These points may have seemed controversial—maybe pure hell-fire—yet I continue to think that they were somewhat germane to that gathering. Not a single question! Since this strikes me as a significant experience in itself, I will take the liberty of using this letter of reflections to explain somewhat more fully the points I made then; clearly, they reflect on the University more than the weekend, but they may still be of interest to you.

Concerning the faculty: we were well imbued during Freshman Week four years ago with the notion that we were at Columbia to become "Whole men". David Truman gave a speech that week in which he pointed out that "pre-meds and pre-laws were possibly only premature," and that "just as important as our obligation to go to classes and understand the great sentiments of history was our obligation to ride on the subway and look into the eyes of the people sitting opposite us and try to understand the sentiments which they were trying to hide." I was tremendously struck by this (i.e. my mind was blown), and decided that my major goal at Columbia was to become a "Whole man". I think I have succeeded, not just in becoming a whole man, but more importantly, in understanding what one is. What I discovered was that a whole man is comprised of mind, heart, soul, muscle, and balls. What I discovered about the faculty, for the most part, is that it is men comprised of mind. It was an unfortunate discovery, difficultly tolerated in an age in which so much understanding, strength and action are essential. I have seen particular contradictions in this area; just to give one, I was quite amazed at a professor who thought enough of me to announce to a class of his that they should all get to know me, and then told me that he did not think that he could nominate me for some award because I did not "look good enough on paper". Such a discrepancy in his words indicated to me that he did not learn well the lesson of the whole man, a lesson which he had often communicated to me. Suffice it to say that as far as the new order goes, the faculty do not make it.

The second point has already been discussed to some extent in the third paragraph of this letter, and I do not think it will be valuable to say more here. The third point was perhaps the crux of the whole struggle between young and old, both on the university and national levels. The reason that capitulation is necessary is that you cannot win, for we are unbeatable. You can throw us into jails, but it is clear, that does nothing; you can kill us, but, although that does something, your suffering will be far greater than ours. You must understand that there is no defense against goodness, and that you cannot even attack our souls. So, eventually, we will win; you will lose. More important, however, than your capitulation is that it be graceful; for, since we are going to win anyway, it will be best that we all derive the good to which we are entitled; if you capitulate gracefully you will share in every goodness, but if we have to fight, you will lose everything. Most important to both of us is that fighting becomes such a bore; we don't want to have to struggle for every damned obvious thing; we don't want to have to prove ourselves to you, or argue with you, or wait around until you come to your senses. The time has long passed when you should have realized what we are about, when we were willing to talk to you and you did not choose to listen. Now we don't just want to talk to you; we want to talk to you and we want you to do what we tell you. You similarly missed your opportunity for argument; but this is also all right. For it gave us the time to strengthen our convictions so that now, should we engage in argument—rational discourse—and your high-powered intellects beat us by rationality, we can still walk away, admitting full well that we have lost the argument, but at the same time realizing that that doesn't really matter, because we are right anyway. It is true that no one has a monopoly on the truth, but you must remember that it is the young who monopolize wisdom. Just as we respect you for realizing the technology which enables you to put a man around the moon, so you should respect us for realizing the wisdom that makes that particular brand of lunacy unacceptable, at least until some other matters closer at hand are cleared up. I will cut the philosophy short to give you an example of the

value of graceful capitulation. The Joint Committee on Disciplinary Affairs has just granted amnesty—too late. That is, the capitulation was entirely ungraceful, consequently entirely unimpressive.
Think for a moment what would have happened if such a step had
been taken, say, last April 29. You will recall that it was the pre-
condition for negotiations. You will recall that the buildings would
have been emptied peacefully and constructively had such a step
been taken then; you will imagine, please, that 1,200 people would
not have been arrested and the University would not have been
shut down, but rather constructively, and vastly, improved. How
do you explain your destructive nihilism? How foolish you all
were; how I hope you have all learned your lesson. Keep it in mind
when spring comes, when a young man's fancy turns to rioting.

On the last point, the most important part of it is its quali-
fication "for all kinds of revolutions". John Maynard Keynes was
a revolutionary in the field of economics; don't you think he
would have been a good man to have in the Columbia community?
James Joyce wrote a revolutionary piece of English literature
with *Ulysses;* would he not be welcomed at Columbia? Dr. Chris-
tian Barnard created a revolution in the field of cardiac surgery;
would he be unwanted by the Faculty of P&S? These are the
kinds of revolutions that should be going on at Columbia, along
with the social and political revolutions which would make this
country a bearable place. I would point out that it was only to this
that anyone else at the Conference responded; (one trustee) stated
that "Some of us don't like revolutions." I would suggest that that
is not the best attitude for a Trustee of Columbia.

So much for my own offering Saturday night. It is quite possible that these points would not interest those who attended a
Conference on the University after Crisis; I will persist in thinking that they are relevant to both the University and Crisis, not to
mention the aftermath. As for my experience later that evening,
related to the message on the shirt I wore, surreal would be too
kind a way to describe it. I wore the shirt neither to talk about
it, nor to cause a furor; it is quite ironic for me to recall that, although I do not usually think too much when I get dressed in the
morning, on that particular morning I was somewhat concerned
that my co-conferees would notice that I was wearing two different socks.

As for the remainder of that evening, there are two reflections
which might be helpful. The first is the reply which I formulated
in my mind for (one of the trustee's) biblical quotations. Having

spent a portion of my life subject to monastic training I was somewhat accustomed to the rabbinical debate, and all I could think of
was this line: "Call me not Naomi (that is, beautiful), but call
me Mara (that is, bitter), for the Almighty hath quite filled me
with bitterness." On the subject of that shirt, there is an interesting passage in Wordsworth's "The Prelude" in which the poet
describes a blind man whom he saw in London, wearing his message on a card that hung from his neck, a card which the man
cannot, needless to say, read himself (Book VII, 11. 637–649). It
might be worthwhile for all of us to consider the message which
we wear on our chests without being able to see it. The second
overall reflection I have had concerning that session stems from the
reaction which I heard a number of the guests enunciate: that it
was a put-on. You would do well to understand that the only put-
on is pride. We have practically nothing to be proud of in the
world which we have inherited. The report of the Cox Commission
begins with the following words: "The present generation of
young people in our universities is the best informed, the most
intelligent, and the most idealistic this country has ever known."
(p. 4) This is, of course, completely true, yet I was sorry to see
that it was not followed by this: "It is also the most angry, frustrated, and fucked-up generation the country has ever known".
This is not a source of pride for us, and should not be for you.

It is for this reason that we rile at pronouncements of the glory
of Columbia, how it is a "dynamic, progressive" campus, etc. It is
clear that Columbia is a terrific university; for my purposes it is
the best, and I view my decision to come here instead of to Harvard as the wisest decision I have made. Until this year, there was
not another academic community in this country—probably not
in the world—that was as alive and jumping, with every kind of
stimulation. The most essential thing to remember about last Spring
is that the Rebellion would never have taken place if Columbia had
not been as good as it was. Columbia succeeded magnificently in
teaching its students to question and seek, and just as important,
to act on the conclusions of the search. So you are certainly right
to praise this University; but not at the price of avoiding the responsibilities which such success entails. Columbia's best students
for example, should be praised, not suspended, for having learned
so well.

In short, we just do not have time to sit back and praise a dynamic compus, for there is too much work to be done; you have
much to do, for instance, if you wish to catch up to your students.

None of us have time to gloss for it takes only a fine sense for the obvious to dwell on Columbia's greatness; its problems need hard work fast. The greatest immorality is to deny oneself the opportunity to fail; this is what you will be doing if you do not join in the struggle to improve this University—we don't need praise.

I was asked upon my return to Morningside after the Conference if there were any concrete, substantive results to the Weekend. To this question I was happy to be able to reply in the affirmative, having copped a roll of toilet paper and three bars of soap as I left Arden House. There were other nice things about the Weekend though; thank God for Erik Erikson in general; and it was nice that Dean Hovde, even though he has forgotten much, stood up to defend me, sucker that I am, after [a trustee's] attack. It was somewhat characteristically Columbian, on the other hand, that the single most important man for Columbia to have at that Conference—David Truman—was not even invited originally, and could not stay for the whole weekend when he finally was invited. That he is leaving Columbia is also typical; for most jerk–democratic institutions strive for mediocrity and will not tolerate the best.

I very much enjoyed getting to know Vincent Kling, who was in my discussion group and seems a good man. After a short period of public-statement type pronouncements, he really began to say some honest things. It was pleasantly surprising to find that he at least understands the nature and difficulty of the struggle, and that we must arrive at a clear definition of our relative powers in the interactions to come.

You might be getting the impression by now that I did not find the Conference particularly worthwhile; if so, you would be right. In general, I have not been impressed by the response of my elders to last spring's opportunity; this is of course saddening, for I am not sure that we will give you another opportunity to change yourselves. I was shocked by Mark Rudd's use of the word "bullshit" in his communication with the Administration last Spring; but I can assure you that I did not even learn the meaning of the word until I had spent a summer working to constructively improve Columbia (College) only to see the final report of our summer's work shelved by the Committee on Instruction. If Columbia College is evil, then it must change; if it is so evil that it cannot change, then it will have to be destroyed. Destruction, needless to say, is nothing to worry about; just as one would not dream of putting up a new building over ramshackle existing structures but rather first destroys them (e.g. the new School for

International Affairs), so must incontrovertible human institutions be destroyed before good ones can be built. I am afraid that the message for most of the powerful in this country is "we will destroy your world, for it is evil and inhuman; whether or not we destroy you will depend on your sense of humor."

I do not think that it will be valuable to have any more conferences, nor any more discussions, nor any more words. Talking is no longer necessary or appropriate; it is a time for action. I could do no better than to refer you to the "Antigone" of Sophocles (11. 718-731) where, you will recall, a conflict is presented between Creon (pro-law-and-order) and his son Haemon (pro-good); Creon wins the argument, but the price of such a victory is clear. In any case, my point in mentioning this is that the play was written almost 2,500 years ago, and 2,500 years is time enough for talk. So we don't want to talk anymore; we want to practice the lesson which we have learned from Sophocles. If this lesson, and all the other lessons that are so obvious to us are not clear to you then I feel badly. But until they do become clear, you are just going to have to take our word for it and act accordingly. Please remember that we are not presenting our view for your agreement or disagreement, for neither reactions are appropriate; we are, after all, presenting nothing more than nature, and one can't fight nature. It would be like responding to someone who demonstrates how two plus two equals four by saying, "Yes, I understand, but I don't agree."

In keeping with his view that one difference between an intellectual "half-man" and a whole man is that the whole man takes action, this student then went on to present a list of recommendations for action to improve Columbia.

In many ways, the conference at Arden House could be considered a failure. In one important way it was successful in that it focused clearly on one of the principal problems facing Columbia and other institutions—the problem which results when human traits and capacities are divorced from each other: rationality from emotions, wishes and desires from the will to satisfy them. As their name implies, "intellectuals" are sometimes partial human beings. The rest of what they could be is too often locked uselessly inside them.

This first chapter has attempted to define some of the problems created by an educational system dominated by one-deminsional teachers and faculty—half-men whose intellectual capacities may be highly developed, but whose affective capacity is often severely stunted. Accordingly, these educators have functioned to foster almost purely intellectual learning in the classroom. The nurturing of the emotional side of the student—love, empathy, awareness, and fantasy—either has been neglected or left to chance.

Additionally this chapter looked into the widely held notion that learning should involve hard, unpleasant work in order for one to earn his place in middle-class society. We looked at this from the viewpoint of high school students and a Columbia University student, and had to conclude with such people as Paul Goodman that it does not follow that learning should be unpleasant or that one should aspire for the same goals for which his parents or teachers strived. Young people today are, for the most part, much more in touch with their feelings than were youngsters of the past few generations. Many of the problems in our classrooms and on our campuses stem from the fact that teachers and faculty deny feelings or refuse to integrate them with the intellectual content of the classroom. Chapter 2 will look deeper into the make-up of the overly intellectual faculty member who tends to deny both his own feelings and those of his students.

2

Educating the Whole Man

*. . . an occupational hazard for the college professor is arro-
gance. This grows out of the easy victories of the classroom where
he works with young people who know less than he does. He
may thus unconsciously come to believe that business, politics and
educational administration would be much better managed if those
in charge would only apply the same intelligence to their work
that he uses in his own . . ."*

Harold Stoke[1]

In this chapter we will explore what it is that makes the faculty
and teacher react in the counter productive, avoidance-of-feeling
syndrome described in the first chapter. What personality traits
are prevalent among the teachers or faculty members who have
been conditioned to avoid feelings and, hence, have become "intellectual half-men." In addition to examining this important source
of educational problems, we will look at a student's view of the
importance of integrating the intellectual with the affective to
produce a more humanistic education.

The previous chapter posed the question: Why is it that learning has to be presented in such a way that it becomes unpleasant
work? The answer was reached that learning doesn't have to be
unpleasant work, but that our educational system seems to make it
that way partly by conditioning teachers and faculty to deal only
with intellectual content at the expense of feelings. This is occurring at a time when students are more deeply than ever in touch
with their feelings and alienated from that which is purely intellectual and non-feeling.

For years, the teachers who have been achieving success in the
classroom have been practicing what I have labeled as "human-

---

[1] Harold Stoke, *The American College President* (New York: Harper & Row,
Publishers, 1969), pp. 115–116.

35

istic education"—that is, integrating the intellectual content with feelings. There is really nothing new about this approach. These teachers, however, are very rare "birds." If a person is lucky, he can recall one or two such humanistic teachers from his past as standing out from a mass of otherwise indistinguishable "intellectuals." What is it about our system that prevents more of these beautiful humans from developing?

Perhaps part of the problem lies in the kind of insecurity we condition into our faculty and teachers in graduate school. We force them to jump over a continuous series of hurdles. Almost before the student is able to clear one hurdle, he must be looking down the track for the next. Carl Rogers, in his excellent book *Freedom to Learn*, details some of the preposterous assumptions that govern graduate education today. Among these are the assumptions that students can't be trusted to pursue their own learning; that the ability to pass examinations is thought to be the best criterion for admission and for judging professional talent; and finally, that evaluation is all important in graduate school because of the belief that education *is* evaluation.

> It is incredible the way this [last] preposterous assumption has become completely imbedded in graduate education. . . . Examinations have become the beginning and the end of education. . . . In one university the graduate student . . . is faced with these major evaluation hurdles:
>
> 1. Examination in first foreign language
> 2. Examination in second foreign language
> 3. First six hour qualifying examination
> 4. Second six hour qualifying examination (both of these in the first graduate year)
> 5. Three hour examination in methodology and statistics
> 6. Four hour examination in a chosen major field of psychology
> 7. Two hour examination in a minor field
> 8. Oral examination on Master's thesis
> 9. Committee evaluation of Ph.D. proposal
> 10. Committee evaluation of Ph.D. thesis
> 11. Oral examination on Ph.D. thesis
>
> Since 10 to 50 per cent of those taking any of these examinations are failed on the first attempt, the actual number of examinations taken is considerably greater than indicated above. Understandably, the anxiety on the second attempt is considerably (sometimes unbearably) greater. Furthermore, these examinations are so spaced

out that during the four to seven years of his graduate work the student's main concern is with the next sword of Damocles which hangs over his career. As if the above list were not enough, it should be made clear that these major examinations are in *addition to* any quizzes, mid-semester and final examinations given in his courses.[2]

The process for elementary and secondary teacher preparation is less rigorous but still over-evaluative and miserably behind the times. In a space age world where progress has been dynamic, education has been relatively static. Schools of education are out of step with the progress the world has achieved. In fact, in many cases they are several decades behind.

But what happens to the personality of the teacher or faculty member who emerges from this system into a career in education? He still remains on probation for several years. If the faculty member cannot produce enough publications or perform enough research (neither of which have much relevance to the classroom or any relevance to the feelings of students), the system will not be favorably impressed and his career becomes jeopardized. Even if he does devote enough attention to research and publications to impress his superiors, and even if they do grant him tenure, he'll be lucky if he ever gains the security of financial independence.

Of course tenure is a very strange concept—an amazing one to those outside academic circles. After some time, a teacher who proves he will not "make too many waves" and upset the system is granted (usually by a group of those already entrenched with tenure) a guaranteed position with small annual increases of salary regardless of productivity. What better way could there be to stifle a system and reward unproductiveness? If, in reality, tenure could assure the faculty member the freedom to be truly creative and to implement the new ideas and changes he sees evident, then perhaps it would be a useful concept. However, it frequently has the opposite effect, tending to bolster the educational institution's resistance to change.

The elementary and secondary school teacher is put in even more constricted surroundings. The conservatism of many of our school systems allows for even less creativity or nonconformity. Pay is miserably low and the good teacher may be quickly lured out of

---

[2] Rogers, *op. cit.*, pp. 174–175.

the classroom where he is so badly needed. Statistics gathered by
the U. S. Office of Education show that we are actually producing
more teachers than we need; however, we still have a teacher short-
age because few trained teachers remain in the classroom where salaries are inadequate. Too many good ones change professions within
a few years.

Leadership in education at the principal and superintendent levels is a sorry state of affairs. Close autocratic supervision with little
freedom for teachers to experiment and innovate is the rule rather
than the exception. What kind of leadership do we see in the principal who is concerned about teachers wearing opaque stockings
and seeing that students' bangs are at least two fingers above the
eyebrows? In Chapter 7, the need for more "people-oriented" educational leadership will be advanced.

What sort of person emerges from this system? George Williams
in his delightful book *Some of My Best Friends Are Professors*
suggests the following:

> The personality that eventually emerges from all this is typi-
> cally underlain with a deep sense of inferiority, fear and maladjust-
> ment, yet overlain by an almost frantic sense of superiority. This
> deep split in the personality is further complicated by a latent hos-
> tility to that which is nonbookish and nonintellectual, and a fluttery
> insecurity that creates morbid fear of any criticism that may endan-
> ger hard-won academic place. Moreover, since only a persistent
> doggedness of personality could have come through the obstacles
> that graduate students must overcome, the professor is (by a process
> of natural selection) a single-minded person without much capacity
> to view the world impartially, much less appreciatively and lov-
> ingly.[3]

John Corson reveals a little more of the typical personality of
the faculty member in his book *Governance of Colleges and
Universities:*

> . . . More than his counterpart in other institutions, he is likely to
> hold as important for organizational decisions such choices as abso-
> lutism versus relativism, objectivity versus commitment, freedom
> versus authority, and sacred versus secular. Hence, a needed deci-
> sion on a practical matter may be deferred until theoretical issues
> are debated.

---

[3] George Williams, *Some of My Best Friends Are Professors* (New York:
Abelard-Schuman Limited, 1958), p. 50.

Concern with such fundamental commitments shifts the faculty member's focus away from institutional needs. Thus, recently the faculty of a major eastern university was unable to decide on a curriculum for a program in public administration because of disagreement on the fundamental role of the state in society.[4]

To be quickly enlightened (or disillusioned) in more detail about this subject, all we have to do is visit a few meetings of university faculty senates. At a large eastern state university, the author found ample evidence of the truth of John Corson's statements. In these meetings there was continual harangue about tightening up of the curriculum, higher and more rigid standards for grading, increasing course requirements, how high schools are not doing their jobs, why athletics, physical education and ROTC should not be accredited courses, the immaturity of students or the AAUP's position on this or that. According to Paul Goodman:

> ... the AAUP is a national craft union, largely of entrenched seniors, that copes with distant crises by dilatory committee work. According to its rules, it will not protect freedom in cases of pragmatic action, but only academic 'inquiry' and teaching—but what kind of inquiry is it that is not essentially involved with pragmatic experiment and risks? The AAUP is ... the pure style of the dominant organized system to establish status and to transform intellect into conversation, with the proviso that nothing is in danger of being changed.[5]

Decisions on important business in these meetings usually take the sidelines to make room for such statements as the one made by a distinguished faculty member arguing against the movement for "pass—fail" courses: "The grading of students happens to be one of the few sacred privileges afforded to faculty members and I'm for preserving grading at all costs."

Somehow many teachers and faculty have the idea that in order to uphold academic standards they must give a high percentage of low grades. One of the rare revolutionary schools of education in the country, at a state university, is being severely criticized by other departments in the university for its small numbers of failures. This idea seems to be ingrained in most universities and school systems.

---

[4] John Corson, *Governance of Colleges and Universities* (New York: McGraw-Hill, 1960), p. 30.

[5] Goodman, *op. cit.*, p. 254.

Teachers and faculty often boast about the high percentage of failures within their departments. The eyebrows lift immediately when
someone confesses that no one has failed in his course. It's amazing
that few teachers or faculty members view the failures of their students as a failure of themselves. Paul Goodman reinforces this
observation:

> For most of the students, the competitive grade has come to be
> the essence. The naive teacher points to the beauty of the subject
> and the ingenuity of the research; the shrewd student asks if he is
> responsible for that on the final exam.[6]

He goes on to say:

> Rushed, [the student] gives token performances, which he has
> learned to fake. No attention is paid to what suits *him*. The only
> time a student is treated as a person is when he breaks down and is
> referred to guidance. In place of reliance on intrinsic motives, re-
> spect for individuality, or leisurely exploration, there is a stepped-up
> pressure of extrinsic motivation, fear and bribery. The student can-
> not help worrying about his father's money, the fantastic tuition and
> other fees that will go down the drain if he flunks out. . . .[7]
>
> Students have to invent a "personal problem" if they want an
> admired faculty member to pay attention to them. As it works out,
> it is an unusual scholar who can ask a fatherly question as a matter
> of course and follow up with practical concern. Teaching is worth-
> while if it is pursuing a subject matter *with* someone, or teaching it
> for someone. If it is merely lecturing on a subject matter or hearing
> lessons, it is better done by tapes and films and teaching machines.[8]

And finally, George Williams makes the following severe indict-
ment of academia:

> Too many professors are cynics who can do nothing but ridicule
> the ignorance of students; too many are determined factualists who
> beat down imagination and creativeness; too many are disciplinar-
> ians who think that classrooms and the process of learning should
> never be fun to students; too many are academicians whose thinking
> moves always in formal grooves and who are quite unable to com-
> prehend differences of interpretation; too many have such high
> regard for "truth" that they discourage all independent thought for

---

[6] Goodman, *op. cit.,* p. 128.

[7] *Ibid.,* p. 136.

[8] *Ibid.,* p. 284.

fear that the young person may be "wrong"; too many are insensitive to the feelings of other people, or unsympathetic toward universal human weakness, antagonizing students permanently by unjustly accusing them of cheating, refusing to believe or accept honest excuses for absences or late work, making no allowances for normal human lapses of attention or deviations from the straight and narrow path; too many of them have developed (as a result of early maladjustments and insecurities) an inferiority complex that results in certain typical personality traits, including compensatory arrogance, morbid suspicion, fear that students will discover professorial weaknesses, timidity that masks itself as unfriendliness, intolerance of disagreement and sometimes downright sadism. Professors are not the only people with these personality weaknesses. But they are likely to have more than other people; and besides, they are so situated that their personality weaknesses, by operating on students at a very impressionable period of life, can do immeasurably more harm than those of most other people.[9]

This is a severe criticism of the faculty member with an intellectual half-man syndrome. Needless to say, the typing of individuals is risky business. Obviously, there are many exceptions to the typical. But the average faculty member becomes so inwardly-focused on his own narrow specialization that, not only will he rarely be concerned about his own inadequacies, but he will often challenge any outsider or administrator who dares to suggest that he should improve or change his ways. This book considers the faculty or teacher as the key link in a vicious cycle that has taken the humanness out of our educational system.

Graduate schools tend to produce insecure paranoic graduates, who become inhuman teachers, who then mold students without feeling, who in turn become insecure graduate students. Paul Goodman brings out the irony of such a self-perpetuating system:

. . . there is almost never conveyed the sense in which learning is truly practical, to enlighten experience, give courage to initiate and change, reform the state, or deepen personal and social peace. On the contrary, the entire educational system itself creates professional cynicism on the resigned conviction that Nothing Can Be Done. If this is the university, how can we hope for aspiring scholarship in the elementary schools? On the contrary, everything will be grades and conforming, getting ahead not in the subject of inter-

---

9 Williams, *op. cit.*, p. 106.

est but up the ladder. Students "do" Bronx Science in order to "make" MIT, and they "do" MIT in order to "make" Westinghouse; some of them have "done" Westinghouse in order to "make" jail.[10]

In the final part of this chapter, I would like to present a student's view of this problem from a course on contemporary problems in education taught by the author and an associate. Class members primarily were conservative New England school superintendents, principals, and teachers. We had exposed the large class to several sample doses of humanistic education techniques (as large a dose as we felt their conservatism could tolerate for the time). Three of the younger graduate students, Carolyn Hanson, Maureen Riley, and Tim Dailey, however, became much more enthusiastic than most members of the class and were frustrated by the reluctance of the majority of the students to get off the intellectual plane and onto a feeling level. They approached us and asked if we would share the class time with them for a project they had in mind. Among the experiences to which we had exposed the class was a discussion of my experiences with other educators at an Esalen (Big Sur) workshop with George Brown who is working under a Ford Foundation grant with classroom teachers to see what can be done with humanistic education in the classroom. Also, since the class was all white and naive about the problems of the black man, we had arranged for a black–white confrontation with black friends visiting in the classroom. Additionally, we staged a role-playing simulation of a campus crisis with the students playing the parts of the faculty, administration, students, trustees, community, etc. Finally, we had invited Gerald Weinstein, who has pioneered in humanistic curriculum development, to spend a few hours "turning on" the class. Apparently these experiences had whet the appetites of these three graduate students and they were pleading for more.

They asked to have a two and one-half hour block of class time for a "Humanistic Educational Happening," and we agreed. The objective was to establish among the members of the class the kind of rapport that would facilitate open and free expression of thoughts and emotions. The happening was to be built on small group discus-

---

[10] Goodman, *op. cit.,* p. 31.

sions of individual members' fantasies about ideal education experiences. The description which follows was handed out to all the students in the class the week before the happening:

We know there are problems in education, both for teachers and for students. Most are dissatisfied because the educational system does not coincide with their picture of what it should be. Many are frustrated because the improvements or changes they visualize are not considered. Still others do not know how to put their ideas into action.

In what kind of educational experience would you like to participate, either as a student or as a teacher? What would the enviroment be like; what would be taking place within the enviroment? What would be happening to people; what would be going on inside them? What would they be doing to/with each other? How would participants feel about the experience? What would they learn; how would they change? Would there be students and teachers, if so, what would be their respective roles? Would teachers, as well as students, learn/change? Who would teach whom?

Next week we would like to participate with this class in trying to bring fantasies of an ideal education experience into some kind of concrete reality. We would like this class period and group of people to become fantasy made real. The kind of fantasies we have been discussing among ourselves seem to be inspired by the concepts and goals of humanistic education. One we have talked about is a class which is a community—a group in which there is an atmosphere of warmth and openness where people communicate freely their ideas, feelings, and sensations—a setting for growth and change. But this is only one person's fantasy; there are many others. We have no consensual fantasy.

Next week we plan to bring our individual fantasies and we ask you to join us and bring yours. Breaking into small groups, we would like to share individual fantasies, synthesizing where possible, and creating, perhaps, a group fantasy. Please bring with you anything that will help you to make your fantasy real. A tape recorder and record player will be available in the room. As a means of facilitating our own fantasies we plan to bring food, music, candles, incense, and pillows. What things would you like in the room?

We are looking forward to our next class together as a time to share with each other our individual desires and aspirations, to more fully understand and appreciate one another, and to celebrate our humanity. We hope you share our joyful expectation.

What follows is Tim Dailey's description and views of the happening and of the need for a more humanistic educational process:

Student restiveness, student rebellions, while upsetting many people and causing others to act in an extreme fashion, have had one direct and beneficial result. Attention is now focused directly on education, even the attention of those only remotely involved. Problems which have lain dormant for decades, criticisms of students and faculties which have been muttered within the school and campus for years but never acted upon, are now being revealed and confronted. No matter what the outcome of all this confusing and provoking outcry, everyone has been forced to think about both the purpose of education and the way in which it should operate.

Inevitably extremes of opinion on both sides result from such a situation, but also inevitably much valuable thought, be it critical of the status quo or critical of the recommended changes, occurs. It is from this contingent—those who take this opportunity to think hard about the problems raised—that will come the synthesis and the real change.

This word "change" is used so often, however, that it should be carefully defined, before we can begin to understand what is happening. For some people, change is synonomous with destruction. To tear everything down and start over would for them constitute the only acceptable change. Revolution, in its literal sense, is what this group means by change.

Another group talks about change, meaning accommodation or adjustment. By maintaining the present structure of education, one can introduce new programs, revitalize old ones, or merely move existing methods around more efficiently. This has been happening very slowly ever since education became institutionalized. In this sense, change refers to orderly improvement.

There is a third group, to whom change, particularly in its revolutionary sense, is a bad word. For the best elements in this group, change means eliminating the bad parts of education, and revering those aspects proven by experience to be valid, important, useful, or worthwhile. Of course, some elements of the system are kept only for reasons of sentimentality, but that is important to these people.

If these differences in the commonly used word "change" in fact exist, it is little wonder that people get upset with each other. Communication is difficult if not impossible when a discussion involves terms which the participants define differently, without informing each other. But a further complication exists, in that the three groups of ideas associated with these definitions represent different ideologies, so that even an explicit definition of change would not resolve differences.

The humanistic educational happening we had in class would be classified as the second kind of change, improvement without starting from the beginning, introducing something new without having to revert to some traditional method. What we did in class, from another perspective, relates to the total problem resulting from the clash of these three concepts of change.

Much has been written about affective and humanistic education. While these refer to somewhat different concepts, in many ways they point to the same goal. I can be more clear by referring to my own experience as a student. School means going to class, listening to the teacher, and doing the assigned homework. Variations of this pattern exist for each level of education, from kindergarten to graduate school. But the essence of this pattern is that one is to be taught. The teacher knows what to teach, how to teach it, and how the student should learn whatever is being taught. The teacher is right, both by virtue of education and by position as teacher.

The result of this is that emphasis is placed on the mind, on following directions and reciting, in one form or another, what has been gained from the directions. One becomes educated when one knows what the teacher knows. A certain body of knowledge exists that must be learned, and in reality this means memorization of "facts." What the facts are from this point of view is another question. In too many cases, the facts are the values and beliefs of the teacher.

A further result of this approach is that communication between pupil and teacher is question and answer. It is not mutual reinforcement of enthusiasm to find the truth, to express oneself. Feeling and emotion are left out, on an overt level at least. But they exist, underground. Because another aspect of this system is that the teacher judges, he grades. When he does this, his feelings about the student affect him, even though he does not recognize it. When the student receives a grade, or anticipates the fact that he will be graded, his feelings are aroused. He knows he is being judged: his worth as a person is on trial. These feelings may not be explicit, but they are there.

One curious fact which belies this pattern is that there is some recognition that education involves the whole person. So schools now provide health services, physical education, sex education, counselors and psychologists. At every level these services are offered, but the difference at various levels is interesting. Another interesting fact, is the way in which these services are used, and by whom.

In the elementary school, where the teacher plays mother or father much of the time (of necessity in some instances and by design in others), the child is evaluated on social ability, manners, and the like. The teacher is also expected to recognize personality problems. One reason this is possible, is that the teacher is with the same class all day. But the interesting thing is, that here no aspect of the child's life is unconnected with his school "progress." He is totally watched.

In high school, teachers generally change each period, so that this guardianship is not possible. The emphasis on such nonmental activities decreases, but a person's education is still partly evaluated on such things as extra-curricular activity, good citizenship, and so on. In a sense, these are only more sophisticated models of the elementary school concerns.

Again, in college and graduate school, there is an ever decreasing emphasis on these aspects of the educational process. I suppose the assumption is made that by this time the student is becoming a mature person, and he can handle such activities himself. Thus, physical education is generally required only for the first two years. The professor also sees the student only as part of a mass; he may not even recognize him.

Also, other institutionalized means of dealing with life apart from classroom learning exist—fraternities, clubs, activities, and the like. But at the same time, when a person reaches college age he is apt to be more consciously concerned with how he feels, with his emotional life, and to make more of an effort to understand and control, or change himself.

As this happens, it is left to the student to deal with these concerns on his own. Furthermore, the purely mental aspects of education are increased in intensity and extent. Learning how to think in logical, verbal, conceptual terms is the goal. The student also has less access to the teacher-professor, less communication with him. He is on his own, literally in too many cases, so that what should be independence, becomes isolation from the guidance of the professor whose teaching is now lecture, not dialogue or discussion.

This means that frustration and apathy are apt to occur, coupled with resentment. I speak from personal experience on this, for myself and for every other student I have known. We have all had this experience. And another problem is competition, which increases as one rises through the educational system.

What does all this mean? It means that when the total person is considered, as he is in elementary school if at all, it is done to judge and evaluate more than to help. But when such a consideration could be most helpful, as in college, opportunities for it do not exist. Students and teachers do not communicate as people. Even when the teacher and student do get together, it is probable that they cannot communicate.

This may be an exaggeration, but it points to a real problem. Affective and humanistic education offer a ray of hope to alleviate this situation. By various methods, they seek to involve the student as a whole person in the educational process. It is trite to say that learning is facilitated by a recognition of the importance of emotions, that a person must feel well to learn well. But this is not usually recognized by teachers. Learning is thought by some teachers to occur best when punishment is the motivation. Doubtless this is true, in a stimulus-response fashion, for some kinds of learning. But real learning, learning which involves not only creative thinking, but learning how to be one's self, does not occur this way.

Therefore, one method which promises improvement in this problem of teacher-student communication and relationship in the classroom, as well as student-student communication, involves teaching people how to form relationships—how to communicate. What I am advocating would hopefully fill the gap which exists in higher education settings, the gap between the presence of services for non-classroom needs and the traditional logical and factual learning of the classroom. What I am advocating would not only facilitate this kind of learning, by taking account of the student as a person, but also allow other changes which might be necessary to occur more peacefully, and more quickly, with less pain and frustration.

Perhaps the whole class should be divided up, with the professor and the students forming small groups. In these groups, students and professor could talk freely about their ideas, how they feel about the course material and about each other, about how the class works as we did in the "Educational Happening." The goals would be honesty of expression, non-judgemental reactions, freedom to speak, concern for understanding how the other person thinks and feels.

Certain conditions must exist for this to happen. The participants must be willing to participate, especially the professor. They must accept the idea that the person as a person is important in the whole process of learning, and in the operation of the classroom.

How could this be put into operation? We decided to invite the class to fantasy, to be free to envision any and all possible alterations in education, and then to try to act these out with each other. We hoped to provide an atmosphere in which this could happen, in which they would feel the acceptance and freedom to do this. In this sense, the project had a dual purpose. First, we wanted to see what could happen if students tried to communicate on this level, by using their imaginations freely. The hope was that this would release us to communicate with each other on a personal level, thus circumventing judgements, harmful competition, and rigidity.

The second purpose was to provide a setting in which new ideas could be produced. The nice thing about fantasy is its unreality, its allowance of all possibilities. This is close to the strategy for change, in which one starts with the widest possible range of alternatives, knowing they will be narrowed down. But the end result is larger than that produced by the traditional method, in which one works outward from a kernel of change, trying to expand a small but realistic beginning step.

If one fantasizes about all the possibilities, there is a greater probability of discovering some really different alternatives. And even if these fantasies can be acted out only under special circumstances, such as the arranged setting we used, nevertheless this provides data on which to build realistic changes.

Did our approach succeed? I think in many ways it did. But before we evaluate the class, let us analyze what happened in one of the groups.

My group, counting myself, consisted of ten people, two men and eight women. Six of them were from the same school system, and were well acquainted with each other. This was beneficial in that immediately over half the group was at ease. On the other hand, this meant that the group tended to stay at a level already achieved, rather than being able to perceive and deal with personal differences.

Three of us began by sitting on the floor, but by the end of the session, more than half the group was sitting or reclining on the floor. Some cushions were available; fruit was in bowls in the center of the group, and people consumed it fairly steadily.

We began, at my request, by going around the circle telling our first names. Not only did I not know their names, but also I felt this would be a step towards setting a tone of informality. Then I introduced my feelings about my educational experiences as a student, saying that they had been, mostly, unpleasant. I thought one reason was because of the human relations of teacher-student communications. I suggested the possibility that if teachers were more open about themselves as people, and encouraged the students to know them, and if not just minds but the whole person were involved in the educational process, regardless of the subject matter of the particular class, then students might be happier.

At this point, I said I had a fantasy about what I would do if I were a professor and this was the first meeting of the class. We would go around the group and tell two things about ourselves, one characteristic we liked, and one we didn't. (I had intended originally, just before this, or concurrent with this exercise, to have the group join hands, as a means of demonstrating physically and overtly that the class was a group, that all were to be included and to participate. I must confess that my nerve failed me at this point and I did not dare try this. I suppose I thought they would think it silly, or unseemly.)

An interesting event occurred, just as I finished describing what I would do if I were the professor. Before I could suggest that we actually try it, one woman stated she thought such a procedure would raise problems of control, especially if students got to know the teacher too well. This problem was discussed by the others at some length, but mostly on an abstract, intellectual, non-personal level. Finally I suggested we probably wouldn't be able to solve this problem today. I went on to say that I thought my fantasy and fantasy in general had one advantage, that it was not necessarily realistic. Therefore it freed us to experiment, and the result might or might not be some concrete solution to a problem.

I then mentioned that it had been my intention actually to act out this fantasy, but I thought maybe from what the group had said they might feel uncomfortable about doing so. They said not, and eventually, after some further discussion, the other man in the group suggested we try it.

I learned from this, that I should have at the outset said "we will" do this, instead of saying "this is what I would do."

So we went around the circle, telling one thing we liked about ourself and one we didn't. I began, and said I thought I was accepting of people, and tried not to be judgemental, but on the other hand I said I was not always honest in expressing my negative feelings. I think I set some precedent, because the next four people said almost the same things about themselves. Most of the group expressed feelings of inadequacy, either in being honest, courageous or energetic. People in the group seemed more able to think of characteristics they didn't like, than positive aspects of themselves. Whether they were afraid of being boastful, I'm not sure. If I judge from my own feelings, it is possible that people in general spend more time thinking about their weaknesses than about their strengths. During this procedure, there was much laughing and joking, which I interpreted to be signs of anxiety and efforts to release tension. This interpretation and the one about concentrating on negative aspects, I did not fully recognize at the moment. I wish I had, because if I had been able to comment to the group as these things happened, it might have helped the group to focus more on how they reacted to what was going on.

At the end of this fantasy, several comments were made to the effect that this couldn't have been done with the whole class as a group, that the small group made people less anxious about talking and more willing to express honestly their feelings. Periodically, however, questions were directed to me as to the purpose of my fantasy, and what would probably happen if it were done in an actual classroom situation. I explained it as being an "icebreaker," in the sense that when people knew and felt comfortable with each other, learning could be more pleasant and easier, less competitive and anxiety producing. I said also I thought with this kind of activity, communication about subject matter would be improved; instead of the teacher telling the students what they should know, the teacher and students could learn together in a more active manner. I'm not sure I convinced everyone, because these questions kept being raised for some time.

One criticism was that my method would be too much for some people. People who are unacquainted with each other would not want to reveal themselves at a first meeting. This to me was interesting, because I have found through experience that being honest and talking about feelings is the quickest way to get to know someone. (Again, this did not occur to me at the time, not until I was writing this. In part this was due to my involvement in the group, and my efforts as leader to keep it going. I was tense about the operation of this experiment, which interfered with my perceptions at points.) From something that was said later on, which will be related below, I take the expressions of doubt about the validity of my fantasy as a real method, to be expressions of their personal fears about being classroom teachers.

The next comment by a group member dealt with her experience in a class she is currently attending, in which she feels quite uncomfortable and anxious. She can't answer when called on, because she feels excluded, looked down upon, and as a result thinks more about this than about the course material. She feels there is no human communication in her class. She therefore thought my fantasy held some possibilities for situations of that kind.

An hour had passed by now, so I asked if anyone else had fantasied during the week, in preparation for this class. No one admitted to having done so. Now that I think about this fact, it indicates to me what happens as a result of the way classes are run. Originality and fantasy are stifled; order is the goal, and the disruptiveness of real feelings is not desired. This is a strong statement on my part, but I think something like this is responsible for people not feeling free in educational settings.

Although there were no fantasies forthcoming, the other man in the group, a fifth grade teacher, told about an exercise he had tried with his class, using a method he had gotten from Gerry Weinstein's visit to our class. He had each child write down his own name, and then under this write a list of adjectives describing himself. The teacher regretted have done this, because several children brought up personal material, upsetting to them, and as a result were quite anxious during this period. For instance, one boy expressed a deep fear of dying. The teacher didn't know how to handle these feelings, and in turn felt quite anxious himself. He thought it bad for these children consciously to have expressed their feelings of inadequacy, fear, and unhappiness.

The group was very interested in this. Another teacher had tried the same exercise with her class, and had been satisfied with it, apparently having experienced none of the same upset. The group members tried to reassure the fifth grade teacher by saying kids were "tough" and that they would bounce back quickly. There was a general agreement that if one is not trained in how to deal with children's deep fears and troubles, one should not bring them out in the open. They should be avoided.

To me, this represents more a screen for fear, than a particularly valid representation of a policy to be followed. From my ex-

perience as an amateur social worker and minister, I've found that
when, for instance, someone had died, and one is called to visit the
relatives, the best and only thing one can do is to express sympathy, be attentive, and let the person talk. Nothing I could say
would lessen the loss or stop the grief. The comfort expressed by
the presence of a sympathetic concerned person seems the most
one can offer. Again, when a child expresses fear, or some problem,
the one thing one can do is to let him express himself, and accept
his expression. By that method, he sees his feeling is valid, not
laughed at or not productive of horror in the listener, but treated
as important because it's his feeling. It is through this procedure
that he sees himself more objectively and as a result, less anxiously.

Another perception comes to me about the teachers' feelings
of inadequacy in dealing with children's feelings. They mentioned
that many times these feelings were none of their business. I think
this is a reaction to a fear of feelings which is probably common to
most of us, but it causes the drawing of sometimes arbitrary lines
between what is and is not our business. Granted, some private
feelings or information may not be the teacher's business, but too
often this kind of policy shuts off valuable communication between people, which might be helpful to both parties. And it tends
to make the teacher seem to be a professional who does not have
feelings, who is unconcerned. This comes from reflection after the
group meeting, but it indicated in part what I learned from this
whole session.

The way in which the group members dealt with each other is
also reflected in the perceptions related in the previous paragraph.
When someone did, however rarely, express a real problem or feelings of anxiety, the group offered support, but did not encourage
further expression of such feelings by that person. At such times,
some tension was evident, indicating to me a desire to avoid these
expressions. This is a feature of most groups at one time or another, and since this was a one-meeting group, one could not expect them to go so far all at once.

Eventually, the fifth grade teacher in the group decided to try
an exercise with us, in which he would give us the first half of a
sentence, which we would complete individually. The sentences
were such as, "My school is . . . ; I wish my parents had . . . ; I will
be happy when . . . ." The sentence about parents brought forth
the most feelings, or the most negative feelings. The sentence about
future happiness was answered by most of the women with "when
I am married," or "when I have children." The school questions

received mostly neutral kinds of answers. This is interesting, because I find it hard to believe schools to these teachers are not associated with some negative, or anxious feelings especially in light of the rest of our discussion.

Nothing was done to explore these feelings, however. When the exercise was completed, the matter was dropped. It was interesting to me, however, that the teacher who had introduced this exercise was the one who raised the most critical questions about my fantasy in the beginning. He had thought it wasn't workable! He was also the one who had tried the exercises in his classroom in which the children brought out so many troubled feelings. He seems, on the one hand, to be afraid of such involvement, but on the other hand, he keeps trying to set up situations in which involvement is demanded.

After some more general discussion, I raised the question, "What did you expect when you came today, and did what you found meet your expectations?" Several said they hadn't known what to expect, but what they found was good. Most seemed not to have understood what we had in mind, when we gave the descriptive handout the previous week. They had envisioned the class doing this together, which frightened them. They thought each person would get up and perform for the whole class. That would frighten me too. The group from the same school had discussed this for the whole week before, and decided to come despite their misgivings. In general, they expressed quite positive feelings about the whole meeting.

One difficulty I experienced throughout the whole session was not being sure of what role to play. I wanted at one time to stimulate the group, by providing feedback on what was happening, and in general to direct the group. At other times, I wanted to be just an observer, an occasional participant, but to let the group follow its own path. As a result of this conflict in aims, and because of my inexperience at this sort of activity as leader, I was not as effective as I could have been. The reader of this will probably have come to that conclusion already, if he has noticed the many opportunities apparent for intervention and stimulation. Many perceptions came to me afterwards, that were not in my mind at the time. The group was able to operate on its own, but as a result, it stayed on a fairly impersonal level.

Taking the session as a whole, however, I was satisfied. For my own benefit, I gained insight into problems teachers experience in their classrooms, and I think I saw some carryover into this group

from these unresolved problems they face every day. I think for the
members of the group it was a good experience, showing them what
a humanistic class could be like, and having people meet new ideas
and approaches. Whether or not they learned anything from this,
about themselves and how to deal with their difficulties, I cannot
say. I only hope they did. I do think, however, something like this
for teachers should be provided, not only for their communication
with each other, but also for their learning how to be better teachers, more at ease, and more free with themselves.

Two further questions remain. One concerns our evelution of
this experience for the class as a whole. The other concerns the
possibility of putting into operation some similar program for other
educational settings.

The three of us who conceived and carried out this project
agree on several points. We think that in general the participants,
the class, found it difficult to get inside themselves. There was a
tendency to put feelings abstractly; and when, in rare moments,
an actual fantasy was shared, this tendency became a need to grasp
at reality. "You'd never get it past the principal." "The legislature
wouldn't give you money." "You'd lose control of your class."
Somehow, we cannot fantasize in the presence of others; no doubt
we all fantasize to ourselves, but to admit it is difficult. What would
others think of us, if they only knew . . . ?

I am not suggesting that all students and teachers should fantasize with each other all the time. But I am suggesting that the fact
that they don't is an indication of a lack of freedom to communicate
what they really think. We must keep to business, they say; we
must be orderly and rational, and above all we must be realistic.
After all, neurotics are the ones who are unrealistic.

Despite these drawbacks, the three of us felt that everyone was
interested, was willing to participate, and evidenced some intensity
of involvement. The video tapes which we made during the class
show this; people may not be talking to the group at large, but even
between themselves they have some discussion about what is happening, what they feel about it. Their facial expressions give away
their attempt to be abstract and impersonal.

From what was said in my group, I can confirm this general
opinion. Problems may not have been solved, but they were certainly revealed. The feelings that teachers have about what they
do are deep and many are anxious. Principals and superintendents
are somewhat the same. They are only human. Why can't they get

together, why can't they work on these feelings openly? There is no simple answer to that, nor any easy solution.

What is needed? This question leads to the second remaining question. If what we did was successful, how can it be applied as a change, or as a means toward other changes? We cannot agree whether the structure of the educational system is at fault, must be changed before communication can be open and free, or whether until communication opens, the structure won't be changed.

It is easy to say, some of both. But I think what is really necessary is a simultaneous attempt; the structure will not be altered until people can communicate, nor will people communicate unless they decide some change is necessary. Many pressures are being felt towards some kind of change, and soon, hopefully, real change will be unavoidable.

Perhaps the place to begin is in our schools of education. If enough teachers come out of these settings willing and able to be more fully human, to communicate about their inner selves and to listen to others, then slowly but surely this attitude will spread.

That may be too optimistic. It is easier for change to come from the top, working down. If administrators recognize a need for groups which facilitate and teach people how to talk to others, their influence can be a great impetus. And how do administrators change to this way of thinking, particularly when they are the ones experiencing the most pressure to conform, to do things the way they have always been done?

I do not know the answer. I cannot offer a program. I do think the utility and practicality of this approach has been demonstrated by what we did with the class. There is a purpose to be served by having groups learn how to tell each other about themselves, to probe each other, to help each other.

I think the idea is spreading. It is not the kind of change that can be blue-printed. Nor is it the kind of change that can be achieved by laws or court decisions, by takeovers or revolutions. It is a change that can occur when some people try it, as we did with this class. When it is offered as an alternative, as a possibility, people seem to respond to it, however slowly and hesitantly. People see that communication and openness are what they want. What we tried fills a need for many people, that hopefully will result in this kind of change becoming accepted.

I hear this student and many others saying quite loudly that: "We are human beings just like you. We have feelings just as you do. In fact, many of your actions indicate that you do not 'feel' as much as we do. We need you and your experience; however treat us as individual human beings, rather than collectively as another class."

Today's youth are extraordinarily energetic, strongly and positively motivated, well educated in certain categories of knowledge, and passionately committed to improving the world in which we live.

Though the violent efforts of the more irresponsible students have clouded over the constructive efforts of others, many constructive things have been accomplished by students. Students have been in the vanguard of the civil rights movement, the Peace Corps, the Teacher Corps, VISTA, the cry for reform on our campuses and, in fact, the demand for relevance and sincerity in the nation.

The views expressed here are not to suggest, however, that youth are infallible. It is nonsensical and, perhaps, destructive to accept the shibboleths and inconsequentialities of all simply because they come from youth. Parents, teachers, and faculty have enormous responsibility for the actions of our youth, especially when we believe in their causes. It becomes our obligation not simply to approve uncritically, but to attempt to share whatever resources we have to make our young leaders and their followers better able to deal with and change the world around them effectively. This is impossible from the pedestal of the "intellectual half-man."

Altogether too many faculty members assume "status authority" rather than "natural authority." The faculty member assuming status authority stands behind the podium, his Ph.D., and professional title, and lectures intellectually "down" at a class or to the back corner of the classroom about what *he* thinks is relevant. The faculty member assuming "natural authority" has earned it not because of his Ph.D. or title, but rather by demonstrating to his students that he shares with them the classroom time for learning and the resources he has available—himself, his friends and associates, the students in the class, his knowledge, his experiences, and his feelings. He demonstrates that he has a combination of these resources which are relevant to the students' goals and purposes in signing up to participate in his course, or in being at the university. It is quite appropriate, as Carl Rogers has suggested, that we call such a person with natural authority a "learning facilitator" rather than a "teacher." As he points out, the dictionary definition of "teaching" is: "to make to know." I agree wholeheartedly with Carl Rogers' reaction which follows:

> Personally I am not much interested in instructing another in what he should know or think. . . . why not be more efficient, using a book or programmed learning? As I see it, too many people have been shown, guided, directed. I have no wish to *make* anyone know something. So I come to the conclusion that . . . teaching is, for me, a relatively unimportant and vastly over-valued activity. As soon as we focus on teaching the question arises, what shall we teach? What, from our superior vantage point, does the other person need to know? I wonder if, in this modern world, we are justified in the presumption that we are wise about the future and the young are foolish. Are we really sure as to what they should know.[11]

In this chapter, we have explored what it is that makes the teacher and the faculty member so willing—in fact so determined—to avoid his students' as well as his own feelings and, hence, become an intellectual half-man. One of the possible answers we looked into was that perspective teachers may have conditioned into them, in our graduate education systems, certain insecurities resulting from the process of having to jump over a continuous series of artificial hurdles in their training. We took a look at the insecure personality traits of the typical faculty member. We found him to be an inwardly focusing individual with basic personal insecurities who, on the one hand, had feelings of superiority about intellectual matters stemming, perhaps, from easily won cognitive victories in the classroom; on the other hand, he had basic feelings of inferiority, maladjustment, and hostility to that which is emotional or non-bookish.

Again, we tried to empathize by looking at the problem through the eyes of a student who presented his view of the importance of integrating the intellectual with the affective to produce a more humanistic education.

Finally, we explored the notion that a faculty member or teacher who assumes what I call "status authority," standing behind the podium with his titles and lecturing "down" at a collective body of students, will have an almost impossible time being relevant to his students. On the other hand, the faculty member or teacher who is

---

[11] Rogers, *op. cit.*, p. 103.

able to assume what I call "natural authority," authority earned from sharing with his students the resources he has—himself, his friends, his knowledge, his experience, his students and his feelings —will find that being relevant comes from being natural and real. Natural authority is gained from sharing a relevant learning experience—an experience in which the students and the teacher become colleagues, learning from one another.

In the next part of this book we will take a look at what some of the pioneers in humanistic education see as answers to these serious problems.

part **II**

Learning to Feel

Introduction to Part II

The only legitimate objective in teaching is that the student shall be changed in such a way as to transcend mere intellectualizing and to become a better, more fulfilled person. I guess we are looking for what you call "joy." We want something to happen to students which inculcates a joy of life they can carry out of the classroom and into life. Pedagogically we want students to have meaningful experiences. Our failures in these attempts have become increasingly evident to me over the years . . . A year ago I would not have believed it, but it is evident that the cult of "academic excellence" has succeeded to the point where it will be necessary to develop special experiences, like T-groups, in which young people will be encouraged to take the time necessary to discover what it is like to be alive and human.

—A humanistic high school teacher—

We will now explore some of the various ways that learning to feel can open up new educational vistas through feeling to learn. The pioneering efforts to develop the human half of man by some of the notables in the field as well as some great work of other less well-known educators will be sampled. Additionally, this part of the book will sample and highlight some of the humanistic education classroom techniques being employed by these innovators and others.

3

Pioneering Efforts to Develop the Human Half of Man

I see the facilitation of learning as the aim of education, the way in which we can learn to live as individuals in process. . . . We know . . . that the initiation of such learning rests not upon the teaching skills of the leader, not upon his scholarly knowledge of the field, not upon his curricular planning, not upon his use of audiovisual aids, not upon the programmed learning he utilizes, not upon his lectures and presentations, not upon an abundance of books, though each of these might at one time or another be utilized as an important resource. No, the facilitation of significant learning rests upon certain attitudinal qualities which exist in the personal relationship between the facilitator and the learner.

Carl Rogers

Let us sample briefly some of the pioneering efforts in humanistic education by such notables as Abraham Maslow, Alexander Lowen, Carl Rogers, Frederick Perls, and those working at the Esalen Institute, as well as some of the innovative work being carried out in classroom frontiers by a handful of educators such as Dwight Allen, George Brown, George Leonard, Terry Borton, Masha Rudman, Gloria Castillo, Sid Simon, Sylvia Ashton-Warner, Gerald Weinstein, and others. Although these educators show wide diversity in their approaches to humanistic education, it will be apparent that a certain interrelation exists in their work.

Humanistic education is an umbrella. It has clustered beneath it a diverse and amazing collection of people: unconventional innovators from the Esalen Institute poking fearlessly into the nooks and crannies of human potential, pragmatic industrialists seeking to maximize the productive output of the brains they employ, utopian thinkers busily creating strategies to keep society viable throughout the twentieth century and into the next, Third Force psychologists and psychiatrists setting forth their image of man as a self-actualizer, uncovering the essence of his humanity, and educators desperately attempting to combat the wholesale failure of the urban public school systems.

The movement is rather undisciplined and inchoate, an unorganized aggregate of highly individualistic innovators. The thin glue that holds them together is the notion that the integration of affective and cognitive processes in the learning experience is a highly desirable, potentially real, but seldom practiced state of affairs.

While there are a few large-scale programs in affective processes there is a veritable ferment of activity taking place throughout the country. More and more individuals, groups, and institutions are realizing the importance and potential of these techniques and they are being tried out in a bewildering array of situations.

ABRAHAM H. MASLOW—
The Underpinning of the Movement

An individual whose work underlies many of the philosophical and psychological frameworks of the humanistic education movement is Abraham H. Maslow. Maslow considered himself to be part of "Third Force" or "Humanistic" psychology. He described this branch of psychology as one which has developed a new image of man, one which accepts the reality of higher human needs, motives, and capacities. The conception of the self as developed in Third Force psychology is one which speaks of man's essence, his intrinsic nature, his humanity, his animal nature. Maslow believed that man becomes fully human when the needs of his inherent nature are uncovered and realized. He felt that man must listen to the small, delicate impulse-voices from within—the hints of his animal nature. These voices speak to him of his essence—his species–nature—as well as his own uniqueness. When the organism discovers his humanity at a deep enough level, it emerges with discovering his selfhood. The fully human, self-actualized person is true to his specieshood while he moves toward the fulfillment of his unique potential.

Maslow's concept of "a hierarchy of needs" is one which has great application to humanistic educational management as well as to education. Maslow's premise is that there is a hierarchy of needs progressing from the lowest order of bodily needs to the highest order of "self actualization needs." A higher order of need does not emerge until the need below that one is fairly well satisfied or saturated. A satisfied need is one that is no longer a motivator of behavior. The lowest order of need includes the bodily wants such as hunger and thirst. When those are well satisfied the second order of need, for safety or security, emerges and becomes a motivator of behavior. If one is hungry, however, the search for food becomes the primary motivator of behavior and higher orders of needs become irrelevant.

This second order of needs involves protection from attack and the elements, a shelter and clothes, an income, insurance, hospital care, and other general forms of security. When these are relatively well satisfied, the social needs, for companionship and other human contact, emerge. When these are met, the next higher order, the ego needs, emerge as motivators of behavior. These important needs are for recognition, status and esteem. After these are fairly well satisfied the highest order of needs, for self-actualization or creativity in the broadest sense of the term, emerge. Few people in our society have this highest order of need well satisfied. Certainly those that have seriously unsatisfied lower order needs, rarely achieve self-actualization.[1]

Some important work which has direct application to "humanistic management" parallels Maslow's work. This is the work of such people as Chris Argyis, Douglas McGregor, and Rensis Likert. In general, they say that managers or administrators should build into their organizations opportunities for teachers or employees to satisfy their own needs while working toward organizational objectives. Chris Argyis and Douglas McGregor point out that most organizations, however, are still treating their people as though their lower orders of needs—which in our present period of prosperity (in spite of low teacher salaries) are fairly well saturated—are not met and hence are primary motivators of behavior. The fact is that unions, worker mobility, guaranteed wages, fringe benefits, social opportunities, welfare, and other security measures generally ensure that the average teacher's or other employee's lower order of needs are fairly well satisfied. Hence, managers and administrators should

---

[1] See Maslow's *Toward a Psychology of Being* (Princeton: D. Van Nostrand, 1962); *Motivation and Personality* (New York: Harper & Brothers, 1954); and "Some Educational Implications of the Humanistic Psychologies," *Harvard Educational Review* (Fall 1968).

be directing much more attention to the higher ego and self-actualization needs which today are the primary motivators of teachers' and employees' behavior.

Chapter 7 will deal in more detail with the application of Maslow's philosophy to educational management. However, the same idea is applicable to children in our classrooms. The teachers who are achieving success are building into the classroom situation opportunities for children to begin to meet their own ego and self-actualization needs. Many of the other pioneers in humanistic education use Maslow's seminal work as a point of departure for their own theories.

GEORGE LEONARD—*Education in the Future*

George Leonard is a utopian thinker who embraces the image of man presented by Maslow and the Third Force psychologists. The main thesis of his book *Education and Ecstasy* is "that the highly interactive, regenerative technological society now emerging will work best, indeed will require, something akin to mass genius, mass creativity and lifelong learning."[2] He is saying that for society to remain viable it will have to produce self-actualized men on a mass scale. He believes that the schools as they now exist retard the process of self-actualization. They are not designed to produce whole men, but rather the fragmentation of man. Schools have forced the segregation of senses and emotions and intellect in order to produce human beings who are well-regulated components.

Specialization, standardization, narrow competition, eager acquisition, aggression, detachment from the self—without them, it has seemed, the social machinery would break down. But Leonard is postulating a new post-civilized, post-literate, retribalized society in which the fragmentation of man is dysfunctional. He feels that society's demands are changing radically, and that schools as they now exist are inculcating human characteristics that will not work much longer.

Leonard visualizes a kind of education that will "return man to himself," that is, one which will encourage rather than stifle aware-

---

[2] George Leonard, *Education and Ecstasy* (New York: Delacorte Press, Dell Publishing Co., Inc., 1968).

ness, one which will help people become truly responsive and therefore truly responsible. These are skills crucial to the survival of the race—not the narrow competition, eager acquisition, and aggression which the schools have been fostering. If the schools encourage students to self-actualize, to move toward the fulfillment of their own unique potential, narrow competition will be impossible. And if the students, in the process of self-actualization, experience the joy and ecstasy which accompanies uncovering one's essence and realizing its potential, then eager acquisition and aggression will lose their potency as motivators of learning.

Leonard postulates that the kind of educational experience that he is advocating requires a "free-learning situation." This is one in which the student is free to go anywhere within the school and do anything he pleases, so long as he does not harm himself or his fellow students. Leonard reports that the children he observed at the free-learning school on West Fifteenth Street in New York City exhibited a joyful intensity while learning. The principal of the school has found that in the free-learning environment the children often help each other, and that they are, in fact, the *best* teachers. Leonard believes that the free-learning situation is educationally more efficient and, in the long run, easier to handle than the traditional classroom.

THE "DISCOVERY SCHOOLS" IN ENGLAND

Related to Leonard's concept of free-learning are the views of Joseph Featherstone about the restructing of infant schools in Britain. Featherstone observed classrooms in which the structure was very similar to that of the free-learning school described by Leonard. There was little organized activity for the class as a whole. The children were on their own, moving about and talking quite freely. Every class had a library alcove stocked with books on a variety of subjects and geared to various reading levels. No standardized textbooks or class readers were used. A vast array of equipment, materials, and miscellaneous objects of all sorts were available for the children to use at will.

On a recent visit to one of these "discovery schools," the Julian Primary School in London, I was amazed by the work of the Headmaster, Mr. E. A. Orsborn, and his group of dedicated teachers. In primary classes of forty children (about the average number in London), teachers experienced few of the "control" problems viewed in the average "overcrowded" U. S. classroom of 25 students. Why? The children controlled themselves. In the free-structured classrooms, children four to seven years old were busily engaged in discoveries such as which numbers come up most frequently when shooting dice, supervising the mating of different colored mice, acting out their own fantasy play on a stage they constructed themselves, and using their initiative to organize their own reading tutorial program in which eight year olds were working with five year olds teaching them to read (also with no control problems)! Both the child who "taught" and the child who "learned" were profiting from the experience—one was learning content while the other was learning how to communicate content. Since each child designed and engineered his own learning, he was able to develop at his own pace and according to his individual needs. In the free-learning environment there is no need for tracking. In fact, with students teaching each other, it is best if there are children of various ages and levels of development in each class. As James Coleman and others have stated, children learn more from other children than they do from teachers, who should be catalysts for discovery. In these classes learning was a pleasurable experience for the children. As they explored and experimented with the environment and one another there was no difference between work and play. I was amazed by the high motivation and self discipline as these children related to self-chosen content.

In the Julian Primary School I saw children teaching other children to read using some of the successful techniques practiced by Sylvia Ashton-Warner.[3] Each child had a little book of his own *words*—words that conveyed to him special feelings or meanings which perhaps had been obsessing him one day or another. These words, vital to the child's life and expression, were learned instantaneously and never forgotten. The children displayed exciting, natural, practical vocabularies. Rather than displaying the shyness and distraction observed by visitors in the average school, these children were completely uninhibited in approaching me and the par-

---

[3] Sylvia Ashton-Warner, *Teacher* (New York: Simon & Schuster, Inc., 1963), p. 26.

ents who roamed in and out of the classes to ask us how to spell a word which was important to them. Certainly, this is a far more desirable way to use and learn words than the inane "Dick and Jane-isms" so common in many classrooms. The headmaster, rather than organizing a PTA remote from the classroom, had declared "open school" policy which encouraged parents to come into school at anytime and interest themselves in the materials, the children, and the environment. In his opinion, more beneficial results came from this in a month than usually result from a year of PTA diatribe. These schools have a good measure of the "education and ecstasy" dreamed of by Leonard.

GEORGE I. BROWN—
Affective Techniques for the Classroom

Dr. George I. Brown of the Department of Education, University of California, Santa Barbara, in conjunction with Esalen Institute, has conducted an important exploratory study of the ways in which affective techniques can be adapted for use in the normal school curriculum. Having completed a successful first year, the project was expanded to include work with elementary school teachers, junior high social studies teachers, and senior high English teachers. This project is one of several financed by the Ford Foundation's Fund for the Advancement of Education in its move toward greater support of the affective education area. The goals of the project were as follows.[4]

1. To collect, describe, and organize available approaches to learning in the affective domain.
2. To select from these approaches those that can be adapted for the public school curriculum.
3. To develop sample lessons and units based on these, including special materials where necessary, and to try these out in the classroom.
4. To examine how these can fit into the conventional curriculum, or how the curriculum can be modified to include them with an end toward better integration of the affective and cognitive domains.

---

[4] George I. Brown, *Human Teaching for Human Learning* (New York: McGraw-Hill Book Co., 1970).

5. To make a face evaluation of these changes.
6. On the basis of the results of this pilot project, to plan broader model programs such as subject area and school wide or district wide curriculum improvement, including a more vigorous evaluation.

The basic definitions which preface the project report follow:

Affective: refers to the feeling or emotional aspect of experience and learning
Cognitive: refers to the activity of the mind in knowing an object, to intellectual functioning.
Humanistic Education: when the affective and cognitive domains are integrated in individual and group learning.[5]

The project was structured around a series of workshops in which the staff studied theories and experienced methods of humanistic psychology, and planned how to integrate some of these affective experiences with cognitive learning in the classroom. The teachers then carried out these plans in their individual classrooms and assessed the results.

One of the best things about the project was that it afforded the opportunity for classroom teachers from various levels to gather periodically at Esalen to develop and experience various affective techniques which had classroom application, and then to return to their classrooms to try out what they had developed. After trying them out, they would gather again at Esalen to share experiences of successes and failures from their classroom experimentation.

An example of the kind of work with which they experimented was the teaching of an English unit for tenth graders using Stephen Crane's *The Red Badge of Courage* as the subject matter, but teaching it in a way that integrated the cognitive curriculum material with affective experiences. Aaron Hillman, the teacher who developed this exercise, wanted his students not only to gain a greater understanding of the novel, but also to better understand human beings, to see themselves in the lives of others, and to further their skills in critical thinking and in communication (verbal and non-verbal).[6]

In approaching *The Red Badge of Courage* in a humanistic way, Aaron Hillman employed diverse means including daily diaries,

---

[5] *Ibid.*
[6] *Ibid.,* pp. 5–12.

readings, discussions, writings, field trips, and affective exercises. Some of the questions explored and exercises used are listed below:

- What is your courage?
- What is the difference between you and manhood?
- A comparison of Civil War and World War II poetry.
- Interviewing someone who has known war.
- Debating whether or not war is inevitable.
- Collecting a series of pictures that represent courage and weaving them into a story.
- Awareness exercises which help the students contact their environment in much the same way the hero contacts his thoughts and actions in the novel "before the battle."
- Having the students form groups of six, and then telling each group to get rid of one member followed by a discussion of how it felt to be rejected from a group as the hero in the novel was rejected from time to time.
- Listening to war music and writing down freely associated thoughts and feelings that are evoked and then sharing them in small groups.
- Having the students (with eyes closed) recall a specific incident in the novel and then concentrate on getting in touch with the environment of that situation—the temperature, the surroundings, etc. The students go through the incident from beginning to end, and then instead of trying to understand it, they are told to drop it entirely and "with a bounce of the imagination" to jump into another character's place and experience the same incident from the beginning, but this time from inside that other person.[7]

This study by George Brown contains the entire curriculum unit on *The Red Badge of Courage* as well as detailed descriptions of other curricula developed by the Ford–Esalen Project staff and participating teachers.

The author had the enlightening experience of attending an Esalen workshop conducted by George Brown and his talented wife Judy. This experience defies description. Esalen and the environment of Big Sur provide a spiritual experience. Contrary to the spectacular articles in the popular periodicals (written to sell magazines),

---

[7] *Ibid.*, pp. 5–16.

emphasizing nudity and promiscuity, Esalen is a vitally important haven for innovation in the behavioral sciences. Promiscuity is the exception at Esalen workshops rather than being the rule (there are few rules at Esalen). Openness, freedom, and self awareness are the rules, if any exist. George and Judy Brown are skilled and delicate group leaders. George Brown is exceptionally skilled in Gestalt Therapy described later in this chapter as is Richard Price, the Vice President of Esalen. I have had the liberating experience of doing work on the Gestalt "hot seat" with both of them.

The Esalen Institute brochure describes its functions as follows:

> Esalen Institute is a center to explore those trends in the behavioral sciences, religion and philosophy which emphasize the potentialities of human existence. Its activities consist of seminars and workshops . . . , research and consulting programs, and a residential program exploring new directions in education and the behavioral sciences.

Michael Murphy, the President of Esalen, is dedicated to the idea of providing a learning haven for aware humanistic "change agents" who can return to society to sensitively attack, in antibiotic fashion, the festering depersonalization which has infected our society. He has also pledged to launch renewed efforts in the area of humanistic education and research. Dr. Julian Silverman, the Research Director of Esalen, brings considerable research sophistication to the group work being done there. Dr. Silverman was formerly the Chief of Perceptual and Cognitive Studies of the Adult Psychiatry Branch of the National Institute of Mental Health.

After admitting that Esalen defies description, a psychologist friend describes Esalen this way:

> I have grown and shrunk there; I have made friends, lost them and regained them; I have known pleasure, pain, loneliness, despair, acceptance, rejection, and peace there. I have seen and found myself there. I can hardly speak of it dispassionately.

GERALD WEINSTEIN—
The "Curriculum of Concerns"

The prime goal of the Ford–Esalen Project was to develop affective techniques that would enhance the existing curriculum of the public schools and thereby facilitate cognitive learning. There is another approach to humanistic education which aims at the development of a whole new curriculum area for the public schools—the "curriculum of concerns." In this approach the subject matter is the learner—his emotions, his feelings, his thoughts. The goal is to assist the student in developing his sense of identity, his sense of power, and his sense of connectedness. The affective domain becomes a "subject," as biology and English are subjects. This is the approach to humanistic education espoused by Gerald Weinstein and his associates Gerald Loney, Richard Nessen, Mark Polon, and Charles Ungerleider of the University of Massachusetts School of Education.[8]

The two approaches to humanistic education in the public schools are compatible; they simply focus on different curriculum areas, both of which are important. A curriculum of concerns does not imply that academic subjects are not more meaningful when the cognitive and affective processes are an integral part of the learning experience. Nor does the approach of the Ford–Esalen Project imply that a curriculum of concerns should not be developed.

In fact, Brown, Weinstein, and their associates are coordinating this important venture very closely, and the Ford Foundation saw fit to financially support continued work for both of these mutually complementary activities.

Gerald Weinstein's fascinating classroom work with "one way feeling" glasses and his "Education of the Self" unit will be described in Chapter 4.

DWIGHT ALLEN—
A Revolutionary in Teacher Training

Dwight Allen, Dean of the University of Massachusetts School of Education, is one of the most effective innovators in teacher training to emerge in this decade. His past work at Stanford University in microteaching, differentiated staffing, and the "student as teacher" has been disseminated through films, tapes, and even through the somewhat unwieldy communication lines between our

---

[8] See Gerald Weinstein and Mario Fantini, *The Disadvantaged* (New York: Harper and Row, Publishers, 1968); *Making the Urban School Work* (New York: Holt, Reinhart, and Winston, 1968); and Gerald Loney, Richard Nessen, Mark Polon, Charles Ungerleider, and Gerald Weinstein, "Curriculum For the Inside: Humanistic Education" *Trend* (Spring, 1969), pp. 18–19.

country's elementary and secondary classrooms. Under his leadership, the School of Education at the University of Massachusetts is now planning a revolution in teacher training with a great deal of emphasis on humanistic education. In his first year there Dwight Allen brought in thirty-five new faculty members, most of whom hadn't been previously influenced by schools of education, plus one hundred fifty new doctoral students, many of whom had been "drop-outs" from irrelevant portions of society. This exciting group of people erased the slate clean and, after tossing out all the old required courses for the first semester, initiated a "planning year" during which they experimented with what a relevant school of education ought to be. Students and faculty worked side-by-side in this process with no status distinctions. Students received course credit for the planning work in committees. If a committee and its work appeared to be irrelevant, it dissolved itself and students either began a new venture or worked on one that appeared to be more relevant.

One interesting change already implemented is the abolishment of all grades and conventional graduate student transcripts. All courses are now "pass-fail," and instead of a transcript showing "3 hours of Ed. 432," etc., each graduate student maintains a portfolio containing descriptions of "relevant learning experiences"—in or out of the classroom. Additionally, credit "modules" are granted for educational, non-course experiences. How much more relevant and useful this system is both for students, the faculty, and future employers than the meaningless transcripts of credits being used by most institutions!

Dwight Allen is a believer in juxtaposition of views, experiences, and approaches. A look at his faculty demonstrates this. He has everything, from historians to psychologists, and a former gang leader. A *Saturday Review* article on this exciting school makes the point.

> The planning committees cover most of the traditional areas, plus a few not frequently found at other institutions. Some groups appear to be working toward contradictory ends; for instance, one committee studying "student centered teaching" is "testing the assumption that effective learning occurs best in the context of a student exploring his own interests," while another is concentrating on means for evaluating teachers according to performance

criteria. Both plans will probably be used next year since, one faculty member recently explained, "we really don't know what works. That's what this place is about."

Credentials at U Mass don't count as much as Allen's perception of people with ideas, talents, or perspectives that could prove useful in shaping a new education school.

For instance, there is a full professor with no Ph.D. who is a nationally known consultant on urban education. One thirty-seven-year-old instructor was a mailman until he earned a B.A. a couple of years ago; he is also a founder and executive director of one of the few successful ghetto community centers in the country. Another instructor without any advanced degrees is a founder of Black Mountain College, an experimental "community of scholars" that flourished briefly several years ago. One associate professor who has a Ph.D. in history from Yale is a former campaign manager for a successful state assembly candidate. Another example of this new eclecticism is a full professor who is thirty-six years old, Phi Beta Kappa, a Rhodes Scholar with a B.A. and M.A. in music, and a Ph.D. in Jungian psychology and social anthropology from the University of Chicago (he wrote, choreographed, and produced a ballet for his dissertation).

This potpourri produces a dynamism and excitement that animates education both as an academic subject and an arena for action and social change.

One device that may be a useful starting point in this respect is the educational "marathon," during which classes are suspended for a day or two so that students, faculty members, and outsiders can attend a number of simultaneous events, ranging from lectures on such topics as "The Bomb, the Beatles, and the Second Coming—The Problem of Identity and the High School Student," displays of educational technology, "concerts" given by the Jungian musician in which musical analogies are used in a lecture on "Becoming Your Real Self," to selections from more than 160 hours of films and video tapes on the New York teachers' strike.

The way these films were made is indicative of the unfettered spontaneity of the "planning year" at the school. On a Thursday in the middle of the strike last fall, a group of students and faculty members decided it was a good opportunity to gather a wide range of views on the problems of urban education. By Friday the decision had been made to take five camera crews to New York, and $5,000 had been raised from a foundation to support a week's expenses. The planning was done over the weekend, and by Monday morning the crews were spread out over the city, filming and interviewing.

The slate has been wiped clean at U Mass, but that does not mean that some of the traditional assumptions won't be reaffirmed.

It is just that nothing is being taken on faith and that everything is being re-examined from an empirical point of view in an attempt to find techniques and structures that speak to contemporary educational needs. Allen and his staff are gambling that they can come up with some relevant responses. They know these responses might not be answers, so they are hedging their bets and wagering on several different horses. None of them may end up in the money, but they wouldn't have been able to find that out unless they took the initial risks of action. As one staff member has remarked, "Education won't be changed by throwing books at it."[9]

Gerald Weinstein whose work is described elsewhere in this chapter is the director of the Center for Humanistic Education located in the University of Massachusetts School of Education. Also clustered around Dwight Allen in this fertile environment is a group of other "humanistically oriented" educators such as Masha Rudman and her "Learning Theater" project, also mentioned in this chapter, and other no less exciting individuals engaged in the joyful endeavor of "learning to feel and feeling to learn."

TERRY BORTON AND NORMAN NEWBERG

Terry Borton and Norman Newberg, working through the Philadelphia Public Schools, developed a theory of affective education based on explicit attention to both the students emotional concerns and the processes involved in learning. This approach was designed to move students beyond the "turn on" stage of initial enthusiasm, and help them learn the logical and psychological processes which would give them control over their own growth. Borton and Newberg wrote two high school courses, one in communication and one in urban affairs, which used this process approach to relate the private world of the students' experience and public knowledge of subject matter.[10] These courses are the first step in an attempt to develop a K–12 track that would provide, within the traditional school framework, the option for a more humanistic approach to education.

---

9 Wallace Roberts, "Voices in the Classroom, Clean Slate at U. Mass.," *Saturday Review*, January 18, 1969, p. 63.

10 Terry Borton, and Norman Newberg, *Education for Student Concerns*, Philadelphia Public Schools, 1969. *See also* Terry Borton, *Reach, Touch, and Teach: Student Concerns and Process Education* (New York: McGraw-Hill Book Co., Inc., 1970.

In speaking of the critics who helped create the climate for humanistic education, Borton suggests that:

> The new critics do not simply attack the schools for their academic incompetence, as did the Rickovers of a decade ago. They are equally concerned with the schools' basic lack of understanding that students are human beings with feelings as well as intellects. Jonathan Kozol has given a gripping sense of the "destruction of the hearts and minds of Negro children" in his *Death at an Early Age*. In *How Children Fail* John Holt has shown that even in the best "progressive" schools, children live in constant fear which inhibits their learning and Paul Goodman's *Compulsory Mis-Education* has made a powerful case for his contention that "the present school system is leading straight to 1984." The intuitive warnings of these "romantic critics" have been backed up by statistical evidence from the largest survey of education ever conducted, James Coleman's *Equality of Educational Opportunity*. This survey correlates academic achievement with attitudes such as a student's self concept, sense of control over his fate, and interest in school. The study concludes that these attitudes and feelings are a combination of many of the factors which educators have usually thought were crucial, such as class size, salary of teachers, facilities, curriculum.
>
> The pressure to deal more directly with student feelings (increasingly a pressure from students as well as critics) has given rise to dozens of different projects.[11]

FREDERICK S. PERLS

> I do my thing, and you do your thing.
> I am not in this world to live up to your expectations.
> And you are not in this world to live up to mine.
> You are you and I am I.
> And if by chance we find each other, it's beautiful.
> If not, it can't be helped.[12]

Fritz Perls, the father of Gestalt group therapy, was one of the leaders in the self-awareness field. His book *Gestalt Therapy Verbatim* and the book he co-authored with Ralph Hefferline and Paul Goodman entitled *Gestalt Therapy: Excitement and Growth in the*

---

[11] Terry Borton, "Reach, Touch, and Teach," *Saturday Review*, Jan. 18, 1969, p. 57.

[12] Fritz Perls in an address to the Association for Humanistic Psychology, Washington, D.C., 1969.

Human Personality are excellent sources of the various "Affective Techniques" and exercises for self-awareness leading the reader up through more advanced Gestalt therapy exercises.

Dr. Perls (both M.D. and Ph.D.), once a colorful philosopher in residence at Esalen working with younger psychologists and psychiatrists and with Gestalt workshops and groups, was until his death in 1970 Director of the Gestalt Therapy Institute of Canada. He was one of those rare individuals who inserted a message in most everything he said.

I had the privilege of meeting Fritz Perls briefly while at Esalen in early 1969. The brief exchange involved an introduction during which Fritz Perls and I shook hands, with me giving my habitual firm hand shake. Fritz Perls winced and withdrew his hand quickly saying, "Not so hard." I began to stammer a reply like "a good firm hand shake, you know . . ." "is a sign of weakness," interrupted Perls quickly. "It's a cover-up for lack of warmth and sensitivity which can be expressed in a gentle hand clasp." So much for my short encounter and personal lesson from Fritz Perls. Of course, he was right. In the enlightening days that followed at Esalen, I was to learn a great deal more about my "cover-ups" and masks.

Fritz Perls did a great deal to advance the concept of group Gestalt therapy to the point where he felt that individual therapy, outside a group setting, is almost obsolete.[13]

Perhaps this would be a good place to make it clear that I am not suggesting in this book that teachers should practice therapy in the classroom. Clearly, the classroom is not the place to dig deeply into an individual's past. Educators, however, have been too shy in dealing with "here and now" feelings which invariably foment between students, and between students and teachers. Certainly, most counselors and psychologists have made their message painfully clear that laymen should not be practicing the professional's trade. Some counselors are quite threatened by the advent of the humanistic education movement. It's as though the teacher's dealing with feelings in the classroom will prevent them from having to be dealt with by the counselor outside of the classroom. Of course, if that happened it would be a blessing, but we're far from that utopian stage when

---

[13] See a paper delivered by Perls at the American Psychological Association Convention in New York City, September, 1966, entitled, "Workshop vrs. Individual Therapy." *Also see* Fritz Perls *Gestalt Therapy Verbatim*, published by the Real People Press, 939 Carol Lane, Lafayette, California, in 1969.

children have their concerns so well worked out with their teachers that counselors become obsolete. Carl Rogers stresses the fact that there is solid evidence that a Ph.D. or M.D. is not necessary for group work: "An outstanding example is the work of Rioch (1963) showing that selected housewives can be given training in a year's time which enables them to carry on therapy with disturbed individuals—therapy which in its quality is indistinguishable from work of experienced professionals."[14] In spite of this, I am still not advocating that teachers practice therapy. What I am advocating is that they have the courage to push forward—and push hard—against the boundaries that are keeping them confined purely within the cognitive realm. They must widen their sphere of influence to include the affective domain as well. Only by stepping out and taking the inherent risks—risks which are present in all meaningful human encounters—will progress be made.

PAUL GOODMAN

Paul Goodman, who has been freely quoted throughout this book, is an individual admirably impatient with our existing educational system. His books *Compulsory Mis-Education* and *The Community of Scholars* reflect his views that we must humanize our educational system before it is torn down completely by the student it has alienated:

> It's in the schools and from mass media rather than at home or from their friends that the mass of our citizens in all classes learn that life is inevitably routine, depersonalized, venally graded; that it is best to toe the mark and shut up; that there is no place for spontaneity, open sexuality, free spirit. Trained in the schools, they go on to the same quality of jobs, culture and politics. This is education, mis-education, socializing to the national norms and regimenting to the national needs.[15]

and:

> There is good evidence that normal children will make up the first seven years of schoolwork with four to seven months of good teaching.[16]

---

[14] Rogers, *op. cit.,* p. 319.

[15] Goodman, *op. cit.,* p. 23.

[16] *Ibid.,* p. 32.

He proposes some possible solutions to our school problems:

1. No school at all for a few classes.
2. No school buildings for a few classes (use the city as a school).
3. Use unlicensed adults of the community (a druggist, store-keeper, mechanic)
4. Make class attendance not compulsory.
5. Decentralize an urban school into small units with 20-50 in available storefronts or clubhouses and equip them with record players and pinball machines for combining play, socializing, discussion, and formal teaching.
6. Use some school money to send children to marginal farms for a couple of months of the year (six children from mixed backgrounds to a farmer).[17]

In addressing himself to the problems of our colleges and universities, Goodman suggests:

> Two modest changes, that are feasible almost immediately, that would entail no risk whatever, and yet would immensely improve academic communities and liberate them in relation to society. First, one-half dozen prestigious liberal arts colleges—Amherst, Swarthmore, Connecticut, Wesleyan, Carlton—would announce that they required for admission a two year period, after high school, spent in some maturing activity. By "maturing activity" could be meant: working for a living (especially if the job were gotten without connections), community service such as volunteer service in a hospital, the domestic Peace Corps, the army; a course of purposeful travel that met required standards; an independent enterprise in art; business, or science away from home with something to show for the time spent. The purpose would be twofold: to get students with enough life-experience to be educable on the college level, and to break the lockstep of 12 years of doing assigned lessons for grades.
>
> Second, abolish grading and use testing only and entirely for pedagogic purposes as teachers see fit.[18]

He suggests that:

> In reconstructing the present system, the right principles seem to be the following:
> 1. To make it easier for youngsters to gravitate to what suits them, and to provide many points of quitting and return.

---

[17] *Ibid.*, p. 34.
[18] *Ibid.*, pp. 125–126.

2. To cut down the loss of student hours in parroting and forgetting, and the loss of teacher hours in talking to the deaf.
3. To engage more directly in the work of society, and to have useful products to show instead of stacks of examination papers.[19]

To be candid, I do not think that we will change along these lines. Who is for it? The suburbs must think I am joking, I understand so little of status and salary. Negroes will say I am downgrading them. The big corporations like the system as it is, only more so. The labor unions don't want kids doing jobs. And the new major class of school-monks has entirely different ideas of social engineering. Nevertheless, in my opinion, the present system is not viable. The change, when it comes, will *not* be practical and orderly.[20]

Finally:

. . . Non-directive interpersonal contact . . . acceptance and understanding rather than cajoling, coercing, ordering, forbidding, threatening, advising, etc. Allowing, . . . students to express their hostility, guilt, secret wishes. In this atmosphere, it seems, it is possible for the students to feel again the spontaneous interest that any young person might take in a reasoned subject matter and to exercise what intelligence they had. It does not matter if this is called "therapy" or not, I would prefer a use of language that would call it precisely the normal state of things: the lively response of normal students to a teacher who knows something and who pays attention to them as human beings.[21]

CARL ROGERS

Carl Rogers is Resident Fellow at the Center for Studies of the Person, La Jolla, California, and he was formerly with the Western Behavioral Sciences Institute. Carl Rogers was recipient of the American Psychological Association's first Distinguished Scientific Contribution Award.

Carl Rogers has written extensively concerning his experience and research in psychotherapy. His book *On Becoming a Person* is a classic. However, he has written also what, in the author's opin-

---

19 *Ibid.*, p. 153.
20 *Ibid.*, p. 154.
21 *Ibid.*, p. 284.

ion, is the best book in the field of humanistic education. This book *Freedom to Learn* is Carl Rogers' first attempt to put down for teachers and educators his pertinent thoughts about learning which have been so popular and rewarding to those in psychology who have read his works. The theme of this book is that learning can be enjoyable when the teacher becomes a "learning facilitator" and deals with feelings as well as with the intellect. The book shows how three teachers—a sixth grade teacher, a professor of college freshmen, and a graduate faculty member—have provided in different ways the exciting freedom in which their students learn. He presents the attitudes which he feels the successful learning facilitator must achieve and suggests ways for achieving such attitudes. He then presents some of his basic philosophy and convictions about learning. From there he deals with the problems of values in the modern world. In the last chapter he presents a plan for bringing about self-directed change through intensive group experience in an educational system.

At the beginning of this chapter Carl Rogers was quoted as saying ". . . the facilitation of significant learning rests upon certain attitudinal qualities which exist in the personal *relationship* between the facilitator and the learner." Carl Rogers and his associates first discovered these attitude qualities through their work in the field of psychotherapy, but they are now finding increasing evidence that they apply in the classroom as well. These thoughts of Carl Rogers are so relevant to the theme of this book that I feel it essential to quote from him at some length:

1. *Realness in the facilitator*
When the facilitator is a real person, being what he is, entering into a relationship with the learner without presenting a front or a façade, he is much more likely to be effective. . . . he can be enthusiastic, . . . bored, . . . interested, . . . angry, . . . sensitive and sympathetic. Because he accepts these feelings as his own he has no need to impose them on his students. . . . Thus, he is a person to his students, not a faceless embodiment of a curricular requirement nor a sterile tube through which knowledge is passed from one generation to the next.

2. *Prizing, Acceptance, Trust*
I think of it as prizing the learner, prizing his feelings, his opinions, his person. It is a caring for the learner, but a non-possessive caring.

It is an acceptance of this other individual as a separate person, having worth in his own right. It is a basic trust—a belief that this other person is somehow fundamentally trustworthy. . . . an imperfect human being with many feelings, many potentialities.

3. *Empathetic Understanding*

When the teacher has the ability to understand the student's reactions from the inside, has a sensitive awareness of the way the process of education and learning seems *to the student*, then again the likelihood of significant learning is increased.

This kind of understanding is sharply different from the usual evaluative understanding, which follows the pattern of, "I understand what is wrong with you."[22]

. . . Only slowly can we learn to be truly real. For first of all, one must be close to one's feelings, capable of being aware of them. Then one must be willing to take the risk of sharing them as they are, inside, not disguising them as judgments, or attributing them to other people. . . .

It would be most unlikely that one could hold the three attitudes I have described, . . . unless he has come to have a profound trust in the human organism and its potentialities. If I distrust the human being then I *must* cram him with information of my own choosing, lest he go his own mistaken way. But if I trust the capacity of the human individual for developing his own potentiality, then I can provide him with many opportunities and permit him to choose his own way and his own direction in his learning.[23]

When a facilitator creates, even to a modest degree, a classroom climate characterized by all that he can achieve of realness, prizing, and empathy; when he trusts the constructive tendency of the individual and the group; then he discovers that he has inaugurated an educational revolution. . . . Learning becomes life, and a very vital life at that.[24]

Carl Rogers advances a number of principles of learning which he draws from his work and the work of other associates which are also most relevant to the theme of this book:

> 1. *Human beings have a natural potentiality for learning.* They are curious about their world, until and unless this curiosity is blunted by their experience in our educational system.

[22] Rogers, *op. cit.*, pp. 106–111.

[23] *Ibid.*, p. 114.

[24] *Ibid.*, p. 115.

2. *Significant learning takes place when the subject matter is perceived by the student as having relevance for his own purposes.*
3. *Learning which involves a change of self organization—in the perception of oneself—is threatening and tends to be resented.*

Why has there been so much furor . . . concerning an adolescent boy who comes to school with long hair? Surely the length of his hair makes little objective difference. The reason seems to be that if I, as a teacher or administrator, accept the value which he placed on nonconformity then it threatens the value which I have placed on conforming to social demands. If I permit this contradiction to exist I may find myself changing, because I will be forced to a reappraisal of some of my values.

4. *Those learnings which are threatening to the self are more easily perceived and assimilated when external threats are at a minimum.*

The boy who is retarded in reading already feels threatened and inadequate because of this defining. When he is forced to attempt to read aloud in front of the group, when he is ridiculed for his efforts, when his grades are a vivid reflection of his failure, it is no surprise that he may go through several years of school with no perceptible increase in his reading ability. On the other hand, a supportive, understanding environment and a lack of grades, or an encouragement of self evaluation, remove the external threats and permit him to make progress because he is no longer paralyzed by fear.

5. *When threat to the self is low, experience can be perceived in differentiated fashion and learning can proceed.*

When [a poor reader] is called upon to recite in class the internal panic takes over and the words on the page become less intelligible symbols. . . . When he is in an environment in which he is assured of personal security . . . no threat to his ego, he is once more free to . . . move forward in the process of learning.

6. *Much significant learning is acquired through doing.*
7. *Learning is facilitated when the student participates responsibly in the learning process.*
8. *Self-initiated learning which involves the whole person of the learner—feelings as well as intellect—is the most lasting and pervasive.*
9. *Independence, creativity, and self-reliance are all facilitated when self-criticism and self-evaluation are basic and evaluation by others is of secondary importance.*
10. *The most socially useful learning in the modern world is the learning of the process of learning, a continuing openness to*

> *experience and incorporation into oneself of the process of change.*[25]

Carl Rogers questions in what possible way can he make real *contact* with his unknown readers. He likes to be heard—to truly communicate himself. Well, he has achieved this—and most phenominally, through a book—*Freedom to Learn!*

Carl Rogers is also associated with the La Jolla Program, formerly the Group for Religion and Psychology associated with the Western Behavioral Sciences Institute. This group is doing a great deal of pioneering in small encounter groups and their applications to different kinds of organizations and professions. Each summer they hold institutes for persons interested in applying small encounter groups to their work. These sessions, held at the University of California, San Diego campus, emphasize direct experience in encounter groups, both for a member and for a facilitator, plus content-centered sessions which stress a "people-oriented" philosophy of leadership. The La Jolla Program is co-directed by Bruce Meador, Douglas Land, and William Coulson, with Carl Rogers serving as consultant.

SIDNEY SIMON—*Value Theory and Practice*

Dr. Sidney Simon, formerly of Temple University, but presently with the University of Massachusetts School of Education, is an exceptionally humanistic classroom teacher who has developed classroom exercises and experiences which lead toward the development of values. In addition to teaching a section of a course on "Education of the Self," Sid Simon has designed a complete course on values. I have had the privilege of sitting in on a few of these fascinating, humanistic sessions.

Sid Simon will ask his students to list the five most important things in which they believe. Eventually he will teach them to test these values against a set of seven criteria which he believes are a fair measure for values. If a belief does not meet all seven criteria, it is less than a value, and Sid Simon calls it a "value indicator." It might

---

[25] *Ibid.*, p. 157–163.

become a value after some hard work, but at that point it is only an indicator of a value. Students are required to make separate value cards which contain a complete description of each of their values. The seven criteria against which Sid Simon measures values follow. Before something is a value:

1. You must be willing to publicly affirm it.
2. There must be an element of pride in it.
3. It must be consistent, repeated, and part of a pattern.
4. It must be chosen from alternatives.
5. It must be based on free choice.
6. It must be thought out rather than happenstance.
7. You must act on it.

Take a minute now and write down a list of the things you believe in most and apply the above criteria to them one by one and see if they are really values (they must meet all the criteria to be values).

A sample list of possible values which stimulates a great deal of thought can be presented for discussion. Take each one and decide how it applies to you. After you have done that, apply the seven criteria to these to see if any of them are values for you. This is a good list for adult classes to bring out the various aspects of values and the criteria as well as to stimulate discussion.

1. What, if anything, does your family do that is special at Christmas, Chanukah, or on holidays?
2. Do you believe that every 12th grader should be given full birth control information?
3. What plans, if any, have you made for your parents for when they become old and feeble?
4. What things, if any, do other people spend money on that you do not?
5. What percentage of the time do you feel that a woman should achieve an orgasm during sex?

When I applied the seven criteria to this list I found I had only two values out of the five possible. The first one concerned the family decoration of our Christmas tree which met all seven of the criteria. The second was that I don't spend any money on cigarettes which met all criteria. Though I believed in number 2, it didn't meet all the criteria. I fell through completely on number 3, and on number 5, my answer wasn't selected from alternatives, wasn't based on free choice, and I hadn't put a lot of thought into it. Sid Simon has a delightful example of a value with regard to number one. In his family on Christmas morning, rather than the typical rush and chaos that most families experience opening the presents followed by an anticlimatic and long Christmas day, the Simon family begins at eight in the morning at the Christmas tree with the youngest child going to the tree and getting the presents that he has made (not purchased!) and taking them one by one to each member of the family who in turn opens his gift and listens while the giver explains why he made that particular gift for that person, what it means, difficulties he had making it, etc. The youngest child takes his turn doing this for each member of the family while the family listens and watches. This is followed by the next youngest child and on up until, sometime in the evening (after breaks for meals), the father's turn to give his gifts comes. How unlike the greedy commercialized version of Christmas that has emerged throughout this country! This is a sample of a value which meets all seven criteria for that family and which undoubtedly provides a great deal of strength and happiness for them.

These exercises with values bring out how few strong ones we really have (strong values are those that meet the seven criteria). Values, even small ones, provide a great source of strength to individuals and families. Another value that Sid Simon's family has is that whenever someone in his home drops something—an egg, a glass, a pencil, etc.—someone else picks it up for him. This is a nice little value to have. When you drop something, rather than becoming depressed or angry, you can receive a little lift when someone rushes to pick it up for you. It is easy to belittle the importance and the strength that can derive from even small values, and we seem to have really few in this modern age. Another interesting exercise which Sid Simon uses in his humanistic values class is to have the students each make a list of the fifteen or twenty things that come to their minds that give them great pleasure or joy. Try this out now (if you can't list fifteen, there isn't nearly enough fun in your life). After this is done, write after each pleasure, the date that you last experienced it. This can lead to a revealing and fascinating class discussion about how we enjoy ourselves and how often. Next, place a dollar sign after each item that costs money. It was amazing to me, as I did this, that very few of the things that I really enjoy cost much money. Pleasure and happiness are inexpensive! Now go through the list again and place a "P" after those activities which usually require considerable planning. Finally, go through the list and place an "S" after those things that you generally share with someone or other people. Place an "A" after those which you do alone. This will tell you a lot about whether you are a "loner" or a gregarious person. This exercise helps lead a student into a clearer idea of what he values, why, how strongly, etc.

Sid Simon has several exercises which force students to think about priorities. After dividing the class into small groups of four, for example, he will ask university students to evaluate the following three qualities in a potential mate and rate them in order of priority one through three: great sex partner; great communicator; great child raiser. After this has been done he will have them think about a new quality they would rate even higher than the one they placed first of the three given ones, plus another new quality they would rate below the one they placed last. This is followed by what invaribly becomes a fascinating discussion in the small groups. This same exercise is done with other things such as occupations: "If you had to rate these occupations one through three, how would you rate them?"

> Pickle inspector
> Wiper at a car wash
> Toll collector

Then pick a worse occupation than any of the three and a better one. Or, "How would you like to be loved?" Rate these one, two, and three: loved more than you love; loved less than you love; loved equally but dull. Another way of forcing students to think of value priorities is to have them place the following things, as they are read off one-by-one, in the chart on page 91. How to do you feel about:

1. A favorite kind of music
2. A favorite season
3. News on TV
4. Favorite kind of ice cream
5. Favorite actor
6. Underwear preference (e.g. Fruit of the Loom over B.V.D.'s)
7. Favorite automobile
8. The man should carve the roast

9. Favorite food for breakfast
10. Favorite deodorant
11. Favorite romantic place
12. Favorite love-making position
13. Favorite type of Christmas tree
14. Favorite variety of apple
15. Part of the newspaper you always avoid
16. Favorite color of hair

Now place the items, starting with the first (don't skip around), in the chart. Use a pencil because you'll have to erase as you fill up the blocks and find the need to change priorities. Each of the four blocks under each category has the same weight or value.

Very clear preference	Pretty strong preference	Doesn't matter much	No strong feeling at all

This is a fascinating exercise which can force students to think about their values and the priorities associated with them. After doing the exercise break up into small groups or dyads for discussion.

Another interesting thing that Sid Simon has his class do is to make a collage name tag in any shape or form using any materials, drawings, cut-outs, etc., which depict something about them, their values, or the way they feel. Each day this is built upon, changed, added to, etc., to reflect the changes and growth the person may be experiencing. In one of these classes I attended, the variety and richness of expression in these name tage collages were amazing. Some were larger than the people, others were three dimensional, and they contained everything from photographs to foliage to velvet figures. But each contained deeply personal and human meaning which came out in small group discussions. It is the large number of nationally unrecognized humanistic teachers hidden in isolated classrooms throughout the country, such as Sid Simon, who make it worthwhile

to hold out hope that someday many more of our students will realize that learning can be fun and deeply meaningful.

MASHA RUDMAN

Once again we focus on the University of Massachusetts School
of Education's hotbed of innovation to take a look at Masha Rudman
and her Learning Theater—a fascinating project enabling teachers
and children to live and feel their learning. What follows is Masha's
own description of the project:

THE LEARNING THEATER

We Call it Education for the Year 2000

Creative, concerned, and perceptive teachers have always recognized that different children learn from and respond to the same
stimulus in very different ways. These teachers have attempted to
vary their teaching styles in order to reach as many students as
possible. They have encouraged their students to report on their
learning in as interesting and effective a manner as possible. And
they have always recognized that the student learns more from
what he generates and discovers than from what the teacher hands
out and pours in.

For the past two semesters we have been conducting a series of
pilot projects aimed at combining all the above practices and principles. We call our approach the Learning Theater. Why "theater"?
What is theater? Shakespeare says that *"all the world's a stage."*
Theater analyzes, influences, and interprets society. It uses the
communication process as an instrument of change. Today's theater
further expands the role of the audience so that it is involved even
more actively in the production. Effective theater stirs all the participants, including the audience, to a new understanding of themselves, a new awareness of the world, and, hopefully, to some action
or reaction leading from the learning situation. This is what education is about.

The aims of the Learning Theater stress student-initiated curriculum, decision making, acceptance of the responsibility for these
decisions, developing a sense of responsibility for one's self and for
the community, and the developing and enlarging of the reper-

toire of communication skills for each participant. The Learning Theater encourages integration of the arts and the use of many techniques of drama, music, art, and new media in order to accomplish the above aims.

Within the concept of learning as theater, every phase of education becomes involved. Teacher education must be changed both in method of preparation, and in final "product." Curriculum development and architectural structure must undergo radical change to keep pace with the thrust of this new system. Dissemination of information and involvement of the community at large are essential factors.

Although successful models of the free learning schools (such as the Leicestershire schools in England, and the Fayerweather Street School in Cambridge, Mass.) have been functioning for years, the Learning Theater moves beyond these models, providing a total learning environment, and completely removing the traditional confines of classroom, grade level, and the narrow image of the teacher. Further, it enables the student to grow and develop by following his positive instincts of curiosity, imagination, and self-fulfillment. Just as the theater's commitment is to communicate to the audience its interpretation, exploration, analysis and understanding of the world, so too members of the learning theater take the responsibility of communicating to and with themselves and each other. The continuous development of the capacity for commitment and responsible decision making is an important factor built into our concept. By insuring freedom of choice and multiple avenues of communication we end the tradition of programming a passive child. To quote George Leonard:

> Every child, every person can delight in learning. Every educator can share in that delight. The methods are available. The needs for reform are clear. The chief obstacles are simply inertia and low expectations. Actually, a new education is already here, thrusting up in spite of every barrier built against it. Why not help it happen?[26]

During the spring 1969 semester, for the first time, we offered a course in the Learning Theater for college students. We began each class with student-led improvisations aimed at increasing communication. Some are in the form of dance, some musically oriented, many are dramatic. There are no restrictions. We then move to a

---

[26] George B. Leonard, "The Future Now," *Look* (October 15, 1968).

group warmup exercise involving identifying ourselves and each other in different ways: "My name is_____; if I were a food I'd be_____." The students have taken the responsibility for sharing their reading with each other. One student, who had read Maslow's *Toward a Psychology of Being*, pre-taped a narrative, and a poetry reading with a Mozart piano concert in the background, danced, and offered to our view a montage of pictures, souvenirs, paintings and graphics, all very effectively communicating the peak experiences of her life, and the ideas inherent in Maslow's book. Other students have shared readings such as *Teacher, How Children Fail, Now: the Human Dimension, The Primary School Revolution in Britain* and others in interesting and meaningful ways.

We have explored learning styles and teaching styles through films, field trips, and demonstrations. If the response of the students is any indication, the idea is working fine. The major revision our students have suggested is that we please hold classes more often!

If we are to accept the responsibility of institutionalizing growth in today's society we must be courageous enough to discard all of our preconceptions about the current institution of education, especially those that dictate the notions of "classes," "teachers," and the stereotyped in-take-regurgitation process called learning.

Education today can be a box: sometimes its walls are "flexible," interchangeable, movable, but the confines of the box remain. Into this box we insert curricula, administrators, teachers and students. Each of these components is separate, integral to itself, and unequal in value or position compared to the others. If the box is shaken, the components might get jarred and bounce against each other, but the box is generally positioned so that it is immovable. Sometimes other components are added, but always in the context of the box. The Learning Theater does not merely open the box, but throws it away.[27]

CRYSTAL-BALL GAZING:
Some possible experiences in the Learning Theater of the future

Andrew is an exuberant five, but under pressure or under the confusion of too-quick changes he may lose his normal willingness to participate. He is at his best early in the morning, so his parents leave him at school a few minutes after 8:00. He has brought a snake

---

[27] Masha Rudman, "The Learning Theater," *Trend* (Spring, 1969), p. 29.

with him today so he heads for the receiving room to get someone to hold the snake while he puts his coat away. The other children who are there (6 children ages 5–12) are delighted with Andrew's snake and he posts SNAKES on the board. After half an hour or so Andrew decides to put the snake in the terrarium. Eight children have signed up for SNAKES and Andrew, with the help of a staff member, posts the meeting time (11:00) for the group to discuss their production.

Andrew finds he has 12 children signed up for SNAKES. He asks an older child to help and the group looks at Andrew's snake and materials for a while. The "teacher" then guides a discussion to find out what is already known and what should be expanded. The small children decide to find out:

1. How snakes grow and shed their skins
2. What they eat
3. Who and what are their friends and enemies
4. What kinds are poisonous and how to tell

Three older children remember the snake in the story of Adam and Eve and want to know more about mythical snakes. A guide is called to help children find resources. The younger children plan a trip to a science museum in two days, and they all plan to meet in three days to discuss the production. Andrew is helped to schedule his own pre-museum activities—the above listed—with others and decides it is time for lunch and play.

*   *   *   *

Eight and one-half year old Mark's day begins at the Computer Center, although most of his day is pretty well taken up with existing projects. His production of caterpillar metamorphoses is being shown today for all the school. It has been in production for a week. Mark is directing this project since it was his caterpillar that was brought in two weeks ago, and it was he who had slides taken of the change. He has a set of slides that he has put in order, and a narrative that he composed in his science studio–workshop. The climax of the slide production occurs when the Monarch butterfly achieves its freedom. Mark has had help from the Audio–Visual Sudio–Workshop in setting up the equipment and in the actual development of the slides, but he took the pictures himself, three each day at given intervals, and he researched each phase in the Science Studio–Workshop. He is now about to enter a more advanced stage in photography because of his experiences in this production. He spends from 8:30–9:30 practicing the narrative in sequence with the slides. At 9:45 his show is presented and taped on TV. He and members of his cast lead discussions and have a question and answer session from 10–10:30.

After lunch, Mark proceeds to the round auditorium where he has agreed to paint some sets for an upcoming production on outer space. Unfortunately, his older sister, who bosses him constantly, is also involved in this production. Mark decides with the help of the production adviser that he needs help on coping with this situation and goes to the Psychology Studio–Workshop to gain some skill in "confrontation." After half an hour, Mark returns to the production board to get an idea of what he will select for tomorrow. He makes some tentative choices and boards the bus for home.

*   *   *   *

For Donna, an eleven year old student at the Learning Theater, each day is in a sense personalized, tailored to fit her needs. At the close of school Friday, the computer has punched out Donna's schedule for Monday to read as follows: Creative Writing Workshop, 8:00–12:00; Sewing Workshop 1:00–4:00; Cast Meeting for Great Depression production, 10:00; Attendance at production Autumn Leaves, 1:00.

Donna arrives at school a little before 9:00, goes to the central room of Theater 2000 Now, and checks her bulletin board and mailbox for any changes in schedule. She then goes to her creative writing workshop which is manned by a group of instructors who, for the most part, are able to give a good deal of individual attention. Under the influence of her production and the book she had read this past weekend, she has written a short story about prejudice and a Mexican American boy. Donna and the instructor discuss the story, discover both its good and bad aspects, and plan what revisions or changes Donna will make when she rewrites it. The instructor also suggests that Donna might want to attempt writing a poem, and they discuss how a poem works.

After leaving the workshop, Donna attends her cast meeting of the Great Depression production. After some discussion, the cast members sketch some rough plot ideas, choose one on which they will elaborate, and split up into committees. Donna joins the script writers and also offers to help with the scenery. The group decides to meet every day that week and schedules a tentative production date for that Friday.

After lunch Donna attends the production "Autumn Leaves." The production opens as the cast gives a choral reading of a poem which they have written about Autumn. The next part of the program is a description through slides and overhead projector of the scientific reasons why leaves change color. After a question and answer session, the production closes with children costumed in red, yellow, orange, and brown performing a dance of falling leaves which they had made up and choreographed with the aid of the dance expert.

*   *   *   *

Valerie is 11 years old, and in the sixth grade. She is obsessed with the desire to become a dancer, and spends two to three strenuous hours daily in serious dance study.

Valerie arrives limping, and goes immediately to her advisor. She has pulled a ligament at her previous day's modern dance class; this has happened before, and she has agreed with the suggestion that some knowledge of the muscles of the leg might prevent future accidents. Her advisor consults the schedule of the day's productions and finds that a group of boys and girls (with interest in becoming doctors and nurses) are working on a production "The Digestive System." She suggests that this group might be interested in a further project on muscles. Valerie finds them almost ready to begin a scene on "the stomach." They agree to help her in a few days time if she will be in their present production; they are short of people. After listening to a discussion on the process, Valerie becomes an enzyme swimming in digestive juices. She promises to help the following day to create, in movement, a demonstration of the peristaltic process.

She spends half an hour at lunch, and at 12:20 goes off to fulfill "Community Responsibility." This is one of the options of the school. Each child can contract weekly for one project which actively contributes to the needs of others. Valerie leads a lower elementary group in creative dance. She has weekly planning sessions with specialists in creative dramatics and in physical education, and draws on their assistance whenever necessary. Not only is this arrangement benefitting the young children, but Valerie's interaction with them and the guiding adults is a satisfying and valuable learning experience to her.

*   *   *   *

The genuine enthusiasm and excitement of the college students involved in the Learning Theater is apparent in these student evaluations:

FROM JUDY GOLDMAN

It's happy feeling for the rest of the day!! The most valuable course I've ever taken—for myself, my major, my future and *now*.

> Sharing . . . . ideas, feelings, experiences
> Warmth . . . . in beautiful people
> New Friends . . . . from new people
> Discovery . . . . new styles, old forms
> Learning . . . . through awareness and fun

How sad more people haven't joined us.

FROM MARJORIE LEWIN

Blind walks . . . writing haiku . . . non-verbal communication . . . what is a piece of string thinking when small boy scouts are learning their knots? . . . one person creates different images to different people . . . can one really tell the color of an object by just feeling it? . . . thinking of six objects beginning with the same letter isn't as easy as it sounds under pressure . . . do I really call my professor by her first name? . . . since the whole course is new and different, why shouldn't teacher–student relationships be different also? . . . Right? . . . Of course, right!
Improvisation:

Did you ever stop to think about what a piece of bacon might be thinking while fried? Or did you ever wonder how a plum felt becoming a prune?

Well, these lifeless things came to life one morning in class when I asked each person to act out a different object. The kids used their whole bodies to enact it and did a very good job.

FROM BARBARA WOODBURY

The 2½ hour class: As teacher, how do we use up two hours this week; as student, it can't be time to leave; I was effectively using the Stanislavski method to play that ornery-bright-disoriented student's alter ego. With John Holt and psychodramas, that alter-ego becomes my ego. A new found ability and courage to articulate outside this accepting community and I take on the Speech Department.

A name game, I'm a Russian Wolfhound, a *Midsummer Night's Dream*, a Moussaka. I know everybody's name and Masha's a pumpernickel. Math equations and xylophone compositions, the strobe light dance. We're all *Getting Stewed With Patch*.

I'm a Maori five-year old pre-reader and my word is zoo. A blind walk with yellow dandelion pollen on my cheek. Thumbs up for Haiku and a Mozart–Ciardi partnership. When did .*you* ever look forward to a book report?

FROM STUART KAPLAN

The Learning Theater—where your next-seat neighbor wishes he were a knish—where a visit from Superman is not surprising.

What is the Learning Theater? It is the greatest innovation in Education since the pencil. Different teaching styles, different learning styles, different ways to communicate. Interact. Become what you really are. Bring out the you in you. And the me in you. And make them into the "we" in you.

Like, WOW!

Where else could you climb your favorite mountain or become your favorite state. Where else would uninformed spectators ask "Is there a blind convention in the building?" Where else can you see people let loose and really become themselves?

It's the Learning Theater.

And It's the Greatest!!

FROM SUSAN BRAINERD

When we first initiated the Learning Theater "course" we had many feelings, ideas, and philosophical notions, but we wondered how to translate these into a viable series of experiences. For the staff of the Learning Theater perhaps the most significant question was "How to determine a focus and structure for the course that would encourage a common group experience and also allow maximum individual flexibility?" We agreed on a focus: observing, analyzing, and experimenting with three interrelated facets of teacher–student involvement—communication, teaching styles, and learning styles.

Rather than begin by trying to explain our ideas about the Learning Theater and impose our focus, however, we decided to involve the members of the class in a variety of experiences that would stimulate their thinking and perhaps bring in fresh ideas. For the first three weeks of class, then, we presented improvisation games, attended a session on the Flander's Interaction Analysis, viewed and discussed films on the Bereiter and Deutsch methods, on the Philadelphia Affective Education Project. We also viewed tapes of pilot projects that members of the Learning Theater had done in schools and at Marathon II. By the following week of class, we all felt it was time to evolve a structure that would help us focus our involvement for the remaining weeks. The groups agreed that the name game and improvisations were valuable for creating a sense of shared experience and expanding our means for communication. We also agreed that each person would read at least one book from the bibliography and devise a project that would help investigate teaching and learning styles. The essence of the readings and results of the projects would be presented in class in any way that would be appropriate to the material and interesting for the class. Thus, each member of the class became a decision-making teacher–learner, with a commitment to exploring his own interests and sharing with the group the results of his learning. This "structure" has far exceeded our expectations for promoting individualized learning and enthusiastic group participation in class.

*   *   *   *

Chapters 4 and 5 will present a few samples of the humanistic education techniques being developed in the Learning Theater.

GLORIA SIEMONS CASTILLO

Gloria Castillo is a first grade teacher in Santa Barbara who is one of those rare humans with the potential to turn a classroom into a laboratory for feeling, experimenting, and learning. She has been working with George Brown and his Ford–Esalen project described elsewhere in this chapter. What follows is an entry in Gloria Castillo's first grade journal. The first entry involves the parents of her first graders with their children in a unique, intimate and sensitive combination of learning to feel and feeling to learn. The second entry shows the great sensitivity with which Gloria Castillo deals with a problem child. The third entry is an example of the everyday creativity which a humanistic teacher like Gloria Castillo can elicit from her children.

March 26

Since the parents were so enthusiastic the first time I had them in, I don't know why I was surprised when they all offered to come back again.

We began with an extension of the crayon activity of last time. While waiting for late-comers and to loosen up the group some, I started them by having them wake up their hands—rubbing harder and harder, clapping, slapping, shaking, feeling what was happening.

From that I had them pour the starch they had on their desks onto the paper taped down. As before, parent was facing child. They were then to move as before—together without talking. I went around the room for pacing clues. Seeing many mothers using only one hand I asked that they simply become aware of both of their hands and then all four hands. They did not have to paint with both. Only become more aware of themselves.

When they were all moving freely and hands were full of starch, I asked them to touch each other's hands only—holding them up between them. From that I asked each of them to dip into one of the colors (dry tempers) that were on the desk and continue to move non-verbally. They could make something of their picture, but a design might be more easily accomplished if they were going to continue without words. I continued to circulate but they did not seem to need any more suggestions. When I noticed paper beginning to curl from rubbing and starch beginning to dry, I asked that they get to some state of completeness when they could. Some will finish quickly, others will need more time. When they finished they had a horrible clean-up task. I asked that they leave their desk as it was for later cleaning and just wash their hands. Children went out to the bathrooms. I had provided wash cloths for the parents.

Since they were getting cleaned up at varying times, I had the children take a blindfold and their parent out to the hill area. Today, unlike last time, it was beautiful—sunny and warm. Early this morning John helped me get things ready. We brought some buckets from home and some driftwood. We put water in the buckets and put them all down in the hill area. Bud brought in two big rocks. One was flat and smooth, the other very sharp and rough. He also stuck great boughs of lemon trees into the fence. They had leaves, blossoms and fruit on them. When we were all ready, the children took their parents on a blind walk. After about 10 minutes, they switched roles. They continued to use the blindfolds, more out of habit maybe. They really enjoyed doing that this time. They ran, crawled, touched, smelled and laughed. It was very joyful and so thrilling to watch.

From that I had them come into the cafeteria. As they came in, they got a sheet and sat down together. When they were all quiet, I asked the children to go through the seed sequence. They each started in their own "shell." When they "felt watered and strong" they began to grow. Upon reaching maturity, they created more seeds and began to die. As they died, they were to change from the plant to the new seed—getting under their sheets again. This went very well.

From that I asked the parents to get under the sheet and assume a prenatal position. As they felt like it, they were to come out of the sheet. They began to talk as they came out. I asked that if they wanted to talk, do it as a baby. They then began to crawl. From there I asked them to get to their knees and really look at their child. I asked them to try not talking as they did this. As they continued in this way, I asked that they try to become acutely aware of their child as a person, an individual. Become aware of how they felt when looking at their child. I then asked them to slowly stand at their full height, continuing to keep eye contact with their child if possible. From that position, I asked them to try to raise their child to their eye level. There were many groans as they tried this. I suggested to a few they put their child on the benches on the side. Either way they soon found this uncomfortable. I then told them to now get in the most comfortable position they had experienced with their child. They then went back to their knees and stayed that way. From there they sat down together. The warmth and affection openly displayed was overwhelming to see. They stayed like this for about seven minutes. Since the hour was more than over, I asked the children to say goodbye when they wanted, and go out on the playground. Bob had agreed to watch the class while I met with Mike, Jane and Bud for a questioning period.

Before leaving, many of the parents engaged in a free play session. Again I was delighted with the joy and freedom they expressed while being with their children. What wonderful people to work with! Mrs. _____ even went out with her son and remained with him until lunch. Bob said several parents went onto the playground with their children upon leaving the cafeteria. It was a long time—up to 45 minutes—before they were ready to leave. Another *Wow* day gone by.[28]

January

Kirk is running around the room wildly. I wonder if his mother remembered to give him his drug. His drug—it keeps down his aggression, but I wonder. Does it also keep down all his feelings? He hasn't touched me. He hasn't let me touch him.

Music is playing softly and slowly. Many of the children are dancing around.

"Kirk, what are you doing?" "I don't know." "What are you doing?" "I am running." And you run away from me. Soon you are back. You are standing. I am sitting on the floor. You smile at me. You run up to me and stop short about two feet away. I invite you to join me. You come closer and then run away.

This time when you come back, you slide on the floor. You still don't come very close, yet closer than last time. "Would you like to slide into me?" "Yes." "Then go back and this time slide into me." You go back. You slide. You do not touch me.

"Did you slide into me?" "No." "Do you still want to?" "Yes." "Then try again." You run off. It is longer before you are back. I wait. You come running up. You slide. Your foot barely touches my knee. "What are you doing, Kirk?" "I'm touching your knee." "What else are you doing?" "I'm smiling." "Would you like to touch more than just my knee?" You don't answer. You get up and run off. Wonder if you will come back. Soon you do. This time you have great big smile. You run towards me, slide, and roll onto my lap. Hold you. We are quiet. You jump up and run to the corner and hide behind the flag.

"What are you doing, Kirk?" "Nothing." "Who is doing nothing?" "I am doing nothing." "May I hold your hand?" No answer. You turn to the wall. I move a step away so you are not cornered but I stay by your side. You run out of the corner and join the rest of the class in responding to the music. I see your eyes looking at me. I see you take a deep breath.

---

[28] Gloria Castillo, Journal of Humanistic Teaching (First Grade), Brown, *op. cit.*, pp. A4–36, –37.

Now the class is lining up to leave. You get in line. You look back at me. You come back and hold out your hand to me. It is warm. It holds my hand firmly. You feel good to me. We walk to class. You leave me at the door. After two or three steps, you turn and smile at me, and then go on your way.

March 13: Writing Lesson—expanding imagination

After reading *On Beyond Zebra*, by Dr. Suess, we had a writing lesson on his letters instead of our usual writing.

It was very interesting and the children were so engrossed in what they were doing. They really paid attention, listened, watched, and followed directions in order to reproduce those strange letters! Bud Robinson came in with a hand-held video camera and they paid no attention to it. They were too interested in what they were doing to care what he was doing.

When we had done six of them and got the idea, I asked them to try to make up some of their own. They went right to work. Soon their pages were covered with weird figures. They had a more difficult time naming them. I drew some of them on the board—as good a job as I could do—and the class tried to name them. The "author" of the letter then chose the name he liked best or made up one of his own after being stimulated by the class.

The next thing was to draw the animal or object that went with the made-up symbol and name. Their pictures were just as creative, colorful and original as Dr. Suess'.

From there I asked them to make up a story about their picture. I brought in the primary typewriter so they wouldn't feel the restriction of having to print after just being freed from it.

Their stories were delightful. Long, original and very funny. I wished to keep them but they didn't want to give them up. I couldn't blame them and so sent them home.[29]

DR. J. L. MORENO—*Psychodrama*

Psychodrama originated some 58 years ago in Vienna with Dr. J. L. Moreno who found that allowing children to act out their problems spontaneously produced therapeutic results. Since that time, largely due to Moreno's efforts, psychodrama has de-

---

[29] *Ibid.*, pp. A4–38, A4–39.

veloped as an action theory and method for understanding and resolving interpersonal problems on a wide range of areas including mental hospitals, correctional institutions, industry, schools, and private psychological practice. Psychodrama is used in many training and educational situations with both adults and children.

Psychodrama originated when Moreno started to practice group psychotherapy using three methods. The first led to psychodrama. About 1909 he began to stage written plays with children and juveniles, but soon he passed over to the completely original practice of "letting them play spontaneously" their own problems on self-creative primitive stages in the Vienna Meadow Gardens. In 1911 Moreno created "together" (as he himself insists) with hundreds of children and adolescents, a "children's theater for spontaneity" where the first recorded psychodramatic sessions were produced. Out of this playing of one's own problems, rather than mirroring the pain of alien things, he developed the Stregreiff Theater for adults.

Psychodrama's wide and varied acceptance is to a great extent due to its adaptability and flexibility. Although psychodrama is practiced more formally in most cases, all that is required for a session is the problem, the group or individual, and a psychodramatist.

The theoretic system which defines the psychotherapeutic practice of psychodrama is found in the hundreds of books, monographs, and articles on the subject. Psychodrama's scientific roots are buried deep in Moreno's philosophies of spontaneity, creativity, the moment, and theories of role and interaction. The sociometric system for understanding human networks and acting on individual and group structure therapeutically is a foundation of psychodramatic procedure.

Psychodrama explores the truth by means of dramatic methods. It is the depth therapy of the group. It starts where group psychotherapy ends, and it extends it in order to make it more effective. The expressed aim of the therapy group is to function for its members as a miniature society to which they can adapt themselves more harmoniously than before. If this aim is taken seriously, other methods besides conversation, interview, or analysis have to be added in order that such an objective—a catharsis of integration—can be filled. The need of going beyond the level of discussion becomes imperative. It is not enough to react to private and collective idealogies of group sessions in a symbolic fashion; the situation must be structured to relate feelings and thoughts to real people.

While the scenes are spontaneous and unrehearsed, each situation is carefully planned to fit the needs of the participants. With psychiatric patients, simple situations are used in the beginning so that the situation doesn't become too traumatic for the patient. He should not fail during his first few scenes on the psychodramatic stage. Support is given if he seems to be floundering. At first, only situations which he can successfully bring to a conclusion are tried. Later on, when he feels more sure of himself and seems ready to meet more difficult situations—perhaps even competition —he can be presented with more involved scenes.

As a form of treatment, psychodrama, combined with group therapy, is very flexible and can be adapted to almost any social and age level. Psychodramatic activities take place in a setting which approximate problem-producing settings very closely. Attempts are made to achieve a realistic view. Group members express insights and interpretations, and form new relationships with each other which can be therapeutic.

Insight is not seen as the major goal in psychodrama, but rather the ability to become spontaneous; that is, to make new perceptions of old situations, or at least to reorganize old cognitive patterns in such a manner that new and more adequate responses are facilitated. The effectiveness of learning through experiencing in the psychodramatized situation can be profound.

Often no "interpretation" or "analysis" is needed, as the subject is fully experiencing a problem situation in all its dimensions, giving his own analysis in terms of action. Students discover they can handle a problem after they find they have done it. Psychodrama comes closer to the "life-line" of human experiences than perhaps any other therapeutic format, for the simple reason that it is lived out more intensively and extensively than the stresses of living would permit on the outside. Every attempt is made to work toward an expanded and integrated self-perception, with its concomitant attributes of interest in others and concern, not with the existence of problems, but with the ability to deal with them —in other words, a freer and more spontaneous person. Acting in the theatrical sense has no place in psychodrama, as the goals are to aid in self-realization rather than to promote the development of façades.

The time factor is a significant issue in psychodrama. Although a production may be focusing on past, present, or future, psychodrama is always the "here and now." The student is giving his current conception of a situation. The problem, objectified with the aid of the group and auxiliary egos, is what is troubling the student at this time. It may refer to similar conflicts in the past, and to similar potential ones which may appear in the future. If the conflict becomes clarified and understood, the subject and group can experience their effective handling of it. If they cannot handle it to their satisfaction, the action may be repeated until the anxiety and conflict of the problem is reduced or resolved. The reality of testing and evaluation is taking place within the session itself. The patients learn to live and to communicate directly. Psychodramatic experience indicates that when a subject has not resolved an issue or conflict satisfactorily, the difficulty will reappear in the psychodramatic session. However, when he has worked out the problem, it becomes apparent in the group session. Later verification in life further aides the subject. Continuous verification and checking back and forth, from life to psychodrama and vice versa, is characteristic of the method.

It is not recommended that intense psychodrama be practiced by the average teacher in the classroom. This description of Moreno's work is presented because variations of it have application to the humanistic classroom.

ALEXANDER LOWEN, WILHELM REICH, ROLLO MAY, IDA ROLF, AND BERNIE GUNTHER—*Relation of the body to the psychological processes*

Alexander Lowen, a practicing psychiatrist and Executive Director of the Institute for BioEnergetic Analysis in New York City, has had extensive experience in psychiatry which has direct humanistic educational application. In work with "normals," his approach emphasizes body movement for the achievement of the individual's potential for more heightened feeling, pleasure, and greater self-awareness.[30]

Some of the most intriguing early work on the relation of the body to psychological processes has been done by Wilhelm Reich.[31] The effects of the psychological process on the body can range from the millions of "goose bumps" raised in sudden fright to the severity of death resulting from belief in a voodoo hex. Since excessive muscular tension tends to desensitize the body, we learn early in life to tense our muscles in order to screen out unpleasant external stimuli or to hold in intense internal emotions. Continual exposure to such threatening events can eventually lead to chronic muscular tension or, in essence, a neuromuscular "body armor." Such tension may be distributed throughout the body, giving a person the appearance of a well controlled automaton or mannikin. Or it may be especially pronounced in the neck, shoulders, rib cage, diaphragm, legs, etc. In either case the person becomes increasingly alienated from his body, possibly leading to a schizoid disturbance. The psychologist, Rollo May, characterizes schizoid persons as "detached, unrelated, lacking in affect, tending toward depersonalization, and covering up their problems by means of intellectualizations and technical formulations. . . ." While noting that the schizoid disturbance is becoming one of the most common psychic disorders of our time, comparable to hysteria in Freud's day, he goes on to say that, "There is also plenty of evidence that the sense of isolation, the alienation of one's self from the world is suffered not only by people in pathological conditions, but by countless 'normal' persons as well . . ."[32]

It is to these "normal" persons that the formal educational system should be addressing itself. Techniques are now being developed by Lowen and others which put a person back in contact with his body and, thus, with his feelings and emotions.

---

[30] See Alexander Lowen, Physical Dynamics of Character Structure (New York: Grune & Stratton, 1958); and *Love and Orgasm* (New York: The Macmillan Company, 1965); and *The Betrayal of the Body* (New York: The Macmillan Company, 1967).

[31] Wilhelm Reich, *Character Analysis* (New York; Orgone Institute Press, 1949).

[32] Rollo May, *Existence: A New Dimension in Psychiatry and Psychology* (New York: Basic Books, 1962).

For example, many persons complain of lack of feeling in the lower part of their body. They seem "unbalanced," out of touch with the earth, "ungrounded." One position which brings out these feelings quite clearly is to have the person stand with his feet about 30 inches apart, turn his toes slightly inward, bend his knees and then lean backward, arching his back and putting his hands on his hips. A person with a well-integrated and coordinated body can assume and hold this position easily. But in many others abdominal respiration becomes difficult and strained, the body tends to twist to one side or the other, the legs tremble, or the person experiences pain or becomes aware of a lack of balance. After becoming aware of his tension points and their psychological significance, the person may, over a number of sessions, become more in touch with himself and report a feeling of balance, self-acceptance, integration, solidity, or of being more in touch with external reality and his internal emotions.

Since almost all of us have something to "kick about," another activity is to have a person lie down on a couch on his back and aggressively kick his legs. While this feels quite unnatural and artificial at first, one soon finds bitterness, frustration, or hostility rising to the surface and finding its expression in the kicking. A healthy person with a well-integrated body will find little difficulty in "letting go" and fully and freely expressing his emotion in an integrated and coordinated way. However, many persons tense up, their breathing becomes restricted, their neck stiffens, and their kicking is fragmented, uncoordinated, and without feeling. After several sessions their movement often becomes freer and more spontaneous; they find it easier to express negative emotions; they feel less tense, less "bottled up." The application of these findings to physical education, dance, or simply the average classroom is obvious.

A different approach has been pioneered by Dr. Ida Rolf. While acknowledging with Reich and Lowen that feelings and attitudes can and do have pronounced effects on our physical structure, she holds that the converse is equally true. Any malignment of the body, whether congenital or the result of some simple accident, can have important psychological or attitudinal effects on an individual. Thus an otherwise benign skiing mishap, fall from a tree, or bicycle collision might result in a slight displacement of a bone and attached muscle structure, interfering with normal movement and, thus, necessitating a compensatory realignment of other body parts. Such rebalancing usually entails a thickening of existing tissues or formation of new fibers of connecting tissue, thus curtailing free movement within the affected area. (Such tissue changes may also, obviously, result from chronic body postures or as the result of some congenital weakness.) The observable effects are seen in habitual immobilization of certain body parts, as in an individual with sloping shoulders, sway back, a chin thrust forward, knock knees, a "frozen" pelvis, or an expanded or sunken rib cage. While these are quite clearly deviations from a healthy norm, these people and their friends consider themselves to be perfectly "normal." A healthy, integrated individual might be defined as one who is physically and emotionally capable of free flow, free exchange, and free movement. However, as Rolf and others have pointed out, emotional freedom is not possible without a corresponding physical freedom. Thus their approach is to "thaw out" and realign the body by breaking down the chronically immobilizing fascial sheaths surrounding the affected muscles. Once freed, the body comes into a more efficient relationship with the gravitational field and the person reports a greater suppleness and ease of movement, less fatigue, and more energy. Objective tests show improvement in body chemistry and cardiac function while "before–and–after" pictures attest to a greatly improved posture.

Though sometimes painful, a series of "Rolf Treatments" can contribute toward revitalizing a person, not only physically, but psychologically as well. At Esalen, I received a Rolf treatment by Peter Melchior, a therapist trained by Dr. Rolf, and I found afterwards, much to my exhilaration, that I was easily able to breathe a much larger and more exhilarating volume of air into my previously constricted chest cavity. I also found that I measured one half inch taller after this body realigning treatment! However, the real benefit was that, psychologically, I felt at least two feet taller.

And still another approach, "sensory awakening," has been developed by Bernie Gunther of Esalen Institute. An amalgamation of sensory awareness, Yoga, Gestalt Therapy, and Zen Buddhism, sensory awakening is a technique for putting us into more direct contact with our environment. By excessive intellectualizing, verbalizing, analyzing, and conceptualizing, we manage to cut ourselves off from immediate experience. Gunther has, therefore, designed a series of experiences which "shift attention from symbolic or verbal interpretation: to *the actual,* what *is.* Too often people *think* they feel rather than feel. Ignoring primary processes, they freeze situations and themselves so that there is no sensory contact with the richness of each event." After first inducing a basic state of relaxation, the exercises then move on to focus attention on simple bodily processes such as breathing, listening, movement and touch. For example:

> Close your eyes and feel your hands; now, slowly stretch your fingers out as wide as they will go, like a cat stretching its paws. Use some pressure to go as wide as you can without its being in any way painful. Hold for 15 seconds in this extreme position. Then, very slowly, allow your fingers and hands to settle back where they want to go. Repeat three times. After each stretch, become aware of any change that may take place in you.

or:

> Close your eyes and feel your shoulders. After taking a few minutes, slowly begin to hunch them as high as you can. This must be done in slow motion. When you reach the extreme position, hold the shoulders there for a few seconds, then slowly let them down. It is important to experience each aspect of the motion. Allow your shoulders to settle where it feels right for them to go. Experience the effects, taking plenty of time. Repeat the movement two or three times.[33]

Having escaped the tyranny of our thought processes we soon discover our excessive reliance on the sense of sight. One exercise that I use with my classes and which is also popular at Esalen is to pair people, instructing one person to close his eyes and have his partner lead him about the grounds, exposing him to various non-visual stimuli. Thus, he has the all too rare experience of exploring the exciting stimuli of the world through the sense of touch and

---

[33] See Bernie Gunther "Sensory awakening and relaxation" (Big Sur, California: Esalen Institute, 1967); and *Sense Relaxation: Below your Mind* (New York: The Macmillan Company, 1968).

smell, such as touching the human face and figure with sightless
fingertips, rubbing up against the bark of a tree, sliding through
clover, sniffing old sea shells, and listening to the sound of insects.

Some typical responses to sensory awakening are: "I haven't
been this relaxed in years." "I feel at one with everything." "I feel
in the floor, rather than on it." "I feel more natural, the way I
would like to all the time." Or, in the case of a knowing student
of Zen, "Nothing special." Applications of this to the classroom
will be brought out in Chapter 5.

Finally, I am growing to believe that the body—its expressions
and movements—really betrays the feelings and hang-ups that we
have. Likewise, use of and exercises with the body can be a key
to unlocking these problems. A surefire way not to get anything
out of any of the humanistic exercises or experiences is to go into
them with the body stiff and rigid, holding one's breath. When
we can learn to express feelings not only openly with words but
with the body also, it becomes an exhilarating and releasing experience. In a group led by Bennett Shapiro I had the enlightening
experience of finally learning how to let my resentment and anger
flow verbally and bodily after holding back for most of my life.
Bennett observed that I just didn't know how to really let my
anger loose and tell someone off. Instead, my fingers gripped and
tapped the arm of the chair, I smiled artificially, and moved my
feet in an uncertain manner. Moreover, I had made a habit of getting back at people in other circuitous, indirect ways which proved
to be much more destructive than would direct expression of my
resentment. After being goaded a bit about this, I was asked to
really take out my anger on the cushion of an overstuffed chair
with my fists and body. Reluctantly, I began pounding on the
cushion harder and harder. I felt foolish at first, but then as I
began to put my entire body into the pounding and gave vent to
shouting obscenities at the top of my lungs, my pent-up anger and
resentment took over and the next thing I realized I had ripped
the cushion apart, torn up the stuffing and inner springs, and had
literally demolished it completely in a matter of one or two minutes. Shapiro still wasn't satisfied that I had freed myself, and after
giving me a few minutes to collect myself, he explained that this
might be my last opportunity ever to let everything out. "This is
the time and place to do it," he assured me. He sneered at me and

egged me on to hit him. I hesitated. The next thing I knew I had knocked him out of his chair with a backhand slap and was wrestling for my life with him on the floor. We stopped, and I was winded, breathing deeply and freely from way down within. I had put my entire body into this and it felt good. Shapiro refused to let me off at this point. He said I needed to learn to express that kind of fury at someone I really felt it toward. I looked around the room uncertainly. I decided that this was the time, finally, to say to a colleague whom I deeply resented what I really felt. I stood before him uncertainly. Shapiro told me to take a bold stand, feet apart and firmly planted, hands on hips. I started talking slowly, and rationally. Shapiro interrupted. "That's diplomatic tactful Hal again." I turned to Shapiro and snapped, "Shut up! I'll do this my way!" The next thing I knew I had seized my colleague by the shirt, almost ripping it off him, and had thrown him across the room into a chair. He started to get up and I threw him back almost knocking the chair over. I told him not to get up until I finished with him. I then launched into him verbally with all the fury of an attacking grizzly bear. When I staggered back to my chair completely exhausted, I knew I had made some real progress in unlocking the sources of many of my problems. My colleague stammered, "That's the first time I've ever trusted or respected you." The fact is that you can't trust someone who is unwilling to tell you what they really feel about you. In order to make me sicken of my old over-sweet ways, Ben Shapiro then had me go around and tactfully apologize to everyone for the violence and trouble I had caused. After doing this for a few minutes, it became vividly clear how saccharine or artificially sweet I had been sounding for a long time, and I sat down, well on my way toward having a new, refreshing ability—the ability to express anger and resentment bodily, verbally, and openly.

AFFECTIVE UNIVERSITY EDUCATION PROGRAMS

Universities throughout the country are offering courses which deal with the affective domain. As might be expected, the Free Universities are doing some of the most exciting work. One of the most impressive is the Midpeninsula Free University located in Palo Alto, California. Running through one of their catalogues one finds the following courses offered: Creativity and Mathematics; Gestalt Workshop; Meditation; Techniques of Massage; Painting as a Journey into One's Self; The Relevance of Esalen to Stanford; Your Ecstatic Home; Tai Chi Chuan; Disciplines in Consciousness; The Harrad Experiment; Yoga; Human Contact; The Undiscovered Self; "You Can Be In My Dream If I Can Be In Yours"; To Be Gentle; Basic Spontaneous Dance; Advanced Group Relaxation; Visual Expression Workshop; Mountain Climbing for Peak Experiences; and The Nature of Human Communication.

Laboratory experiences have a tendency to turn people on, and when they are carried out in a teaching–learning context they may well turn students on to teaching careers. A group of 30 inner-city junior and senior high school students in Detroit were given lab training in conjunction with a program in which they served as tutors to still younger students. Now 25 of the 30 have decided on teaching careers and are looking for relevant apprenticeship experience. At the University of North Carolina several groups of non-education honors students had a similar experience and over half then expressed interest in switching to the School of Education.

Race relations, being perhaps the most emotionally volatile issue in America today, has come in for a great deal of attention in laboratory settings. Desegregation of the Delaware schools was accompanied by a three year program in which black and white teachers and counselors could meet to openly discuss hopes and fears, problems and potentials, attitudes and experiences. The focus of the program has now changed from desegregation to integration. Other racially oriented programs have involved Vista volunteers in New York, Community Action Groups in San Francisco, college students in Florida, policemen in the Great Lakes Area, professional education associations in the deep South, etc. Additionally, the "Strength Training Clinic" which was conceived by Gerald Weinstein, Chuck Kerney, Joe Samuels, and Charles Ungerleider of the University of Massachusetts, School of Education's Center for Humanistic Education, simulates the experiences which white teachers will face in the ghetto classroom.

A number of other universities have created lab-oriented programs of research and training slanted both toward the needs of their students and large organizations. Another development, in smaller public and private colleges, has been the creation of lab-type programs to serve special student needs. At the United States International University (formerly Cal Western) in San Diego, Larry Solomon has developed an intensive study program for underachieving high school graduates. Revolving around intensive small group experiences, the program helps the student to "acquire the attitudes, motivation, study skills, and communication skills necessary for him to be better able to achieve the potential he possesses."

At San Jose State College, Pat Williams, Director of the Institute of Industrial Relations, has trained student facilitators who lead a special series of workshops for college students in the Bay Area. And at campuses across the country, faculty members are experimenting with new, non-authoritarian, student-directed classes in education, psychology, sociology etc. A few universities, growing on a cluster-college basis, have even considered the creation of a Human Potential college.

For the past several years, the United States Office of Education has funded COPED (Cooperative Project for Educational Development), a network of lab-oriented behavioral science teams from seven universities facilitating planned change in fifteen school systems. In addition, Title XI NDEA funded an Institute on Social Studies and Communication which involves the introduction of affective techniques into pre-service training, placement, curriculum development, and in-service training. Like the COPED project, it is coordinated through NTL and, in this case, involves five cooperating schools of education and related school systems, and includes parents, students, teachers, administrators, community residents, and university faculty members.

At San Francisco State, Janie Rhyne, combining art, psychology, anthropology and Gestalt Therapy, offers "art experiences" as a means to growth and self-awareness. She recently reported on a couple of sessions with black teenagers who were "looking for ways to pull themselves out of their ghetto-bound defeatism and assert their own worth and dignity. . . . The sessions were chaotic and I didn't know when the boys left the studio what impression they had. A few days later they called me and asked where to buy clay and other art materials. They wanted to have 'art therapy' groups for themselves, directed by themselves, to meet their own needs."

At this point, I will attempt to pull together what seem to be some common threads among the various pioneers in humanistic education which have been surveyed in this chapter.

First, is the notion that each person has needs which must be met. Students often know what their most pressing needs are. When they are in a free-learning environment, they will involve themselves in activities which fulfill their individual needs. When relating to self-chosen content, the student is highly motivated and able to work independently. When learning is a function of the inherent needs of the individual, there is no difference between work and play. Learning becomes a joyful experience.

Second, is the belief that man has unrealized potential. The whole man is an integration of mind, body, and feelings. Most human beings are fragmented and compartmentalized. Toward the goal of nurturing whole, self-actualizing human beings, it is imperative that schools recognize the importance of emotions in the learning experience.

Third, is the conviction that man must change to survive. The post-industrial society that is emerging demands men who are aware of their emotions and in touch with their senses. For society to remain viable it must begin to produce self-actualizing human beings.

Present trends toward increased leisure time; growing population and urbanization; rapid growth in the human service occupation sector; increased mobility; more racial, generational, and international contacts and conflicts; increased need for interdisciplinary communication to meet increasingly complex problems; greater opportunity for involvement in the creative arts; greater estrangement from our bodily functions through excessive reliance on technological devices, etc., call for a more concerted institutional effort of education in the affective domain. This call is being voiced by such disparate camps as humanistic psychologists, and the varied pioneers whose works in expanding the human potential for openness, honesty, warmth, and freedom were traced in this chapter, to corporation executives desirous of improved efficiency through better communication, cooperation, decision-making, and problem-solving. While one group is predominantly humanistic, concerned with internal growth, and the other pragmatic, concerned with external results, they both share a conviction that man's life on earth can be made more rewarding through concerted efforts at humanistic education. Make no mistake, however; humanistic education is no panacea; it will not correct all of the world's ills, solve the pressing social problems of the day, or guarantee each of us a full, rich, and more joyful life. But it is a step in the right direction.

4

Humanistic Education Techniques

Touching and going
Two thumbs open showing
their owners are shy.

*　　*　　*　　*

To touch is to know
the inner conflict of self
I know your battle

—Two haiku (17 syllable, 3 line poems with 5 syllables in the first line, 7 in the second and 5 in the last) written by students in the Learning Theater after an improvisation exercise of communicating by touching thumbs.—

*　　*　　*　　*

This chapter will survey briefly some of the humanistic education techniques being developed and used by teachers in various levels of classrooms throughout the country. Though many of these techniques have been used by the author, most of them were not developed by him. Where possible, credit will be given to the developer of the technique being described. It is hoped that the techniques described in this chapter will prime the pump of the reader's creativity not only to try some of these techniques in the classroom but to build on these, improve them, and innovate his own.

THE GROUP

T–group, sensitivity training, basic encounter—while each has its own connotations, the terms are often used interchangeably by layman and professional alike. "T–group," being the most neutral term, generally refers to a group of individuals, sometimes co-workers, often strangers, meeting together to learn more about themselves and their impact on others. They do this by opening themselves up, "telling it like it is," about themselves and about the others in the group as they perceive them. They "encounter" each other simply as individuals, putting aside for the time being the roles and status differences which usually inhibit honest and personal dialogue. After setting some ground rules (e.g., talk only about your feelings, no set agenda, stick to the here-and-now, and be honest) the group leader usually plays a relatively non-directive, facilitating role. After the initial intense minutes of hesitancy, anxiety, frustration, and fear, people are often surprised to hear themselves telling relative strangers things which they had previously not said to their spouse or closest friend—or telling their supervisor things they had previously only muttered to themselves while shaving in the morning. Leland Bradford, of the National Education Association, working with Ronald Lippitt, of the University of Michigan, and Kenneth Benne, of Boston University, were the people primarily responsible for the development of the T–Group and the National Training Laboratories at Bethel, Maine.

"Basic encounter" is most commonly used in reference to training in which the focus is on personal growth rather than on the development of interpersonal skill. Primarily a West Coast phenomenon, the term conjures visions of Carl Rogers, Bill Schutz, Esalen, The Center for Studies of the Person, joy, and drama. Basic encounter groups are usually composed of strangers or couples desirous of expanding their potential, overcoming personal problems, or discovering joy. Thus, the focus is on the individual, his problems, and potentialities. Sometimes referred to as "group therapy for normals," basic encounter groups often lapse into psychologizing and discussions of here-and-now situations. Sessions are usually free-swinging and experimental and personal growth is often fostered by dramatically achieved insights.

Within the primary mode of verbal encounter, other techniques, both verbal and non-verbal, may be used when appropriate. If two people reach an impasse in the group discussion they might switch roles and "play the other person;" or if there seems to be some latent competition, they might seek to crystalize their feelings by wrestling, "pushing" or "pressing;" in other cases they might retire from the group for a "dyad" or two-man encounter group, or continue their discussion within the group but without using words. If a person feels terribly inhibited, immobilized, or constricted the group might form a tight circle about the person and have him or her break out of it. Or conversely, if a person feels shut out, excluded, or ignored by the group, he or she might be told to break into such a circle. If a person appears mistrustful he might be asked to fall backwards into someone's arms or, if fearful of dependency, he might be instructed to close his eyes, go limp, and allow himself to be passed around a circle from person to person.

Such simple techniques tend to dramatize and crystalize feelings and attitudes which previously were not fully accessible to the individual in question. The effects can be quite remarkable. For example, participants often remark that they feel more alive and excited than ever before. They often experience a feeling of release and joy. After my first visit to Esalen, I found myself seeing new goodness in many things, from the trees and nature to my work and former adversaries. A friend of mine had a similar experience after returning from a trip to Esalen. Someone stopped him in the hall and remarked that he seemed to have gained some weight in his face; he laughed realizing that his habitual body tension, usually most pronounced in his facial muscles, had been dramatically reduced.

Dr. William C. Schutz (whose best selling book, *Joy*, describes many of group activities discussed in this book) has trained a "gutsy" but skilled group of encounter leaders, many of whom are now leading their own groups as well as training others around the country. Among those that I know of are Seymour Carter, Betty Fuller, Steve Stroud and Anne and John Heider.

Other techniques which can be used sequentially, concurrently, or in place of basic encounter include mediation, group dream analysis, inner imagery, guided fantasy, creativity training, role playing, marathon, psychodrama, massage, etc.

"Sensitivity training" is the term most often used to describe T–groups devoted primarily to enhancing interpersonal competence. Participants are often co-workers and task-oriented. While basic encounters tend to be gutsy and affective, sensitivity training is usually more cerebral and cognitive. The emphasis tends to be on group process rather than personal growth; on education rather than therapy; on steady accumulation of skill rather than sudden insight. While personal problems certainly arise and are dealt with, it is within the context of improving the group process. Chris Argysis points out that in sensitivity training the best learners possess a higher degree of health (i.e., self-awareness and self-acceptance), than the average; they have a relatively strong ego, low defenses, and an ability to communicate thoughts and feelings with minimal distortion. Open and honest feedback is the *sina qua non* for sensitivity training, thus the healthier the participants, the better the feedback, and the more successful the group.[1]

The role of the group leader ("facilitator," "trainer," "educator") is to encourage the flow of information between participants. Rather than assume a superior, hierarchical position from whence he dispenses knowledge, he helps create an environment in which the participants generate their own data. According to Argyris the educator's role at the outset is to help the members become:

> . . . aware of their present (usually) low potential for establishing authentic relationships.

> . . . more skillful in providing and receiving non-evaluative descriptive feedback.

> . . . [able to] minimize their own and others' defensiveness.

> . . . Increasingly able to experience and own up to their feelings.[2]

This is often a slow, painful, and frustrating experience, for educational and organizational norms usually put the highest priority on strictly "rational" modes of interaction. Feelings are often looked on as necessary evils which should be somehow ignored—swept under the rug. Unfortunately their denial in no way mitigates their effect. They continue to rear their now ugly heads in the form of unspoken antagonisms and antipathies, distrust, hidden agendas, dissatisfaction, tension, verbal fencing, etc. Every meeting becomes a battle of wits, every innovation a potential threat, every memo a call to battle.

By legitimizing feelings as a topic for discussion, sensitivity training brings many long-standing problems out in the open where they can be dealt with. It allows people to experiment with new forms of leadership, communication, and problem solving. For ex-

---

[1] Chris Argyris, "T–Groups for Organizational Effectiveness," *Harvard Business Review* 42 (1964), pp. 60–74.

[2] *Ibid.*, p. 67

ample, many of us have stereotyped ways of motivating our subordinates, e.g. by brute force ("this will be finished and on my desk by noon Monday!") or wheedling and cajoling ("Say, John, the boss has asked me twice about that memo you're working on, can you get it to me by Monday?") or by sarcasm ("Since it has highest priority, I'd like it by Monday unless, of course, you're too busy with other more important things."). We are often unbelievably insensitive to the impact this has on others and often do not consider the possibility of other approaches. By allowing leadership and communication styles to emerge in the group and by providing honest feedback the members are able to achieve more insight into their behavior and its impact on co-workers. They can, if they wish, begin experimenting with other styles. This often leads to a greater repertoire, allowing the individual to exercise more flexibility, openness, and sensitivity in his dealings with others. In addition to creating a warmer and more satisfying work environment, there are also more tangible outcomes such as increased productivity, a more efficient use of time and people, and lower turnover.

Such group activities also have application in classroom settings. Some years ago the author was a member of a graduate psychology class entitled Group Dynamics taught by Gordon Lippitt. The class met weekly for three hours and was run as a "sensitivity training group." The student requirements were: to keep a diagnostic diary; to write a report on a reading from a list furnished by the leader; and to evaluate each day's session on a prepared form. I will never forget the first day that our group met with Gordon Lippit. We all gathered nervously around a long table sizing each other up. Gordon Lippitt announced that we were all there for the purpose of learning about our own real strengths and weaknesses, those that were usually hidden by the masks we wear, gaining a better understanding of how we deal with others and with groups, and to experiment with possible new modes of behavior. He said there would be only three rules which would govern our behavior: There would be no set agenda except that agreed upon by the group; there would be no designated leadership; and no one would have to do anything he didn't want to do. He then sat back quietly and waited and waited and waited for what seemed to be hours of the most painful silence I had ever experienced. I was the first to be drawn into the powerful vaccum of the unstructured situation. I suggested that since we were going to be together for a semester, perhaps we should introduce ourselves, tell what work we were involved in, and our reasons for taking the course. I proceeded to launch into an introduction of myself touching lightly, and to my mind modestly, on my accomplishments and motivations for taking the course. After finishing I suggested that we should go clockwise around the table following suit. The next five people went through their introductions as I proudly listened. The sixth man, an executive from the Internal Revenue Service, looked at me and said, "I resent Hal Lyon telling us that we should introduce ourselves clockwise around the table! We were told there was to be no designated leader in this group and he obviously is attempting to assume leadership and impress us all with his qualifications for assuming it. I for one am not impressed!" Someone else said, "I felt that way also." Another said, "Well, I'm glad he had the courage to break the silence and start something or we might have sat here for an hour!" I had become the subject for most of the rest of the three hour session. My motives were torn apart, analyzed, criticized, praised, and finally partially accepted. I received more open and direct feedback in those few hours than I had in the past ten years of my life. Finally, the man who had first called my hand jumped on me in an undeserved verbal assault. Two people immediately leaped to my defense and accused him of hitting below the belt. Someone asked him if he always attacked people when they were down. The attention then shifted to him, and he became the subject, much to my relief. Throughout the course of the semester everyone had ample opportunity to become the subject under discussion, including the group trainer. After a time the group began to care about its members, and toward the end of the semester they became very supportive of its individuals—as though preparing them for survival back in the real world or more appropriately, the "unreal world," where masks are the rule. This experience was for me the beginning of a long and slow realization and acceptance of the fact that my aggressive sense of urgency about achieving and proving myself to others in every endeavor was really a very strong over-compensation for basic feelings of inadequacy which I had held since childhood. Now that I have finally accepted this (and I am still learning about myself and changing and hope I will continue to do so), now that I accept the fact that

I am no superman, I have a fairly comfortable feeling about doing my best and accepting it with inner satisfaction instead of with a driving compulsion to always do better to please others. Feedback from my friends has also told me that they are much more comfortable with me as a human with faults than they were with my assumed role as a faultless superhuman. I have also learned that it is much more satisfying to be real—dealing straight with others about aggressive feelings and resentments—than it is to be my former super-sweet self who wanted everyone to like and accept him, and who found indirect circuitous ways of dealing with aggression and resentment. I attribute this life-changing insight to my experience in groups. I have also conducted a university course in business administration using the "T–group" as format. Additionally there are many useful occasions when a block of sensitivity training can be integrated into the conventional class setting. The potency of the concentrated weeklong "T–group" is lost when the group meets only weekly, nevertheless some excellent effects can be achieved using this technique.

THE MICRO-LAB

In a time of micro-miniturization, the mini-skirt, and minute steaks, one could hardly be surprised at the advent of the micro-lab. The micro-lab is a speeded up, watered down, smorgasbord of laboratory techniques. While not attaining the intensity of a basic encounter experience, it is very useful in giving persons some first-hand experience with the process or in breaking the ice at the beginning of a meeting or conference of strangers. In contrast to the rambling, somewhat self-directed nature of the encounter group, the micro-lab is fast moving and completely controlled by the leader. It can be used with groups ranging in size from 5 to 500 persons because the basic unit is a grouping of about 5 to 7 persons who form a circle, sit on the floor, and encounter one another for segments of 7–10 minutes in a mode determined by the micro-lab leader. For example, the leader might start with a segment of basic encounter (i.e., feelings, honesty, and here-and-now); then a segment of non-verbal communication; then a segment in which each person tells what he dislikes most about his body, followed by one in which he describes what he likes best; then each person might go around the circle, look each person in the eye, touch him in some way, and tell him exactly how he feels about him; then more basic encounter; etc. Also, taking out aggressive feelings through pillow fighting is an effective mode to use in micro-labs. The author has led several such labs and can attest to the surprisingly large and positive effect they can have in a very short period of time.

EVALUATION OF GROUP WORK

It is exceedingly difficult to measure changes in interpersonal behavior. Thus, despite an impressive amount of research on human relations training, the results are not conclusive. While some studies show large, positive changes, others report no significant effects, and others show even negative changes.

In addition to research-based evaluation there is, of course, a great deal more subjective opinion available on the merits or demerits of T–group type experience. Personal testimony is sometimes wildly enthusiastic; it is usually very positive, sometimes neutral, and very infrequently, it is negative.

Another sign of success is the increasingly large investment by big business in laboratory training for top executives and the growing number of heavily lab-oriented schools and departments of business administration, management science, or organizational behavior at top-flight universities.

Despite this phenomenal growth there have been some important setbacks. The Peace Corps has run hot and cold on its use of T–groups in the training of volunteers; the U.S. State Department recently phased out a major training activity for its personnel, reportedly because of lack of funds; however, the main backer of the program left government and the program folded shortly thereafter. In some schools around the country personnel returning from lab experiences have encountered serious difficulties with their administrations. The root of these and similar problems is not always clear. One reason why these activities are not appreciated in institutional settings is that the members develop new feelings of independence from the organization and their superiors. They are able to think for themselves and even to sever their connections with the institution rather than give in to stereotyped practices. In this way these activities become threatening to top management.

For this reason, it is essential to start at the top and involve top management in the process from the beginning. I found this to be an essential element in the success of a program I initiated in the U.S. Office of Education and an essential element in the failure of several other programs in other organizations. Another possible cause of problems is that affective techniques, like other controversial innovations, have friends who outrageously oversell their merits and enemies who denounce them as Communist plots. Another factor could be that some experiences have been designed and conducted ineptly, inappropriately, or incompetently. Still another and probably far more prevalent cause has been a failure to follow up or properly integrate the affective experience into the organizational pattern. For example, there are undoubtedly cases in which an employee returning from a two-week lab has "openly" and "honestly" called his boss a "son of a bitch"; such feedback, regardless of how sincere or accurate, is rarely appreciated.

The more intensive encounter group sessions tend to cause some individuals to gravitate dynamically from the cognitive (associated with conservatism) pole of the continuum to the affective (associated with liberal) pole when the healthy place to be is probably somewhere in the middle. The responsible group leader prior to sending his group back into society, will encourage them to clear a few "affective" channels for honest and open interaction with husband or wife and a close friend or two, rather than to expect most of the world to be ready for such concentrated honesty and openness.

One further caution: When one spouse enters an encounter group or T–group without the other, both should reach an understanding beforehand as to what is the husband's business, what is the wife's, and what is jointly held. Then an agreement should be reached on what may be opened to the group and what will be kept private. Without such an agreement, I have seen serious marital problems which developed between the couple when one attended without the other.

Another problem which arises when an organization decides to use group training is that often the organization will select the wrong mode of training or an inappropriate mix of people. Each of the varied modes of group training is designed to meet a different need. When an institution desires to focus on organizational or management problems, it needs to have a program individually tailored to its needs. This might include a mix of basic encounter experiences, non-verbal exercises, and marathons which are focused primarily on individual growth, openness, and self-awareness. However, the prime emphasis would most likely be on training experiences which are geared toward organizational change and management rather than on individual growth. These might include confrontation or racial encounter sessions between blacks and whites (these sessions can be very effective in convincing "conservative" whites, through open venting of hostility, of the seriousness of white racism in the country today), T–groups with emphasis on opening communications, and retreats for managers at the same strata. By the same strata I mean managers of equal rank or status in a system rather than a manager and his subordinates. It is my experience—especially when the objective of the training is personal growth—that most training is much more effective when it takes place in a setting away from the organization and when it involves people who do not have a superior-subordinate relationship. The individual in the program should be able to be relatively anonymous. When co-workers are thrown together in group training, the opening of intimate details can occasionally make it difficult for individuals to maintain relationships on a daily working basis in the organization. I prefer, for example (starting always at the top of the organizational hierarchy), having group experiences in the summer or at some remote retreat for district superintendents followed by the same kind of experience for principals from different schools, and then, perhaps, sessions for English or physical education teachers, rather than having a principal attend sessions with his own staff. His meetings or retreats with his own staff can come later after the individuals achieve a certain amount of self-insight and growth.

The point is that not all training is appropriate for all organizations or people. Unfortunately, on some occasions, an over-zealous school administrator will see group training as a panacea for his school's problems, and will call in someone to apply a randomly selected repertoire of exercises or gimmicks to his organization. For instance, a big city school principal hired a consultant to conduct racial encounter sessions for the blacks and whites in the same school. After stirring the pot, the consultant left only to have the lid blow off a month later because of poor follow-up and little planning for more than the initial confrontation. When carefully used, group training potentially offers one of the most promising modes for dealing with the conflicts and tensions which exist among administrators, teachers, and students today, for changing the attitudes which have prevented our schools from progressing with the times into the twentieth century, and for making the classroom alive by integrating into it the affective with the intellectual. Chapter 8 gets deeper into evaluation of humanistic education.

"EDUCATION OF THE SELF"

I will present in some detail a description of a block of instruction which uses the student himself as the content for the course rather than any other body of cognitive material. This is a course designed by Gerald Weinstein and his associates, Sid Simon, Gerry Loney, Dick Nessen, Mark Polen, Chuck Ungerleider and myself. We first presented the course to two mixed groups of approximately seventy undergraduate and graduate students. The basic idea for the course is that the self is examined as seen by the student himself, by others, and as the student would ideally like to see himself. The student works, after the initial few meetings, with small intimate permanent feedback groups which help him to negotiate change and develop strategies which will help him to move closer to his ideal self. Rather than stopping at the self-awareness stage, I feel it is important that this course go further—to help the individual negotiate with himself and others and to work toward changing his behavior if change is perceived and desired by him.

One of the end results of this course is a "self kit" which contains anything the student feels exemplifies himself. The contents vary from photographs, to art, to journal descriptions of how he sees himself in various exercises compared with how others see him and how he would *like* to be seen. Additionally, at the end of the course, the students can stage a "Carnival of the Self" where each student has a booth at which he puts whatever he desires of himself on display. Half the students visit the booths sampling the exhibits and wares while the other half put on their displays. On another day they change places, the other half putting themselves on display while the previously displayed group tours.

The process of how Gerald Weinstein has organized the planning for this course is worthy of note. Each week the planners have a seminar with others who are interested in humanistic education. A "post mortem" of the past week's class is held and ideas on how to improve upon and follow up the "unfinished business" from the preceeding session are hashed over. New exercises are brainstormed, experimented with, and experienced. Ideas from visitors or other group leaders are shared and tried out. Finally the planners expose and encounter the invariable interpersonal problems and frictions which have developed among themselves. Graduate students participating are given three hours of academic credit for their efforts in the planning seminar.

One of the models designed by Gerald Weinstein that we use in this course to ensure that individuals get beyond the self-awareness state involves the following series of steps:

Step 1: Confrontation

This pertains to any type of confrontation between the student and any exercises, the student and the leader, or the student and another person. For the example which follows, we'll use a simple small group meeting and the students' confrontation with it.

Step 2: Determine my unique responses

What is unique about the way I respond to this confrontation? (e.g., I spoke first, sat against the wall, and looked people in the eye.)

Step 3: Identify the patterns of my response

I usually initiate the action in a conversation. I also usually sit against the wall. I try hard to always look people in the eye.

Step 4: What are the functions of my patterns of response

I initiate the conversation to impress people and take the leadership. I look people in the eye so they will think I am sincere and interested in them. I sit with my back to the wall so I won't feel surrounded and insecure.

Step 5: What are the consequences of my patterns of response

When I speak first, people think I'm overeager and it deprives others of a chance to be first. They dislike it. When I look people in the eye, they like me and give me attention. When I sit with my back to the wall, it limits who I can sit next to.

Step 6: Try an experiment with new behavior

I will try to sit in places other than against the wall and see how it feels, I will try not being the first to speak to see if I am valued more or listened to better. I'll try not looking people in the eye to see how it goes.

Step 7: Evaluate results of experimentation

I find that it makes little difference in how I feel if I sit in different places than against the wall, plus I have the flexibility of sitting next to whomever I please. I think others enjoy the chance to initiate the conversation and I find them attending better to what I have to say. People don't appreciate me looking down or away while they are speaking.

Step 8: Choice

I will start sitting wherever I like rather than against the wall. I will hold off initiating the conversation unless there seems to be a long lull. I will continue looking people in the eye.

This eight step process is used by the individual as a model for the course. In the first two or three lessons the students are exposed to a variety of exercises which begin mildly and increase in threat as they progress. The first few lessons emphasize step 1 or the confrontation. They are asked to catalog their unique responses to the exercises in a journal.

In later lessons the class meets in small permanent feedback groups where they concentrate progressively on going through the eight-step process. For example in about the third lesson the emphasis is on determining patterns by doing such things as having each individual stand in the middle of the group while the group calls out rapid-fire adjectives that describe the individual's patterns as they see them. They might feel, push, or touch the individual in this process of trying to determine his patterns of response. At the end of the session each individual reports his reactions to the patterns cited. A description of the first few lessons follows.

FIRST LESSON *(Confrontation and Determining Unique Responses —Steps 1 and 2)*

At the first lesson the individuals, working in two subgroups with two leaders, go around a circle giving a name they would like to be called during the course, followed by the fruit or vegetable they felt most like, and their expectations for the course. This is a mild warm up exercise which usually relaxes the group. I decided to be Hal, felt like an over-sweet mango since I was having trouble being less than sweet and showing anger. I hoped I could become more sour, like a lemon, and tell people off when they deserve it. Others followed suit in this fashion, finding it much easier sharing their honest feelings using the fruits and vegetables.

The next series of exercises is done in a large circle, and it consists of physical warm ups. The instructions given are as follows: "Place your palms together in front of your chest and press as hard as possible." (Allow one minute.) "Next pretend that there is something very heavy in front of you and push it as hard as you can." (Allow one minute.) "Now, walk easily in place. Now put some strut in your walk. Increase your speed now and wave your arms as though they were birds' wings; walk faster and flap faster; take off, soar, crash land."

"Now mill around the room without making contact with anyone; stop milling; look at the people around you; choose one; shake hands using your left hand; explore each other's left hand with your right hand. Change partners several times."

I now begin a series of communication exercises with the class which I find useful in a new group. "Choose someone who interests you; sit back to back and explore how you feel about each other and communicate through back movements and speaking only." "Next face each other and communicate just using eyes." "Now close your eyes and using just your hands; have a conversation. During that conversation say hello; take a walk, have a fight, resolve the conflict, say goodbye." I now have the pairs give each other feedback about their communications modes and which seemed most effective. It's interesting that usually people will communicate some intimate or significant things non-verbally that they were reluctant to communicate verbally.

Finally, I ask them to think of two nicknames which they have been called in the past, getting in touch with how they felt about the names. Now the partner whispers in a variety of tones of voices the names into his partner's ear. When his voice elicits an association or memory from the past, stop the partner and share the association. Then the roles are reversed. This is an effective exercise that I was exposed to in a group at Esalen led by George Brown.

Timing is important in these exercises. It's essential to watch the group to be sure that they have sufficient time to discuss the exercise and perform it.

Next, the pairs are asked to look for other couples who interest them and gather into groups of six or eight. One person from each of the pairs forms an inner circle and their partners form an outer circle. I ask them to think about a time in their lives when they were most free. After giving them a little time to get in touch with those feelings, I have them share the experiences with the inner group. The partner on the outside watches the reactions of his partner while he speaks. The groups then break up and the partner gives feedback to the partner who has spoken. The group reconvenes and outer and inner circles reverse roles. The group splits again and the person who has spoken gets feedback from his partner. You can also do this exercise having them think of when they were most lonely, however this is usually a little more threatening than the "free exercise." I finish this in dyads, having each partner say to the other the one most outstanding thing he's noticed about the other during these exercises.

We frequently finish these sessions with a massage train. Everyone sits in a circle of chairs facing in the same direction with hands on the neck of the person in front of him so as to form a train. Each person gives the person in front of him a rub, relaxing him as much as possible. After two minutes they turn around, reverse the train, and massage the person who has been massaging them. This is a delightful exercise to end a session. It gives everyone a good, warm, relaxed feeling. I use it frequently to begin or end classes.

Following each lesson, Gerald Weinstein has the students enter into their journals information they have collected about themselves in regard to the eight step process (i.e. after the first lesson they record the confrontations they have had (step 1) and their unique responses (step 2) as they saw themselves, as others saw them, and as they would ideally like to be).

SECOND LESSON—*Confrontation and Determining Unique Responses*

We begin the second three-hour block of instruction with a massage train again. We ask the students to change their manner of massaging in relation to the following words: gently; with more pressure; playfully; lovingly; teasingly; tenderly; and savagely. This is a nice warm up for the next exercise.

Milling exercise

"Mill around the room without contacting anyone. Imagine that you are walking in water. Splash around a bit. Get the feel of the water. Now the water is rising to cover your feet. It's up to your knees now. Feel the difference in the way you walk and move. The water has risen to your thighs now and is at your groin. Feel the water with your fingertips. The water continues to slowly rise and is at your chest; now only your head is above water. Feel the space around your head; keep moving. Now the water completely covers your head but you are still able to breathe. The water is beginning to recede now, your head is completely out of the water. Feel your space; you're dripping. The water is at your waist; now at your groin; now at your thighs; now at your knees; now at your ankles; now you are standing in a puddle again. Relax."

A Trip Through Your Senses

"Find your own space somewhere in the room and occupy it. Close your eyes. Feel the space around you and try to get a picture of the shape and area of your space. You are in an envelope of space which moves with you. Make yourself comfortable in your space. Now, concentrating only on your sense of touch, discover as many textures about yourself as you can." (Give about two minutes for this.) "Continue to discover even more undiscovered textures." (Give another minute.) "Relax. Now tune in to your sense of smell to the exclusion of all other senses. How do different parts of your body smell?" (Allow about one minute.) "Now attend only to taste. How great a variety of tastes about you can you discover?" (Allow a minute.) "Relax. Now listen to the sounds of yourself; at some point put your hands over your ears. Can you hear your blood moving, your heart beating, any other noises about your body? Relax."

"Look around the room. Now choose a partner. Go with your partner to your space. Share with each other the senses as in the previous exercise. Sharing with your partner the single most outstanding impression you have of him as a result of this experience." Though it can be too threatening to some groups to taste partners, an interesting alternative is to have each person tell his partner what he thinks he would taste like.

Personal Universe.[3]

"Sit again in a large circle. Face toward the wall and get into your most secure position making yourself very small. Feel your space around you. For the next 50 years you cannot move your body and your space will be your universe. Begin to explore your universe." (Allow at least 5 minutes for this exploration.) "If you choose, let the sounds come out which are characteristic of your universe. Let the sounds become louder. Start to emerge from your universe. Return to the circle. Share experiences with others." When I first performed this exercise, I soon realized that even without moving or seeing, my universe was quite extensive and fascinating, and I had enough things to interest me for perhaps a few years. For instance, just exploring my teeth with my tongue could occupy me for a day or so. Getting into an itch was quite an experience. The sounds of the world around me became amplified and were very interesting. The sounds that we emitted, those of our own personal universe, were a fascinating mixture of almost supernatural and deeply emotional utterances.

Geography of the Self

This is another interesting exercise designed by Gerald Weinstein:

"Mill around the room and form groups of exactly four people. Sit together in a group. Pretend you are elementary school children in a geography class. Remember the old geography book that you used? Will the boys please pass the geography books? What do the books look like? What kinds of headings do you find in the book? Table of Contents? We are going to explore for a while the geography of ourselves by asking questions which might be found in a geography book, but into each question insert the word 'your.' For instance, Where are *your* urban areas located? As each ques-

---

[3] This is an exercise that Gerald Weinstein adopted from an idea of Janet Lederman.

tion within your group is generated, all members of the group should try to answer it only for themselves before the next question is asked. Record your questions and your responses." Some of the types of questions and answers to this exercise are described in more detail in the section on Geography of the Self beginning on page 142.

The students are asked to follow up this exercise by preparing, outside the class, a personal geography map which is later brought to class and shared with the feedback groups. These maps can be artistically or otherwise depicted in any way the student desires.

Additionally, the students are asked to include in their journals a section entitled "Unfinished Business," which is a list of things that they might want to do or say to someone or to themselves but which they have not yet accomplished. These could be either positive or negative things. Finally they are asked to tie each of these exercises and responses to the eight step process described earlier.

THIRD SESSION—*Confrontation, Determining Unique Responses, and Patterns of Responses—Steps 1, 2 and 3*

Gerald Weinstein begins the third three-hour block of instruction with the choosing of permanent feedback groups in which the class will spend much time for the remainder of the semester. The instructions go like this: "Mill around and select a partner. With your partner, each choose three other partners and sit together with your group of eight. Discuss why you chose each other; look at your group and compare it with the others; what things are unique about your group; how does your group compare as to male–female ratio, age, etc."

"If these were going to be permanent groups, would you choose to remain where you are? Vote by secret ballot."

Groups which are very dissatisfied with their composition are given the opportunity to join together or negotiate new groups. It seems to help make people more comfortable if it is explained that the feedback groups function as an anchor for the individuals, a place where one could depend on consistent honest feedback, rather than groups which meet together to do exercises each day.

Composite Portrait

Each feedback group divides in half and, using pencil and paper, makes a composite drawing, i.e., makes a figure which is a composite of characteristics chosen from real characteristics of the members of the group. The students give the figure a name and a personality and indicate on the drawing which characteristic was taken from whom and why.

This is a fascinating exercise which gives the group a chance to openly discuss and deal with their physical appearance. The process usually begins with the hair, and anyone feeling strongly about his or her hair can either volunteer it or say why they think it isn't attractive. Everyone's hair is looked over and then someone's is selected. In one group viewing necks, a girl said in response to someone's comment that she had a pretty neck, "Oh no, I don't have any neck at all. My mother always told me that." The group used her neck to make the point to her that she did have a lovely neck in spite of her mother's old feedback. It was amazing to me to find during this exercise how many mothers seem to tear down the physical image of their daughters. Strangely enough this seems to occur more frequently with daughters than with sons. One attractive girl said that she had always thought her nose was ugly because her mother told her that when she was a teenager. The fact was that she had a nice nose which went very well with her face. It's as though there exists some sort of sexual envy or jealousy from certain mothers toward their daughters, causing them to depreciate their daughter's physical appearance.

When breasts were discussed in one group, two girls volunteered theirs but one soon declined in favor of the other who apparently thought enough of the attractiveness of her breasts that she didn't wear a bra. Her's were chosen.

The work groups are merged again to form feedback groups and they share the composites with each other, explaining how the characteristics were chosen, why, and to whom they belonged.

Then each person in turn tells what it is he or she is most ashamed of about his or her body. The level of intimacy which this question reaches after the last exercise is quite deep. In one group a student said he was most ashamed of his penis because he thought it was too small. Apparently, this had been a deep concern of his for some time, and the opportunity to be open about it seemed to take a tremendous load off his shoulders. Several of the girls in the group told him that they felt penis size made absolutely no difference whatsoever in lovemaking, but rather it was the person himself and how real he was that counted. A girl then volunteered that she thought her breasts were too small, and she received from the group quite a bit of supportive feedback about the attractiveness of her figure. In most cases the problems most people felt about their bodies had been grossly blown out of proportion, and these features were found by others to be quite acceptable. This kind of supportive feedback is usually prevalent in this exercise.

This exercise is completed by having each student write in his journal what part of his body was chosen and whether any choice surprised them. Additionally they were asked how they felt when some part of their anatomy was rejected. Finally Gerald Weinstein asks the class to consider these questions and jot down their responses:[4]

1. Think of your body being twice the size it is now. How would you feel?
2. If you now were half the normal size, how would that feel?
3. If you could add anything you wanted to your normal body, what would it be?
4. If you had to give up some part of your body, if it were absolutely required that you do this in order to live, what would it be?
5. If your body were entirely fragmented before you, laying in a bunch of pieces, how would you layer the pieces in order to construct a pile in which the most valuable piece were on top and the least valuable piece on the bottom.
6. If you had the opportunity to multiply something already existing on your body what would it be and how many would you choose to have?
7. If you could build a new body but it couldn't be out of protoplasm, what material would you select?
8. If you could change your body's color, which would you select?
9. If your body couldn't be used as a body anymore but had to be used for another function that would be useful to mankind, what would that function be?

An interesting variation of the "composite portrait" exercise which we use in later sessions is the making of a portrait using

---

[4] These questions were adopted from an idea presented by A. F. Osborn in *Applied Imagination* (New York: Charles Scribner's Sons, 1957).

personality traits rather than physical characteristics. As always, the students are asked to tie their reactions to the exercises to the eight-step process.

LATER SESSIONS *(Steps 4 through 8)*

The remainder of the semester is devoted to getting the students through the eight-step process so that they can take their patterns of response (step 3), determine what functions these patterns serve for them (step 4), find out the consequences of their patterns of response (step 5), try on or experiment with new behavior (step 6), evaluate the results of the experimentation (step 7), and finally make a choice about how they want to be (step 8). In other words, instead of stopping at self-awareness, we go beyond and give the student some tools in the form of exercises and environment, some help in the form of his feedback group, and the opportunity to negotiate and achieve change in his personality.

In the later sessions we usually begin the class by demonstrating a few exercises which might be relevant to the particular steps which are being emphasized. The majority of work in the later sessions, however, is done in the permanent feedback groups. We are quite flexible about where the students are in the eight-step process. The main thing is to provide the opportunity for getting all the way through the process to include the "choice" step. What's more, the permanent feedback groups will develop their own individuality, group solidarity, or cohesion. In fact they will begin to develop their own repertoires of exercises and procedures for dealing within their own groups and with other groups. (Some of the groups even began to bring favorite foods or wines to share on occasions, while others have extra-curricular meetings at members' homes.)

Though the feedback groups daily develop new and effective exercises on their own, I will describe two more exercises which I feel deserve special mention.

"I see you..."

This exercise is done in small groups and begins with two rules. One is to stay with the "here and now," that is with present feelings and observations rather than with the past or the future. The second rule is the "I and thou" rule, or being specific rather than general in directing a comment, feeling, or observation directly at a particular person rather than at the group.

The exercise begins with the class regrouped in new small groups with members sitting in a circle looking at each other for a minute or two and then directing "I see you . . ." comments at particular members. For instance, after looking around, one member may say, "I see you fidgeting with your feet." or "I see you looking away when I look at you." After doing this for a few minutes the groups are instructed to expand the statements to "I see you . . . and I perceive that you are . . ." For example, "I see you fooling with your fingers and I perceive that you are nervous." This is done for five or six minutes and then the groups are instructed to find a person's eyes and look into them until told to look for someone new. The class is allowed thirty seconds and then told to look for a new set of eyes to look into for the next thirty seconds. In this way they rotate through all the member's eyes in their group. This exercise greatly accelerates the process of recognizing conflicts, tensions, and feelings, both hostile and affectionate, which exist between people.

The final part of the exercise takes the student through the first two steps "I see you . . . and I perceive that you are . . ." and then adds "and it makes me . . ." For example, "I see you fidgeting with your fingers, and I perceive that you are nervous, and that makes me feel uptight." This is followed by a quick response from the person being addressed. This is a fairly threatening exercise and should be used in the later stages of group work. It's a very effective exercise especially if the "here and now" and "I and thou" rules are enforced.

"In the manner of the Person"

One final exercise which we find useful in the later sessions of the course is an exercise we call "In the manner of the person."

This is an exercise which was developed quite by accident by Gerald Weinstein and the planning group. It has several levels of application and is not only fun to play, but is also helpful in giving feedback to each other and in helping individuals to identify the consequences of their patterns of response. The exercise is done in the following manner: One member of the small feedback group leaves the room while the others pick a person to be "it." The member who has left is called back in, and it is up to him to identify the person who is "it" by going around the group and asking each member to do things "in the manner of the person" who is "it." For instance, he can ask a member to tell off another member "in the manner of the person;" or have someone walk and then dance "in the manner of the person;" or even more complex, have someone rationalize an action "in the manner of the person." To add an interesting twist the person the group picks to be "it" could be the person who went out of the room. It's better not to allow guessing until after everyone in the group has the opportunity to do something "in the manner of the person." In this exercise people get a unique kind of feedback about how they "come over" to others as they watch themselves being acted out in various interesting situations by the other group members.

Gerald Weinstein and his colleagues are continually working to develop curricula that have direct classroom application, and which go beyond the fun and games stage, beyond the self-awareness stage, and get into making changes in the classroom, in learning and in individuals. These concerns which are also shared by most of the other serious pioneers in the field are reflected in an article in the November 15, 1969, issue of *Saturday Review*, "Sense About Sensitivity Training," by Max Birnbaum:

> . . . human relations training is capable, if properly employed, of producing substantial educational change. It holds tremendous potential for improving education by dealing with its affective components, reducing the unnecessary friction between generations, and creating a revolution in instruction by helping teachers to learn how to use the classroom group for learning purposes.
>
> The pity is that this promising innovation may be killed before its unique properties have a fair chance to demonstrate their worth. The opposition to its serious exploration is strong and is apt to grow. Among those who oppose sensitivity training are those who say, ". . . it smacks of therapy," which to a very small degree it does . . . , the members of the renascent John Birch Society, who would equate it with brainwashing . . . as well as some of, . . . it's enthusiastic but frequently unsophisticated school supporters . . . and some of the, . . . newly hatched trainees, long on enthusiasm or entrepreneurial expertise, but short on professional experience, skill, and wisdom.[5]

---

[5] Max Birnbaum, "Sense about Sensitivity Training," *Saturday Review* (November 15, 1969), p. 82.

Though there's little question about the need to move in this direction, the moves should be thought out and planned, and they should lead somewhere. Gerald Weinstein and his associates are moving, and they are also thinking out and planning their moves into productive areas.

THE GEOGRAPHY OF THE SELF

Gerald Weinstein and his associates at the University of Massachusetts Center for Humanistic Education have developed and tested in the classroom other effective humanistic education techniques, several of which will be reviewed in the next few pages. The first of these is a sketch of possible classroom techniques on personal geography or the geography of the self. The author has tried many of them out with his children and with students with delightful results. Children expand their openness into new areas that often have been repressed or sublimated to the detriment of a healthy personality development. Additionally, these exercises allow the child to fantacize openly, be creative, and have fun doing it. An effective way to do these exercises is to have the class divide itself into groups of four. Each member of the group will then take his turn making up a question about the geography of the body. Each question will be answered by each member of the group and then by the originator of the question before a new question is asked by the next member. For example, in an Education of the Self class in which I recently took part, one student asked, "If your body were a country, what would be its imports and exports?" One member answered, "My imports would be affection (my country needs lots of it and it also exports a lot of it); love, but that's very scarce now and since we're having trouble getting it, we're taking in more affection than usual to make up for it; ideas—I take these in, work on them and then export them as finished or partially finished products. My principal exports are affection, some love, loyal friendship, some ideas, practical suggestions or solutions to problems, and energy which I export in great quantity because I have a great surplus of it in my country." Some of the questions and adaptations of this which were "brainstormed" by Gerald Weinstein and his associates are presented here as idea stimulations for teachers or parents to try out on their students or children:

1. Take a fantastic voyage, an exploration trip over your body—a group of tiny explorers—a Lewis and Clark expedition over your body. What would their journal be like? Write an imaginary journal of their discoveries.
2. Smile 'til it hurts—see what muscles are affected. What goes into a relaxed smile? The strain of masking or armoring?
3. An odyssey into your inner space. How big is the inside of your head. Get a sense of your message network—what's coming in and going out?
4. If your body were a continent where would your rivers be? Your population centers, your mountain ranges, cliffs, and caves? What are the chief products of your body continent— natural resources, materials for productions, energy centers, power plants, recreation areas and parks?

   What do you like to show to the tourists? If people were living on you, who would they be—where would they be living— what would they be doing and where—how would they feel about their environment—what places would they like best, least?

   If your body were the world, where would the cities be located. (Song "Tatooed Lady," "Under her kidney is a birds-eye view of Sydney.")

   Where are the boundaries of the body?

   If your body were a country, where would you live or not live?

   What are the climates? Seasons?

   Which parts of the body are slippery?

   What are the capitals of the self and why?

   What are the major products?

   What are the differences between the surface and beneath it?

   What are your wars and conflicts (cold and hot)?

   Where are the colonies? Who owns parts of you?

   Where are the tension (trouble) spots?

   What about the "iron curtain" and how it emerged?

   Where would you rest or play?

   When are you most at sea level?

   What do you use to make a living?

   Where are the uncharted regions—the frontiers?

   How and who will explore these?

   What are the seasons of your life?

Suppose you were going to explore uncharted regions of body, what would you need?

Write a journal of a germ traveling over your body.

How does someone get inside you? Who do you prohibit from entering or leaving?

What passport is needed? Are there border regulations? How about alien registration?

What's the history of your country and its people?

How many kings and presidents in your country?

Is your country a satellite or an independent state?

What country is your body most like?

Ever had any revolutions?

Would you like to leave your country?

How would you do it?

Can you take a "legitimate trip"? Do you have an early warning system?

What percentage of your budget would you spend on defense?

What percentage of your natural resources would you use on defense?

Where are the slums of your body? What percent of budget would you spend on improving these?

What music does your body speak and what are the instruments?

5. Make an inventory of body language.

"Get off my back"

"Pain in the neck"

Why do some parts of the body fit more into body language than others?

Organ language—"tearing my heart."

6. Feel, in detail, your hair, skin, feet bottoms—listen to your organs speak over stereo (record on stereo tape recorder using stethoscope).

Where are the hinges on your body?

Matter states of your body—liquids, solids. Elasticity.

What are your body rhymes—what are the rhythms of your life? Create through musical instruments your life rhythm.

What's it like to lose your baby teeth?

What state are you most like?

7. Why are so many love functions "dirty words"? What parts of your body have become the enemy? Which body parts or areas are the friendliest?

What are the beautiful parts of your body—the ugliest? Where did you get your notions of beauty? How will you look ten years from now?

Could you draw artistic patterns from the movement of your internal organs?

What is the day and night of your body—the body asleep?

8. How many transplants could you take and still be you? How would anybody know? What would you have transplanted?

Suppose you had to be 15 for the rest of life?

Suppose you were 50 times bigger or smaller?

Who are the minorities? Who rules?

This is not a unit on anatomy in the biological sense—but an expedition through your body and its relation to how you feel about you, your body and self image. What is your body trying to tell you? Learn to read it? How does your body influence your image of yourself? What are your relations with your body? How do you get along together? How connected or disconnected are you with it? Can you find new ways to come in contact with your body? Look at your body as a stranger or your body as an unplayed instrument. Expand your body's sensory capacities. How have you taught your body nonsense? What chinks have you put in some of your body armor?

What is the effect of eye dominance over the other senses? How do you keep the world at a distance? How much of you have you been cutting off? How can you bring to life the dead or numb areas of your body? (This is real physical education.) What do you mean by: "out of touch"? and "sexuality"?

Trying some of these with your children and students will make it apparent that any single question can lead to a fantastic exploration of values, feelings, and concepts altogether too frequently ignored, or buried, or numbed.

ONE WAY FEELING GLASSES

Another concept developed by Gerald Weinstein is the concept of "one way feeling glasses."[6] He has demonstrated this concept on

---

[6] Gerald Weinstein, "One way Feeling Glasses" (unpublished manuscript, University of Mass., 1967).

television with children from New York City schools. This technique is useful with many different age levels. I have used it very effectively with graduate students and with teachers.

Gerald Weinstein will enter, for example, a sixth grade inner city classroom with a box full of old dimestore glasses. In one classroom he explained to the children that he had very special "one way feeling glasses." "When you put these on, you see things suspiciously." He asked for a volunteer to try on the glasses. A small boy in the front of the classroom came up and put them on. He looked around and smiled. When asked what he saw through the suspicious glasses, he replied, "I wonder why you're here today, and the teacher is out loafing or goofing off?" Gerald Weinstein told him, "That's exactly the way suspicious glasses work!" The boy looked around the room, and said, "I wonder if those two boys in the back of the room are talking about me?" Several other children used the suspicious glasses with equal success.

Gerald Weinstein then pulled another pair of glasses out of the box and said, "These are 'I know they really care about me no matter what they say or do glasses'." Several children tried them on with revealing results.

One of the pairs of glasses, the "self righteous glasses," provided some interesting results. When asked who might wear "self righteous glasses," one child replied, "Batman." Another said the counselor. When asked more about this, he replied that whenever you go in to see the counselor, he asks, "What trouble have you been in now?" Another said, "The principal." When asked what the opposite of "self righteous glasses" might be one student replied, "People are not too different from me glasses."

When the students in the class all put on "strong point glasses," and looked around at their fellow students, the classroom became alive with feeling as students began honestly telling their associates, in most cases for the first time, about their strengths. A warm pleasant feeling seemed to spread among these ghetto hardened children as they heard reinforcing feedback about their strong points from others in the class.

When asked what kind of glasses "a new kid" coming into the class ought to have, the students replied "power glasses" to make it through the struggle. A new student in the class emphatically agreed, and this touched off a discussion on how he had been accepted by the others. This ended with the conclusion that he was now definitely a member of the group.

The author has used the "strong point glasses" technique with graduate students with amazing results. After having each student, in turn, put on "strong point glasses" and give each of the others' strong points, the author passed around a hand mirror and asked each student to tell what he saw in the mirror, still wearing his "strong point glasses." This gave students the rare opportunity of openly and honestly stating what they felt their strong points to be. It was a most intimate, warm, and satisfying experience for the entire group of 15 students.

This technique of one way feeling glasses has infinite variation and application limited only by the teacher's imagination and self enlightenment.

THE CONCEPT OF SUBSELVES

Another very useful technique being used by Gerald Weinstein and his associates, adopted from the work of Stewart Shapiro of the University of California, Santa Barbara, is a way for the students to conceptualize the different subselves or characters which make up their personalities. For example, I have had my graduate students list the subselves which they have in common with one another such as the "critical subself," the "loving subself," the "protector subself," the "reserve subself," the "show time subself," etc. I then arranged for the students to put on individual plays dramatizing some or all of the subselves which they felt existed in themselves. Each student then took turns changing back and forth (changing chairs when he changed roles) in the roles of his various subselves in different situations. Other students empathized and helped the student by playing the role of a friend's various identified subselves as they saw that particular side of his personality. Students discover in this activity that it is necessary to have the various subselves negotiate in order to work out the drama. These dramatizations are often very revealing and helpful to the role players. Caution is in order as this technique can be very powerful if the students are allowed to go deeply into real life situations with their subselves. This practice is often used in Gestalt Therapy. At

Esalen, the author was a member of a group where group members played the roles of their personality with such intensity that decisions and commitments vital to their lives resulted. One girl was wrestling with the problem of living with a domineering mother who over-protected her and sabotaged her every romance in an effort to keep "her baby in the fold." This girl divided up into the subselves, "Mary inner," an extroverted, strong girl, with high libido and "Mary outer," a shy, dominated, dependent person. She was led by the group leader through the playing of the roles of these two very real subselves switching from one chair to another as they argued. "Mary inner" in a burst of aggression shouted at "Mary outer" that she had ruined her life staying around mother when she was entitled to romance, fulfillment, and a life of her own. "Mary outer" argued back feebly that Mother would probably have a heart attack and die if she didn't stay at home. After thirty intense minutes of encounter, "Mary outer" backed down and admitted that she really admired "Mary inner" much more than herself, and though she thought her own reservedness and tact was important to their joint success, she decided that "Mary inner" should "come out" and be predominant much more in the future. We were all astounded to see the vivacious and extroverted "Mary inner" (a much more attractive person) around for the rest of the workshop. In this case real transformation had taken place. In the normal classroom situation, a much milder playing of the subselves role is in order, and this can be controlled by staying with the "here and now."

I'd like to turn for a moment to a "behavioral" approach to humanistic education advanced by Allen Ivey and Stephen Rollin. Is such an approach possible?

ALLEN IVEY AND STEPHEN ROLLIN—
Intentionality. . . . A Behavioral Approach

Can a human relations program written from a behavioral point of view permit and encourage an individual to engage in free choice? This is the task that Dr. Allen Ivey and Stephen Rollin have set for themselves. Recognizing the power and potential of behavior modification techniques drawn primarily from operant or Skinnerian and social learning psychology theory, they have drawn up and tested a curriculum in human relations which uses methods not usually associated with the human potential movement.

The primary objective of their "performance curriculum" is the developing of the *intentional individual,* who is defined as a person who can act freely and spontaneously in response to his surroundings or environment. The individual who acts with intentionality has the tools to generate alternate world views, to "come at" a problem from different vantage points. He readily grasps and considers alternate perceptions of himself and others. The intentional individual constantly *acts*—he may manifest this action in a variety of manners by drawing on a wide variety of behavioral alternatives open to him.

Ivey and Rollin feel that words may not adequately describe the intentional individual and offer the following illustration of what happened when one of their students in elementary education acted with intentionality:

> Susie had a beautiful lesson in human relations. She wanted to share with her fifth grade students some of her ideas about listening to others. She sat on the floor and asked the children to play gossip . . . to pass a message around the circle by whispering.
>
> After the message had gone around a few times, Susie asked the children to discuss what had happened. The children engaged in an excellent discussion of how one learns from listening to others. The children continued the discussion on their own and Susie became a participant with them as they explored the topic. As the children became more involved, Susie dropped out of the discussion and became an interested listener. She was particularly pleased when Craig, usually a negative discipline problem, pointed out that "listening is not necessarily hearing."

Ivey and Rollin point out that in this brief example Susie is demonstrating several specific behaviors which she had learned in her experience in the performance curriculum. First, she was *relaxed,* natural and easygoing in her manner with the children. Her *non-verbal behaviors* indicated support and interest in the experience. Training in *decision making* appeared when Susie demonstrated alternative teacher behaviors of directing, participating, and following. Susie demonstrated *attending behavior* skills in that she was able to listen carefully to the children. These specific behaviors had been emphasized in the human relations classes she had experienced.

Perhaps most important in this lesson is that Susie planned only a few behaviors; for the most part, she did what "felt right" to her at the moment, and that included some planning ahead as well as much spontaneous activity. Not only did she affect children, but they also affected her. Susie's and the class's experience of this session was one of enjoyment and accomplishment.

Given these specific objectives, Ivey and Rollin established a program for human growth which is structured in its early stages so that the individual can have something with which he can interact. In its later stages, the program is organized so that students can utilize constructs in their own fashion and eventually develop their own unique world view and teaching style.

The basic model adapted for the performance curriculum is an "each one, teach one" approach in which a relatively specific area of human relations behavior is identified (e.g., relaxation, attending behavior). The participants then follow three basic steps: 1. they learn the skills of that specific area; 2. they teach the skills to one other individual; and 3. they generate alternative ways to teach or demonstrate this skill to several others; and 4. they act on the alternatives they themselves have decided. The skills are organized in a hierarchial fashion and the individual does not proceed to the next higher level until he has demonstrated his ability to perform at the present level.

At the beginning of the behavioral skills "hierarchy," Ivey and Rollin stress the value of alternative views of each skill. They may use audio or videotapes to demonstrate the skill in question, group or individual procedures similar to those described elsewhere in this book, or written materials. When students reported they had been successful in teaching a specific skill to someone else, the facilitators rewarded most highly the efforts of the student which were unique and most clearly "belonged" to him.

Ivey and Rollin have developed performance curricula in over 30 specific areas ranging from relaxation and self-control of physiological response to listening skills, and empathy to organizational change. After an introduction to the specific behavior in question, each individual must find his own definition of the behavior in question if he is to achieve the central objective of intentionality inherent in the program. As such, each specific behavioral goal simply becomes a vehicle leading to the larger concept of intentionality.

It might be helpful to guide you through a sample hierarchy so that you can get a feel for the construction of a specific program in human relations. The basic framework that was used was the Systematic Desentization Hierarchy of Joseph Wolpe and Arnold Lazarus. Ivey and Rollin in looking for a model for their program felt that the hierarchial approach of Wolpe and Lazarus provided an ideal base to build their program around because of the clear, concise, and compact nature of the hierarchy approach.

The first issue in hierarchy building is to identify the skill (e.g., relaxation, attending behavior, non-verbalization, innovation etc.) that is to be taught, and define that same skill from a behavioral vantage. The next step is to generate the terminal objectives, that is, what would you like your students to have when they have completed the hierarchy in terms of either skill, understanding, or knowledge. The step that follows is to take the broad concept and analyze factors (not statistically) to discern what its component parts are from a behavioral point of view. It is most important to order the factors from the most general factor to the most specific, while also including an opportunity for the student to learn the skill, teach it to another, and teach it to a class of students after developing a hierarchy from which to teach. The final step in the building of a hierarchy is to establish multiple instructional alternatives for *each* step within the hierarchy. The instructional alternatives should provide an opportunity for the student, if the alternatives make little sense to him, to establish an approach to the specific behavior that is most congruent to his own nature. As Ivey and Rollin pointed out earlier, the interest is in multiple world views and multiple approaches to a specific issue or behavior.

In conclusion, then, what Ivey and Rollin have intended to do in their Human Relations Program is to establish a curriculum that is simple to master, conceptually clear, and one that will provide a basis for students to learn any number of specific human relations skills.

THOMAS CLARK—*Caring and Communicating*

As you consider developing a humanistic education approach, you should realize that it is not as easy as obtaining a new curriculum guide and trying it out in the classroom. It's really a total way of life in which the teacher will undergo some pain and change in the process of becoming a humanistic educator. Additionally, it means a deep commitment to students—deeper, perhaps, than many teachers are willing to go. One of the most dedicated university faculty members I know, Dr. Thomas Clark—who makes himself "on call" to his students 24 hours a day—makes the following observations about "caring and communicating."

Being involved in humanistic education is simultaneously simple and complex. It involves attempting to be human and realizing that "role teacher" is not a professional costume which is donned as one enters the classroom and hung on a hook as one departs.

Attempting to be a humanistic educator means that you are working with what might be called a C^2 formula. First you have to be honestly concerned, care, or give a damn about the individuals who are your students. Second you have to learn how to communicate that concern. It is this combination of concern and the attempt to communicate it which seems to be the basis of what is called humanistic education.

Further, it means treating the subject matter, course, or discipline as a "means" rather than an "end," which has been the way most teachers have been taught. The subject matter can become a key to further self-development or self-understanding if treated as such. This does not mean that the discipline becomes a vehicle for a "sensitivity session"; it does mean that the subject matter may form a cognitive link which, in a genuinely supportive environment, unites or enables two or more individuals to share an idea, thought or emotion. This use of the idea or subject matter can be an extremely "affective" experience.

Being a humanistic educator implies working with each student as a unique individual and it implies being concerned with more than the impersonal "conditioning" or the "memorization–regurgitation" cycle that often characterizes the university classroom. It involves seemingly simple things such as learning students' names, why each is taking your course, what each expects to get from the experience, and what each is willing to contribute to the group. This simple technique, which usually entails approximately one class session, may begin in a very simple way the process whereby a group of individuals transcends the impersonal set of bored characters which is all too frequently a phenomenon. Implicit in this process is a certain reciprocity or shared communication wherein the teacher tells the students why he is teaching the course, what he expects to learn from the experience, and what he intends to share with the group. If this process is followed, it means that you no longer view the learning experience as simply "education of the head."

Humanistic education is *not* "value free." If it is to be in any way a personal, humanizing experience, one accepts the fact that both students and teachers have a world view or value set through which each interprets facts and catalogues information. It means that you are candid with students regarding your values, beliefs, and attitudes. It does not mean that you expect students to mime or conform to your values; it does mean questioning frequently but "judging" rarely.

Educating for humanness frequently causes the teacher to use a problem-centered inter-disciplinary approach to problem analysis. (This is probably more common for individuals working in the areas of the arts, humanities and social sciences.) For example, when teaching the theoretical constructs of bureaucratic structure, I find *Mutiny On the Bounty* to provide as much insight as Peter Blau's *Bureaucracy In Modern Society*. Or I find simply asking each student for a vignette recounting an experience with what he perceives to be a bureaucracy, may immediately personalize the learning experience for each member of the group.

I also find that the Beatles' "Eleanor Rigby" or Simon and Garfunkel's "Sounds of Silence" and "Dangling Conversation" used together with Edward Albee's *The American Dream* and *Zoo Story* can often carry a message far more provocative than several texts in social psychology or analytical works on the absence of human communication in contemporary society. (This work at the interface of several disciplines may cause eyebrows to be raised by "specialist" colleagues who defend the "territorial" concept of the disciplines, but so what?)

Perhaps the real difference between humanistic and cerebral education is the ability to present yourself honestly in relation to the subject and the students. Part of this process is being able to openly admit that you are a learner (probably, one with more experience) as opposed to being a pro-fessor. This is not an easy task, but it does separate the learners from the pro-fessors.

A Cautionary Note: When you adapt the role of a humanistic educator, you become a combination facilitator–resource–confessor. If you demonstrate that you are concerned with the development of students as unique individuals—fellow learners—you may find your time commitment tripled, because you are now engaged in three roles. Further, you may be inundated by students who, discovering that you are human, will seek your assistance as a resource for special help with projects, independent study, and action research. You may also find that you are perceived as an "empathetic ear" and that your assistance is sought in the resolution of a myriad of personal problems. Frankly, this means that the telephone might ring from 6:00 a.m. until 2:00 a.m. and that you will frequently have unannounced visitors at the dinner hour (which may be anytime from 5:30 to midnight). This can be part of the joy of teaching, but it may become debilitating unless you allow necessary "breaks" to recharge yourself as a resource.

The university reward system has not yet fully considered this phenomenon of facilitator–resource–confessor role, but this is a topic for another essay.

HUMANISTIC GAMES

James M. Sacco and Michael A. Burton, of the University of Massachusetts School of Education, have developed some humanistic games for classroom use. In the words of Jim Sacco:

> My first day of teaching elementary school I was impressed by the number of bright, but anxious faces I saw in front of me. I must loosen them up, I thought. My smile created a small ripple of cautious smiles back, but there was still fear. During the next month, I discovered in my own personality the quality that could eliminate the fear and anxiety—my own mischievousness. When the kids sensed I had something new going that day or something a little bit zany, their curiosity and impatience was aroused. The form of this Organized Mischief was usually a game or an introduction to the unit under study.
>
> The games outlined below are not elaborately rationalized, but they are intended to serve a teacher's everyday needs. Category A lists Theatre Games and Oral Exercises. Category B includes games in which writing is involved. Category C deals with Sounds and Songs games. Category D is a small-scale physical education program. Category E contains intellectually competitive games. Category F offers math games, and Category G, science games.
>
> Finally, suggestions are offered for teachers who want to design games themselves. The initial steps in the process are introspective ones—recalling what makes you giggle, what active role you take in enjoyment of all kinds, what TV comedians give you the biggest laughs, what fantasies you have had about the classroom, what you can learn by meditating in developing a lesson plan, what most

excites you about your own learning now, and what catchy phrases, nonverbal communications, and game set-ups you can glean from your own and your students' favorite TV shows. The second phase requires thinking through the game, deciding in the process whether you will use its discipline to serve the cognitive goals of your classroom, or use it simply as a new experience.

An outline of some of the games designed by James Sacco, Michael Burton, and others follows:

A. THEATRE GAMES AND ORAL EXERCISES

The Little Theater

The teacher's sense of the dramatic is very important in creating a little theater. With sweeping hand movements, he delineates an area of the class as the theater. The children move their chairs around that spot.

I will give two examples of how I employed the theater. One afternoon I assigned a bossy girl in the class to be Lucy and a shy boy to be Linus. I asked them to play a scene in which Lucy and Linus disagreed over which TV show to watch. They had to improvise the dialogue as they went along. The warm affect and easy identification which the kids have with *Peanuts* gave me a means of entering their inner world. Oftentimes, one girl would come up to me and say "I can't stand it, I just can't stand it."

The teacher must ask the children who are role-playing to take their parts seriously and not let the ones who aren't in the play distract them.

On another occasion, I asked three children to role-play a situation in which an unpopular student had just come into the class. I picked a well-liked boy for the reject, while I chose the one who was being rejected in actuality for the role of the well-liked boy. During the improvisation, one student exposed the scene and said, "That's what's happening to John."

I also had them role-play students who were demonstrating at a college campus. The son of the town's policeman I cast as a demonstrator while the son of a dean at the University of Massachusetts was cast as policeman. The discussion which followed was a serious one about why students are so stubborn and why they are demonstrating.

The Listening Game

The purpose of the game is to have the student summarize the statement of his conversation before making his own statement. For example, with third grade students, I would start a conversation and demonstrate how to summarize what my conversation partner said. Then I would say what I had to say and expect him to summarize what I had to say.

Once the class has experienced this discipline, the teacher can use it at times with individuals she feels are not listening to her· or to other students.

The Adverbs Game

The purpose of this exercise is to increase the variety of descriptive adverbs in spoken and written sentences. The teacher divides the class into two teams. The game is started with a sentence like "She walked aimlessly . . ." One team has to pick it up from there and continue." . . . She walks badly, carefully, drearily, etc." in alphabetical fashion. Once an adverb is used in the game, it cannot be used again. The teacher allows a half-minute maximum for the student to come up with an answer. The team with fewest misses wins.

I've used this game with third, fourth, fifth, and sixth graders. You can play the game with verbs or nouns or adjectives, depending on grade levels and abilities.[1]

The Free Association Game

The purpose of this game is to experiment with free association and to learn the cause–effect relationship between the total thought patterns and the words we choose. To begin this game the teacher throws out a word and the class freely associates. Then, they reverse it and the class throws out a word to the teacher. The teacher can demonstrate how his freely-associated words are related to his present concerns.

For example, I choose the number 815. I look at my watch. I have an 8:15 appointment. I choose the word *flabby*. I was thinking of a chubby friend I'm going to see this morning. I hum notes randomly. The song "As Time Goes By" distinguishes itself. I'm still looking at my watch.[2]

The Color Metaphor Game

The purpose of this game is to identify feelings and perceptions by naming them as colors. The teacher uses himself as stimulus. For example, he asks, "What color do I make you feel?" or "What

---

[1] The game was suggested to me by Masha Rudman, an instructor from University of Massachusetts.

[2] Idea came from Bill Schutz' *Joy*.

color do I remind you of?" A student responds by saying "green." The teacher asks, "What am I doing that makes you think of green?" The teacher then makes the face of a hairy monster about to attack someone. Again he asks "What color do I remind you of?" and "What is the color of that feeling deep in the pit of your stomach?"

Color metaphor games can be played by groups of two or more or a whole class together. The teacher should be aware that negative feelings about other children can come out in this game, and he should consider how to handle this expression of feeling.[3]

The Animal Game

The purpose of this game is to give the students a vehicle by which they can express their perceptions of the teacher and of each other. The teacher first uses himself as the object of attention. "What animal do I remind you of?" He notes down on the chalkboard the different choices and asks why a choice was made (listing the "why" also).

He then emphasizes what his positive qualities were by double underlining. He encourages the students to do the same with a statement like "It's good to know what strengths others see us having, so we can build on them."

B. WRITING GAMES

Dream Workshop

The purpose of this exercise is to share fragments of our dreams and produce written material based on them. The teacher sets up a dream-sharing session, with the lights turned low, in which students are seated in a circle on the floor, recalling dreams, daydreams, fantasies, and communicating them to the class. The students then go to their seats to write about a dream of theirs or a story based on a dream they had.

How Could You Sell An Idea?

This game plays on the TV-commercialized generation's sense of salesmanship through sloganizing. As an example, take the concept "The primitive African tribesman has a power of reasoning the same as an American's;" make a written and/or illustrated commercial to sell that idea. The teacher gives a concept to each member of the class to be handled as in the example above.

---

[3] Suggested by Gerry Weinstein, Professor at Univ. of Massachusetts.

Regular Spelling Test, But . . .

The purpose of this exercise is to provide a vehicle whereby students can laugh at themselves and at their teacher while taking a test. The teacher uses spelling words in a sentence which has to do with two students in the class—a boy walking home with his "secret" girl friend, or two girls giggling and talking about that cute boy Ronnie. The teacher lets the students then make up sentences about each other or about the teacher and his or her girl or boy friend. (They usually want to get back at you for outraging them with *that* girl.)

The Story Composition Test

The purpose of this exercise is to make an informal psychological evaluation of the students in your class. The teacher locates and cuts out pictures from magazines on a limited number of personal and interpersonal topics, such as lonely people, happy people, parents scolding children, parents praising children, children crying, a boy running away from home. The teacher selects a picture for each student and has each write a story about it. The teacher can design his own evaluation system after looking at the stories.

C. SOUNDS AND SONGS GAMES

Sound-Off

The purpose of this game is to express feelings without words. The teacher assigns an emotion to each student and has him make a gesture or non-word sound which expresses that emotion. When students are adept enough, the teacher can rate each performance on a running point chart. Sample emotions that can be given are tired, bored, excited, helpless, scared, angry, or disgusted. A variation of this would be to have students close their eyes and wait until expressions come naturally to their faces. Ask one student observer to identify the emotion behind the expression.

Another variation would be to have students close their eyes and let sounds come to their lips naturally. Ask the student observer to identify the emotion behind the expression.

Sound-Off-Role-Playing

The purpose of this game is to give students practice in gestural, facial, and nonsense sound communication. The teacher gives each student a "sound" expressing a feeling such as one of those from the preceding game. The teacher then sets three role-players in a situation around the "family breakfast table," for instance, where they must communicate using only their assigned sound. This is ended by a class discussion on the limitations or greater ranges of capacities to communicate non-verbally as compared with verbally.

Song Feelings

The purpose of this exercise is to have students verbalize feelings about which music of different types and at different places arouses in them. The teacher prepares selections from sitar, rock, folk, classical, religious, and commercial music. She gives instructions, describes and employs a rating system which distinguishes between superficial response ("It's okay.") and genuine feeling ("I feel peaceful."). She uses the blackboard to record responses.

D. THE NEW GYM

Relaxation and Response to Music

The purpose of this game is to release physical tensions and increase the student's awareness of his body. The teacher starts with deep breathing exercises in which only the diaphragm, not the chest, expands and contracts. The teacher has the students lie on their backs and coordinate stretching their bodies in any way they feel they need, stretching on the inhale and going limp on the exhale. Next the teacher plays a soft classical symphony. She has the students raise their hands above their heads and move them through the air in response to the music. Next she has the students get up and, with their feet in one place, move their whole bodies in response to the music (eyes closed throughout). Finally she has them move around until they meet someone with whom they will move together as a pair.

Trust

The purpose of this exercise is to develop ability to let yourself relax physically into the arms of another. The class is divided up into pairs. Each of the two individuals stands looking in the same direction. The one in front spread-eagles his arms and lets himself fall back on the other person, who catches him before he hits the floor. Then they trade off. One student gives another a head-roll. Hands clasped underneath the other's neck, he rolls the other's head around and up and down. Then he relaxes the other's arms by shaking them out and massaging the tense places.

The Blind Walk

The purpose of this exercise is to make the student depend on his senses other than sight for receiving the world, and to let him experience dependence on another. One student closes his eyes and

another takes him on a walk outdoors. No talking is allowed so that
they must develop some communication system other than speech.
The leader takes his partner around on interesting side trips to
explore objects non-visually and to experience different sensations,
like running, feeling water, mud, grass, trees, rolling, swinging on
swings, going down a seesaw.

Supporting Someone Else

This exercise lifts the burden off another person's shoulders.
One student, with a strong back, stands back to back with a second student. The lifter grabs both his partner's hands from over his
head, squats, and lifts his partner gently off the ground. As the
lifted person breathes deeply, the lifter bends slightly on inhale.

E. INTELLECTUALLY COMPETITIVE GAMES

The Bowl Quiz

One purpose of this game is to test the abilities of quick recall,
analogous thinking, problem solving, and question framing. A second purpose is to teach the value of group consultation. Students
are instructed to chose two teams of five students each. The teacher
has prepared in advance questions based on current events, language
arts, mathematics, science, or other topics. It's good to include some
"fun" and some "dumb" questions. He also prepares some answers
to which students can make up questions. On ten-point tossup
questions, the teacher has students push imaginary buzzer buttons
on their desks; for bonus questions, she has the captain of a team
answer. Bonuses are worth 20 points. The play continues until the
questions are used up (about 25-30 minutes).

A variation is Scrabble Bowl Quiz. Its purpose is to get students
to work in small groups and to make up different words with the
same set of letters. The team with greatest number of words in
five minutes—on a two out of three basis—wins.

Ten Steps

The purpose of this is to teach mathematics with the built-in
capability of moving through the program as quickly as possible,
depending on student's individual learning ability.

Ten levels of competence are established. The teacher writes
one sample test question on a poster for each of the ten levels and
places them by rank along the wall. The teacher prepares three
different tests of ten examples each to evaluate whether or not the

student has mastered a particular level with 80% accuracy. Before a student can move up more than two consecutive levels, he must assist someone at a level lower than his to pass one level. The first five students through the ten steps plan the next series in consultation with teacher. The next five students administer the present ten steps until all have negotiated it.

F. MATH GAMES

Pencil and String Geometry

The purpose of this game is to make students use some imagination in drawing geometric figures. The only tools allowed are a piece of paper, pencil, and a string. A sample problem would be to draw a triangle with all three sides equal or draw a triangle with two sides equal and the third side one-third smaller than the other two.

To Grandmother's House We Go

The purpose of this exercise is to introduce the idea of vectors. A piece of graph paper is divided into four quadrants so that the coordinates have both positive and negative numbers to identify them. Label the axes, and change the labels from day to day to show that they are arbitrary. Give the students the coordinates of the starting place and of Grandmother's house. Choose various lengths for the arrows and then let the students try to "get" to Grandmother's house. The person or team that gets there with the fewest arrows in an allotted time wins.

Dot Pictures

The purpose of this exercise is to encourage looking at graphs as pictures. Divide a piece of graph paper into four quadrants and label the axes. Start giving the coordinates of a picture that is to be made up of dots. A student may guess what the picture is to be at any time. If he is correct, he wins; if he is incorrect, he is eliminated from participation in guessing that picture.

Math is Hiding

The purpose of this game is to reveal mathematics in common objects. One point is awarded for every object that is named and for which the mathematics connected with it is explained. For example, the floor. Someone had to measure the floor to figure out how many tiles were needed to cover it. The student is then asked to solve a similar problem as a demonstration.

Human Rulers

The purpose of this game is to produce spatial awareness of the body. The student is asked to use a yardstick to measure parts of his body and is told that later he will be asked to measure other objects using only his body as a ruler. The length of a finger may be used for short measurements, the person's height for longer lengths. Sample objects to be measured are books, chairs, doors, the room, etc.

G. SCIENCE GAMES

What Would Mother Nature Do?

The purpose of this game is to encourage the answering of science questions by using simple experiments. The class is divided into teams. The teacher prepares some simple experiments, but before each one is carried out, a question is asked as to the outcome. Students vote and the votes are tabulated for each team before the experiments have been done. Examples of possible experimental questions are: Will a razor blade float in water? Does it depend on how it is placed in the water? Will it continue to float if soap is added to the water?

What's in the Bag?

The purpose of this exercise is to develop the testing of scientific theories. Place various common objects in small bags and seal the bags. Let the students figure out what is in the bags by doing anything they can think of except opening the bags.

Paper Buildings

The purpose of this exercise is to emphasize the importance of the shape rather than the type of material used in construction. The students are allotted ten sheets of paper and some tape to make their constructions. Examples of building projects are: Build a platform that will support two books at least six inches off the floor (use of cylinders). Build a bridge between two desks that will support a book (put lots of folds in the paper).

Science Is Our Friend

This exercise makes students aware of both the pros and cons of science. One team names something in science that is helpful to people; the other team has fifteen seconds to name a use of the same thing that harms people. No points scored for correct, or completed, answers; points only for stumping your opponents. A sample round might go as follows: Team 1—Airplanes are used to transport people. Team 2—Airplanes are used to bomb people. (No points.) Team 2—Trains are used to carry people. Team 1— No answer. (Point scored for Team 2.)

Scavenger Hunt

This exercise helps students realize the science in everyday things. Team 1 picks an object that demonstrates a scientific principle. Team 2 has to find an object that demonstrates the same principle; then Team 1 must find still another object that demonstrates the same principle, etc. A point is awarded every time a team continues the chain. For example: Team 1 picks radiator. Team 2 picks light bulb (it also gives off heat) (point); Team 1 picks sun, (also gives off heat) (point). Team 2 is stumped (no point, end of chain). Then begin again.

In all these games it's a good idea to rehearse the rules of the game, making sure they are clear. Think of new variations and new games by recording notes from your own meditation, daydreaming, or brainstorming. Let your rough-cut ideas germinate for a time. Recording side comments by students about TV or Charlie Brown or off-the-cuff ideas from the classroom can produce excellent ideas for games. Watching Johnny Carson or Captain Kangaroo on TV with the sound turned off is an interesting stimulus. Finally, cultivate your own sense of the mischievous and ridiculous, for in these lies the secret of successful games.

* * * *

I have presented a wide variety of these games in an effort to make the point that humanistic education techniques and games can be integrated into every kind of classroom from math to social studies, to English, to physical education. These are presented as idea stimulators with the hope that teachers will "piggy back" on them and build many more of their own.

THE UNIVERSITY–STUDENT CRISIS ROLE PLAYING GAME

This is one of my favorite exercises which Robert Woodbury and I have been using in both graduate and undergraduate university courses. A role-playing situation of a student protest in its various stages can give students a first hand understanding of the various pressures felt in such a situation. We usually begin this exercise by discussing the difficulties of governing a university, and pointing out how the president of a university must be all things to everyone: the students, who are demanding an ever-increasing role in the governance of the institution; the faculty, who really defy governance; the community, to whom the president must sometimes be a mayor ex efficio; the alumni, who often are more worried about the caliber of the football team than they are about the quality of the academics; the non-academic employees, who recently have begun to assert new power through collective bargaining (strikes have forced several universities to close down temporarily); the trustees, who often know little about education and make the mistake of attempting to apply their knowledge of industry to academia; the legislature or regents who are necessarily remote but vital to the welfare of the institution; and the parents of students, who expect the president to protect their "child" from the evils of sex and "grass." All of these people put different pressures on the university president, making his job much more difficult than that of a corporation president who can often measure his productivity by the profits he makes and who must answer to a board interested mainly in profit.

We then usually build the scene at a fictitious state university, "Abalone University," where the editor of the student newspaper, after having written numerous unheeded editorials about the evils of the university and the lack of involvement of students in decisions, finally puts out a completely obscene issue of the paper attacking the administration and the trustees. Needless to say, some attention is finally paid to his paper. The trustees, several of whom have been mentioned by name in the accurate, but gross, issue of the paper, phone the president and instruct him to take immediate action to nip this action in the bud. The university is also in the midst of a large fund-raising campaign based on the theme that Abalone University has been free of strife. The president has set up a meeting with the editor of the newspaper which is to take place in thirty minutes. We then go around the room dividing the students into the following role-playing groups: administration—they are instructed to pick a president, dean of students, etc.; students—they are asked to pick an editor of the paper, S.D.S. leader, president of student body, president of a conservative student group, etc.; faculty—they must choose a president of the faculty senate, faculty advisor to the student paper, etc.; community leaders—they select a police chief, mayor, publisher of town newspapers, etc.; trustees; alumni; legislature and governor's staff.

We set the scene a little farther by telling them that the president is now meeting with his key staff deciding on his stance for the meeting with the editor of the student paper. The student editor is meeting with the president of the student body, S.D.S. leader, etc., deciding on their stance and demands. Trustees and any others can send public or private messages or notes to any other group through me, which I deliver and announce for everyone's interest.

The tensions begin to build and we sit back to watch the fun. We usually build the pressure in a fairly natural way by having a mob of students gather at the campus gate singing and blocking traffic to which the police chief typically overreacts. The pressure begins to build on the president as trustees and alumni call in their concerns and as the student group with which he is meeting begins to vocalize their demands. (We usually arrange for the student group to be larger than the others, and we usually include some of the middle-aged members of the class to play students and some of the more radical students to be administration.) I have watched presidents literally sweat through their shirts and students become almost violent as they get into the roles. Frequently it is difficult to turn the group off. We generally hold a thirty or forty-five minute critique and discussion at the end when we deal with such questions as why the president "talked down" to the students, how they felt, what pressures they felt, and when if ever do means justify the ends.

There are many variations of this exercise that can be played, limited only by the instructor's imagination. Ample grist for feelings mills usually emerges as the students talk about how they felt and negotiated in their respective roles. On one occasion, I ended the session by having the students close their eyes and get into comfortable positions. I then asked them to visualize a teacher or administrator whom they hated or particularly disliked and to get in touch with and experience their feeling about this person. I then had them think of an animal for that person, and an animal for themselves. Next I had them think of as many things about the disliked animal as they could that they appreciated. These were written down. Next I asked them to close their eyes again, and as their own animal, take a fantasy walk through paths in the forest until he comes to a large clearing where he finds the disliked animal. They were to walk to the middle of the clearing where they came face to face with the disliked animal and were to fantasize what took place for several silent minutes.

We then discussed and shared our fantasies and looked at the various alternative ways of dealing with people we dislike. This exercise is viewed by my students as a most relevant learning experience, and I also enjoy very much doing it.

LEARNING THEATER ACTIVITIES

In the past chapter, a brief description of Masha Rudman's Learning Theater was presented. Working with Masha is a group of dedicated teachers and graduate students such as Myra Sadker, Susan Brainerd, Barbara Woodbury, and Larry McCullough who are sharing these techniques with various classrooms not only in Massachusetts but in other states as well. What follows is, first, a description by Masha Rudman and Myra Sadker of Learning Theater activities in a junior high school English class; and, second, the use of the Haiku as a humanistic exercise:

> As part of a Learning Theater experiment in expanding students' repertoire of communication, a group of us at the University of Massachusetts' School of Education worked with a junior high school English class in Granby, Mass. The School administration and teachers were most cooperative about giving us this opportunity to experiment. We were permitted to work with one advanced 7th grade English class on Conrad Richter's novel, *Light in the Forest*, the story of a boy torn between two cultures, the white man's and the Indian's.
>
> We began our experiment by imposing a traditional assignment. The class was requested to read the book. After discussing the story and the student's reactions to it, we asked the students for other ways of communicating their responses to each other. Their initial suggestions were symptomatic of how early creativity and willingness to explore can be stifled, for they were mere regurgitations of previous assignments. They suggested book reports, compositions, and panel discussions.

However, when the class began to lose its verbal set, there was a real sense of excitement as each member began to realize all the avenues of communication that were open to him. They suggested writing a song about the book, making up music without words, putting together a dance, making a slide show, a light show, a film, or a movie. As all the different possibilities were mentioned, enthusiasm increased. The students became aware that there was a mode of expression to fit each individual's needs.

After discussion of procedure and of the various resources available, the class decided to split up into three groups; one chose to represent the novel through a play, another through music, and the third through dance. Myra Sadker guided the drama group, Dave Lepard the music group, and Jan Craft and two dance students guided the dance group. We use the word "guide" purposely, for that is all the adults tried to do. We were not organizers, nor disseminators of information, but were merely resource people and facilitators of the process.

The drama group was composed of six boys. They indicated their understanding of the novel by their selection of scenes and their manner of interpreting them. The boys did not write their lines, but improvised them, and they showed a strong sense of identification with their roles.

THE HAIKU

The Haiku is a three line, seventeen syllable poem, with five syllables in the first and last lines and seven in the second line. The Haiku packs a lot of concentrated feeling in a short and sweet message. It usually deals with nature but this is not necessary. In a class led by Masha Rudman in which I participated, she began by describing what Haiku was, and then priming our imaginations by asking us to call out spontaneously any words that the word "blue," for example, brought to mind. These were written on the blackboard by Masha. In a class the following words were cited in response to "blue":

cool	sad
wet	clouds
eyes	deep
pool	Bill
Mark	

The class was then asked to make *phrases* using the above words associated with "blue." The following resulted:

> Oft unspoken word
> Sad blue of her eyes
> Burning loneliness
> Something of value
> Rippling bubbling
> Working blue sound

The class was then asked to attempt to compose from these phrases a Haiku. The delightful result was the following:

> Oft unspoken word
> leaves a burning loneliness
> seen in sad blue eyes.

Several classes in Learning Theater were asked to write Haiku about their feelings following an exercise in which they paired off in dyads and communicated without speaking, first, only by touching thumbs and, second, sitting back to back. The following Haiku were written by the students:

> Uncertain moving
> Groping for understanding
> Everything feeling

> —

> a warming pulse beat
>   our fingers and hands entwine
>   sudden belonging

> —

> What's going on here
> Exploration and meeting
> Why can't I play too

> —

> Everyone but me—
> I look through the glass window
> Please let me taste, too

> —

Response to touching
Unusual back to back
Says what we don't say

—

Without words we speak
understanding and soothing
    I think I know you

—

some crinkling dandies
gingerly embarked dancing
in pinks and yellows.

—

Two lives together
Under one sky in one world
Forever at war.

—

I know I couldn't
hoping, wiggling, loving
reach over the wall.

—

What was that I felt?
Nice and soft and slow and warm
Oh a laughing clown?

—

Communication—
Different, soundless, meaningful
Continue it—how?

—

Me? Communicate?
Dastardly imposition
Violates my soul

—

Touching and going
two thumbs openly showing
their owners are shy

—

Strangers meeting here
Wonderful joy briefly comes
And then you are gone

—

Impasse at first touch
I thought I know who you were—
Why can't I read you?

—

Pressure not forcing
peaceful feeling
between two strangers

—

Stump of flesh and nail
pressing against soft, entwined
another, almost

—

Separate but close
Warmth against one another
Searching for nearness

—

scratching squirmily
laughing, then distant and still
Feeling touches warm

—

Laughing silently
I wiggle my head to yours
And our feet caress

—

To touch is to sense
the inner conflict of self
I know your battle

—

Two souls reaching out
never did find each other
One went away sad

—

Meeting the first time
At first tentative, opened
To lovely new worlds

—

Warm, loving, playful
Flowed between us, lifting up
Soaring heart balloons

—

Playful finger imp
Skips along the rhythm path
Tickles to my toes

—

Tall—the funny mop
Wiggles, runs across the floor
Making laughing puddles

GESTALT AWARENESS TECHNIQUES

Many of the techniques being practiced by "humanistic teachers" today have their origin in Gestalt Therapy. The idea of a whole integrated man rather than a split or "half-man" is what gestalt is all about. An excellent book, *Gestalt Therapy, Excitement and Growth in the Human Personality*, by Frederick Perls, Ralph Hefferline, and Paul Goodman is highly recommended. However, the book, *Gestalt Therapy Verbatim*, by Perls, is really my favorite. Gestalt Awareness techniques have considerable application to the classroom situation. Additionally, they can be useful in assisting teachers to achieve greater self-awareness and sensitivity to their own feelings as well as those of their students. The following techniques are gleaned from the above mentioned books and from practices experienced or observed. They are presented here as thought provokers, fertilizer for the soil of teachers' minds:

ORIENTING THE SELF

1. *Making "here and now I ..." statements*
The individual makes a series of statements beginning with the words "Here and now I am aware of . . ." or "At this moment I feel . . ." or "Now I am tensing my hand. . ."

2. *Noticing Resistances*

While making up "here and now" statements, the student should notice what causes him to stop doing them (e.g., impatience, feeling silly, boredom).

3. *Analyzing the different parts of a painting and putting them back into an elastic gestalt*

Trace the outline of the main figures. Abstract the colors. Follow the receding planes. Trace out the patterns of lights and shadows. Note the texture of the brushstrokes. *Then* look at the story.

4. *Sensing Opposed Forces*

Imagine yourself in a situation the reverse of your own, where you have inclinations and wishes exactly contrary to your usual ones. Do so without evaluating whether what you are doing is right or wrong. For example, instead of wishing to sleep, wanting to go out and play tackle football.

5. *Imagine the motions around you as if they occurred the other way around*

6. *Reverse functions*

What if the purpose of a sofa was to sit on you, instead of you on it.

7. *What would the situation be if you were fifty pounds heavier?*

What if you hadn't gotten out of bed this morning?

8. *Attending and Concentrating*

Attend to some body-feeling, such as a twinge or itch, and observe how the rest of your body-feeling recedes into the background.

9. *Stare fixedly at any shape*

Now let your gaze play around the shape, always returning to it in the varying backgrounds.

10. *Let your attention shift from one object to another*

Notice figure and background in the object and in your emotions. Verbalize "I like this" or "I dislike this about it," as well as differentiating "It is this in it I like, but it is that I dislike."

11. *Differentiating and Unifying*

Attend to a piece of music. If you are "unmusical," play it over and over again. Notice the appearance of a single instrument. Notice dialogues between different instruments. Attend only to rhythm— only to quality or texture of the sound. Feel when harmony makes you tense—makes you relaxed. Wave your hands like the conductor tensing and loosening the muscles as appropriate.

12. *Attending exercise*

Listen to people's voices. Do they sound contemptuous, sexy, soothing, harsh? Is there deadness in it? Excitement? Are the words he speaks and the "message" of his tone of voice in contradiction to each other?

13. *Use the process of destructuring* (taking things apart) *and restructuring* (putting them back together again), in relation to your touching, smelling, and the feeling of your own muscles in action.

14. *Select some memory which is not too distant or difficult*

For example, in fantasy revisit the house of a friend. Close your eyes. What do you actually see? The door—somebody opening it? Furniture? Other people? Do not try to ferret out what is in your "mind"—what you think ought to be there—but simply keep going back to the remembered place and noticing what is there.

15. *Do the same memory sense experiment but . . .*

Include this time all auditory, taste, touch, smell sensing as well as emotional tone associated with experience. Are there some people you can't remember? Some voices you can't hear? Some people you only see photographs of rather than real, live emotion-filled pictures?

16. *Sharpening the Body-Sense*

Make up series of "Now I am aware . . ." statements, paying attention to the physical details—the spontaneous experiencing on the surface. "Now I am aware that my hand is on the book. Now I am aware that I am sitting in the chair. Now I am aware of the car driving past, etc." Try first to attend mainly to external events—sights, sounds, smells, but without suppressing other experiences. Then, in sharp contrast, concentrate on internal processes—images, physical sensations, muscular tensions, emotions, thinking. Then, take these internal processes one by one and concentrate as fully as you can first on images, then on muscular tensions, then on emotions, etc.

Concentrate on your "body" sensation as a whole. Let your attention wander through every part of your body. How much of

yourself can you feel? To what degree and with what accuracy
and clarity does your body—and thus you—exist? Notice pains,
aches, and twinges ordinarily ignored. Walk, talk, or sit down; be
aware of the details of muscular feeling without in any way interfering with them.

Notice which tensions or aches make combinations—or structures. Sit or lie comfortably, aware of different body sensations and
motions (breathing, clutching, contracting the stomach, etc.). Notice when you hold your breath. Do any tensions in the arms or
fingers or contractions of the stomach seem to go with this?

17. *Experiencing the Continuity of Emotion*
Pick some bodily feeling and exaggerate it (smiling, for instance).
Let the emotion associated with that physical sensation (the contempt of a "put on" face) arise. See if you can focus that expression (contempt) on some person you call up in fantasy.

Lie down and try to get the feel of your face. What expression do you feel? Is it serious? Smiling? Sad? Concentrate on it and
see how quickly it changes by itself.

Take a book of paintings. Take a quick glance at each picture
and see what emotion it arouses. Move on to the next one. Also do
the same in a gallery.

Take the most unpleasant experience you've ever had. Relive
it in fantasy, using the present tense. Can you feel the same emotions? Experience the most terrifying, humiliating, embarrassing,
guilt-producing, shaming, event in your life.

18. *Varieties of listening to your inner voice*
Tape record and play back your voice. Recite a poem aloud without affection. Recite the same poem internally. Listen to your subvocal speech. Listen to your subvocal thinking. Notice the tone in
your internal voice. Is it complaining, cajoling, nagging, childish?
Try to keep internally silent, to refrain from subvocal talking. Try
to be without words while you inhale. Upon exhaling, let the
words form themselves subvocally.

19. *Using the awareness so far developed*, form sentences that express your here-and-now situation successively in terms of the
body, the feelings, the speech-habit, and the social relations. For
example, a student might say "I am resting my elbow on my
desk. . . . I am feeling bored and a little tired. . . . I am speaking

with a droning voice. . . ." In other words, when you are not stimulated by the excitement of someone else, you have to struggle to stay awake.

20. *Breathing*
Notice your own breathing and the breathing of others, especially the stops, yawns, deep breaths, irregularities. Differentiate the parts of your own breathing. Can you feel the air going into your nose? Down your throat? Can you feel your ribs expanding? Your back getting bigger? Is your exhalation simply effortless, elastic—return of ribs and muscles to a resting condition? Yawn and stretch frequently, using the cat as your model.

21. *Manipulating the Self*
What kinds of questions do you ask yourself? Do you feel yourself as split into two parts? Obviously, you don't know the answer to your question or you wouldn't have to ask. Is there someone of whom you'd like to ask the question? Is the reason you don't ask because you are shy, or he is too busy, or you don't want to admit ignorance?

When you reproach yourself or nag yourself, for whom are you substituting yourself? Whom do you want to reform? In whom do you want to rouse the guilt that you are pretending to produce in yourself? Whom do you want to punish? Whom do you want to punish you? Is pity often a mask for condescensions and does punishing involve pushing yourself around? How would you get others to do a task for you which you do not want to do? Would you make promises, plead, bribe, threaten, or command?

How do you react to your own compelling? Do you make excuses? Do you give in begrudgingly and do a half-hearted job? Do you respond with guilt and pay the debt with self-contempt and despair? What do you evaluate about yourself? Doubt about yourself? Can you transfer these attitudes to Person X whom you doubt? Who makes you suspicious?

22. *You are your body*
Lie down, close your eyes, and feel where the tensions are in your body. Don't get a "picture" of your body, because that is only a concept. *Wait* until you can feel the tensions. Concentrate on some pain you have. Try to identify with both the headache side of you and the "I gotta get rid of this headache" side of you. Is the head-

ache holding down something? Concentrate on where the pain is. Take responsibility for having the headache, instead of taking an aspirin. Make up "here and now . . ." statements about the headache and differentiate the areas of pain.

23. *Intake*

Examine your intake of food. Take one meal a day alone and stay in contact with your food. Do you begin thinking of what you must do next, daydreaming, lifting up the next morsel? Are you impatient with having to eat? Greedy?

Examine your intake of printed material. Is it light reading, skipping over the difficult parts? Do you copy down exact notes from the book. Compare this process with your eating habits. Do you enjoy reading or just tolerate it?

Examine your visual intake at movies. Do you fall into a kind of trance and drink in the scenes?

Impatience and greed stem from frustrated aggression. Next time you feel impatient exteriorize the aggression by voraciously eating something—bite, don't gulp. What do parents or ministers or friends make you eat? "Stuff down your throat?" Do you reject it? What "loved" person might you be disgusted by? Concentrate.

24. *Projection*

Call up some person in fantasy who you think rejects you. Tell him what you like, don't like, about him or her. How are you talking to him? Self-consciously? Guiltily? Harshly? What qualities don't you like in him? Are you rejecting him for the same reasons you felt he rejected you?

Instead of saying "My conscience demands . . ." or "My boss expects . . ." try saying "I expect of myself." Are you being very harsh with yourself?

Put yourself in the shoes of aggressive people, people you admire, people who initiate, and see if the identification doesn't fit. Put yourself in the role of the commanding teacher.

DISCOVERING SELF CONTROL

Lucy Backer, a first grade teacher in Amherst, Massachusetts, has developed a lesson for confronting children with the important realization that their learning is up to them—that they are in control. Children need to know that they are the ones who are in control of their behavior, emotions, and learning.

> Without an explicit rational stimulus to guide him, the child can perceive little more than do or don't behave this way now, in this particular situation.[7]

The teacher teaches the children a song, *If You're Happy*, which has a lot of rhythm to it causing them to shake their heads as she leads. This is followed by a discussion of the following related questions which are geared to make the children develop evaluation thinking and understand self control:

> What made you shake your head? (The song?) But, if you didn't want to do it, and didn't feel like doing it, could the song really make you do it? No, you, yourself can control it. Everyone shake your hands just as hard as you can. Now, stop. What made you stop? (You did.) But that is only because you do what the teacher asks you to. If you decided to be different and continue doing it, I couldn't really make you stop. Only *you* can control yourself. This time I want everyone to shout just as loud as you can and when I hold up my arm, stop. What made you stop? That's right, yourself. You used self-control. Do you know that you are the only one who can make yourself learn? *You* are the one who controls it. Your teacher is just a helper. All she can do is *help* you learn. What other ways can you use self-control to help you learn? What can you control about yourself that will help you learn?

Discuss using self-control at home and in connection with other children.

Suggested questions

Why is it important to use self-control at home?
What are some of the ways you can use it?
What do you want to do when someone grabs a ball from you, pushes you, cuts in front of you in line?

---

[7] Mario Fantini and Gerald Weinstein, *The Disadvantaged* (New York: Harper and Row, Publishers, 1968).

Tell the following story to the children, trying to make it a participatory experience by eliciting responses and suggestions from them.

Let's pretend we are all going for a hike through the woods. What are some things we might see there?

That's right (flowers, trees, some animals). Now, when we see the flowers, we smell and touch them. We climb some of the trees. Sometimes we run, skip, or walk slowly on our way. All of a sudden, we see a huge, poisonous rattlesnake. We know we must be very, very quiet because if we frighten him he will bite someone. We must control ourselves and not move a muscle, or make a sound.

I know everyone in this class has good self-control, and won't move or make a sound until the snake slithers away; then we are able to finish our hike.

Then have the entire class re-enact the story. Retell it, as a teacher and class; pantomine it together.

Instruct the children to open workbooks to a picture of a boy running into the street to get his ball. Discuss the picture, helping the children to draw inferences from their interpretations of the picture.

Suggested questions

What is happening in the picture?
Why did Tony run into the street?
What could have happened if one of the cars couldn't have stopped?
What does Dan's face tell us about how he is feeling? Why?
Which boy showed self-control? How?
Why was it important to use self-control in that situation?

To speak of "self-control" in a book on humanistic education which is primarily about freeing one's self might seem to some to be an enigma. However, I have included this discussion of discovering self control because I feel it is very much related to the concept of learning to take responsibility for yourself. Going from environmental support to self support is what the long and painful process of maturing is all about, and taking responsibility for yourself is a cornerstone for all growth. A student who is beginning to discover "self control" is beginning to learn to take responsibility for himself. He is less likely to be self destructive or destructive of others as he realizes that he is responsible for his own control and actions. In all the groups I lead, I make it clear before beginning with the group that though I will attempt to provide an environment in which the members can discover themselves and grow in the process, *I* will not take responsibility for them. They can make of the opportunity whatever they will, but they must take responsibility for whatever good or bad experiences they have. If they are not willing to accept this, they shouldn't stay in the group. Once one discovers what "self support" and "taking responsibility" really means, one truly is freed—freed from the suppressing bonds of being dependent on everyone else for cues, for approval, for disapproval, and all the other dependencies which make most of us slaves to all those whom we see sitting as judges of our behavior. Freedom is growing from external approval to genuine internal approval.

In this chapter we surveyed some of the humanistic education techniques being developed and used by teachers in various levels of classrooms throughout the country. We took a look at group training—the T–Group, sensitivity training, the encounter group, micro-labs, and marathons. We looked in some detail at a university level course of study, "Education of the Self," which uses the student himself as content. We also looked at some of the other exercises such as "Geography of the Self" and the "One-way Feeling Glasses" developed by Gerald Weinstein and his associates. We looked at a "University–Student Crisis" role playing exercise and the varied activities of The Learning Theater, and had a glimpse at Gestalt Therapy Techniques.

The humanistic exercises or techniques presented in this chapter are meant to be catalytic. It is hoped that they will serve as idea stimulators of your creativity—stimulators not only to try some of these techniques in the classroom, but also to build and improve upon them as well as to dream up some new ones of your own.

part III

Feeling to Learn

5

Applying Humanistic Techniques to Classroom Situations

Joy is burgeoning. Methods for attaining more joy are growing and are becoming more effective. We are developing ways to make our bodies more alive, healthier, lighter, more flexible, stronger, less tired, more graceful, more integrated. We have ways for using our bodies better, for sensing more, for functioning more effectively, for developing skills and sensitivity, for being more imaginative and creative, and for feeling more and holding the feelings longer. More and more we can enjoy other people, learn to work and play with them, to love and fight with them, to touch them, to give and take with them, to be with them contentedly or to be happy alone, to lead or to follow them, to create with them. And our institutions, our organizations, the "establishment"—even these we are learning to use for our own joy. Our institutions can be improved, can be used to enhance and support individual growth, can be re-examined and redesigned to achieve the fullest measure of human realization. All these things are coming. None are here, but they are closer. Closer than ever before.

William Schutz

It is hoped that this chapter will help to bring some of these things even closer. This part of the book is based upon my work with a group of fifteen selected students (ten graduate and five undergraduate) who spent a semester in my course, "Affective Education," attempting to develop practical applications of humanistic techniques to classroom situations. The group of students first experienced the various techniques described earlier in this book. After "getting in touch" with these experiences, they individually or in groups planned their "own thing" using a repertoire of humanistic techniques: encounter, non-verbal communication, sensitivity training, fantasy games, and other affective experiences geared to the particular classroom applications of their choice. The applications were experienced by the entire group and then critiqued. Most of the applications were then tested in school classroom situations.

The tangible product of this course was the repertoire book of techniques which follows in this chapter, compiled by the class members. The intangible product of the course is fifteen humanistically enlightened individuals who are now either teaching their own humanistically oriented classes or working as missionaries to influence others to deal with feelings in the classroom and in curriculum development.

The requirements that I stipulated for the course were:

1. The planned application using "humanistic" techniques to achieve a classroom objective. Each student had to lead the entire group through his planned experience and then write up the experience for the others.

2. A diagnostic diary written by each student after each class, recording significant feelings or learning experiences. Disclosure of the contents of this diary to others was at the discretion of the writer.

3. Two attitude surveys, given at the beginning and end of the course, attempting to measure change which might have taken place in the students. The first of these was the Philadelphia Self-Survey which attempts to measure discrepancies between the self as perceived by the individual and the ideal self. The second was the Rokeach Test of dogmatism or rigidity in attitudes. I have given these same measures to quite a large number of students before and after humanistic education experiences. The before–after results of one of these tests are presented in Chapter 8.

It is hoped that the reader will not only feel motivated to use the ideas which follow but, hopefully, will "piggy back" on them to develop new and more effective ones. Educational dissemination systems are so poor that if we are ever to bring about change we must do all we possibly can to share the wealth of ideas sprouting here and there. The following statements are presented almost exactly as written by the students:

FEELING ABOUT THE CONSEQUENCES OF OUR ACTIONS—*Ken Beattie*

In an effort to try to get students in touch with what they feel about the consequences of the actions, I decided to combine a role-playing situation with the viewing of the movie, "An Occurrence at Owl Creek Bridge."[1] The objective was to have the students examine and compare their feelings about a situation experienced in two different contexts. The situation was first experienced in such a way as to leave the students relatively remote from the consequences of their behaviors. The situation was then re-experienced after the consequences of their behaviors were made more immediate to them in a "feeling" way. The actual class was conducted as follows:

The members of the class were assigned to one of the eleven roles needed to dramatize the issuing of an order by a general to hang a traitor during the Civil War and the passage of that order down through the ranks to the executioner who carries out the order. The scene of the dramatization was then set for the students: during the Civil War a traitor is to be hung. The general must sign the order to carry out the execution, his aide must carry the order to a messenger who will deliver it to the colonel and so on down the line to the sergeant who must bark the order to the executioner to drop the plank from under the feet of the victim. The students playing the various parts are assigned to different rooms or locations so that the general and most of the persons in the upper part of the chain of command do not actually witness the execution. The dramatization is then begun. At its end, the students are asked to record their feelings about the parts they played.

The students are then shown the film, "Occurrence at Owl Creek Bridge," a film that evokes strong emotions in the viewer, mostly in the form of sympathy for the intended hanging victim during the Civil War. After working to bind up the viewers' emotions in the struggle and hope of the victim, the film shocks the viewer with an unexpected ending. The purpose of showing the film was intended to bring the students' "feelings" into intimate contact with the fate of the victim in their dramatization.

After viewing the film, the students again dramatize the events leading up to the hanging of the victim. Again they are asked to record their feelings about having played the roles they did. They then discuss a comparison of their feelings in the second dramatization with their feelings in the first. (This constitutes the classroom exercise.)

As is often the case with learning strategies, this exercise did not produce the expected outcome. Although the film did make

---

[1] Distributed by Contemporary Films, Hightstown, N. J.: McGraw Hill Inc., 08520.

the students more intimately aware of the consequences of their actions in the dramatization (an awareness both emotional and cognitive), an examination of their feelings did not show an increased reluctance to contribute to the dramatized execution. Rather, after viewing the film, the students attempted to escape from responsibility for their actions' consequences by making themselves personally more remote from both the consequences and their actions themselves. This they achieved by subordinating their own identities to their make-believe military-type roles disclaiming any freedom to act in accordance with their feelings and therefore suppressing these feelings.

As an attempt to realize the objectives I stated above, the exercise could be called a failure. However it did have value by way of adding additional emphasis to my plea for educating people to base their decision-making on an emotional as well as cognitive projection of the ultimate consequences of their decisions. Evidently, this involves not only becoming more aware of the feelings one might have about future consequences, but also involves being able to face up to these feelings and allowing them to move us. The exercise was a success from the standpoint of causing all the students to examine their feelings and behavior and then to realize how they had disassociated from their actions in the actual role playing. The reason given by most for their exhibiting less feéling after viewing the film was that they became discouraged and disillusioned when the hero was actually hanged after they thought he had escaped. This emotional response on their part caused them to withdraw or disassociate from their actions in the final role playing. Certainly the military creates a vital need for soldiers to act in this way. Though this exercise did not have the effects or affects I expected, it did create an interesting opportunity for us to examine how we feel about the consequences of our actions.

This experience has practical application to many grade levels either as an isolated experience or as a way to more vividly understand a particular work of literature. The film can be rented from Contemporary Films, a division of McGraw Hill.

FEELING THROUGH SOUND—*Susan Brainerd*

Too frequently the "experiences" designed to foster Affective Education appear as gimmicks because there seem to be no underlying principles. As far as I know, no one has begun to devise ways in which teachers can diagnose the causes, in people or in the environment, of what appears to be unsuccessful classroom experience. For Affective Education, "unsuccessful" means that classroom experience is denying the real growth potential of individuals toward full "being-ness." We have focused on discovery of feelings about self and others and objects in the environment. How can we put the interacting self and environment into more fulfilling relationships?

In his book *Psychology of Being*, Maslow describes "Deficiency-motivation" and "Growth or Being-motivation." These concepts can be useful in classrooms to determine the focus of the organisms' responses to the environment. More important for Affective Education, however he describes "peak experiences" as those experiences in which the person is most fully alive. People who usually do not find truly fulfilling experience in most of their daily lives can have "peak experiences" and grow to more understanding of the relationship between self and environment through them. People who seem growth-motivated or "self-actualizing" find the qualities of peak experience in most of their everyday lives. Knowledge of the interactions in peak experiences, then, may help us learn how to guide teachers and students to more fulfilling experiences.

Aesthetic experience as described by Dewey in *Art as Experience* has many aspects in common with "peak experiences," but also aspects which seem to go further in developing experience to its full consummation and benefits for "enlivened perception." "Enlivened perception" brings the organism to new modes for more satisfying interaction with the environment. (See *Gestalt Therapy*, pp. 227–232.) I will give some aspects of the overlapping elements of "Peak experience" and aesthetic experience and then describe two important aspects of aesthetic experience that make it useful for enhancing growth motivation. It can be incoherent and deny meaningful relationships between the two, or it can be dynamic, cohesive, and complete and promote the welfare of the two. One or the other, either negative or positive experience, is happening all the time.

Following are a few elements common to "peak experiences" and aesthetic experiences:

1. The experience is undergone for its own sake. This is called terminal experience in that the process is more important than product, and process must determine the product.

2. The organism functions as an integrated unit: sensory, motor, emotional, and intellectual capacities being inseparable and working together rather than against each other.

In experience, the sense material from the environment is taken into the organism, arouses relevant past experience which in turn provides the organism's next response. If the organism is functioning as an integrated unit, both the present and past are reconstructed in terms of ongoing reality; if not, neither the organism nor the environment "learn."

For the poorly integrated organism and/or environment experiences must be found that can promote reintegration. Basically, the student must be allowed to have enough freedom from "curriculum" to find these, but since he does not have freedom from himself, he must also be guided. Reintegration is the goal of Gestalt Therapy and one goal of other forms of therapy, and guidelines for providing experiences which can accomplish it can be found in these. For elementary teachers, however, knowing about experience and how to integrate the environment may be enough, for children seem rarely to operate with the kinds of long-term disintegration that we find in adults.

3. In both peak and aesthetic experience, the person is able to maintain both involvement and detachment. Dewey speaks of "doing and undergoing" in ebb and flow, both necessary even to the person interacting with a work of art. The peak experience seems to be thought of as a more undergoing process, and this is why it just "happens." If we understand better how to help people form patterns for doing and undergoing, they can begin to be at once more completely involved (because there is no fear of being overwhelmed by the experience) and be more able to understand clearly the nature of the experience and respond appropriately for the individual. (The following is common only to aesthetic experience as portrayed in Dewey, but could be common to any experience that has the above pre-characteristics.)

4. Once the impulsion to experience brings the organism into full contact with the environment, there must be resistances which impel the organism to use thought to overcome them. This thought (about alternatives rather than following narrow, rigid modes of operating) will make clearer the meaning of the experience.

The difference between resistance and threat is an individual distinction and must be handled on that basis. Anything that immediately threatens the individual will cause response to that threat rather than integrated response to the total experience. Thus, both the human and material environment must be composed to remove threats to the individual.

5. Emotion in or to or about something—the immediately sensed material and the arousal of past experience—is the energetic

force in experience. This emotion must be gathered up and carried forward, not quickly dissipated, if the experience is to be carried to completion. Emotion thus used is *expressed* through objective materials which then become media. This is a characteristic of aesthetic experience only, because when emotion is thus expressed it becomes the form of experience itself to be communicated directly as experience to someone else. Take art. The more fundamental but originally expressed, the more unified but varied, the more complete, the "greater" the work of art. But anyone can express directly through media at least something of their experience. Every new school program that truly excites the students uses varied media which can more nearly embody the form of experience than the research paper, which has its rules outside the form of experience. Any program which neglects this aspect, neglects the real desire of humans to communicate directly with one another.

Through the expressive or aesthetic or communicative experience comes more understanding of self and a decline in alienation from the environment. The other aspects of experience are required for any fulfilling experience that promotes the growth of the individual and are pre-conditions to the aesthetic (expressive or communicative) experience. The more varied means a person has for implementing these conditions, the healthier the person.

For eons, education in the arts has centered on "how to" use the media. This must change to "why use the media." Children must come to them for means for expression before they become valuable to education. It seems to me that it is never relevant to say, "Just learn how to play this piano, and later you will find some need for it."

The following experience with Orff instruments has been designed to promote aesthetic experience. There is a great deal of room within the structure for individual choice of response, and every different group of people exercises this choice. I, as teacher, have an objective: to help others gather meaning from their world of sound. This objective, however, is consistent with experience for its own sake—the only utilitarian purpose of either being more "enlivened perception." There is a product—a musical improvisation—but the experience determines the nature of the product and whether it is to be "made" at all. If individual members do not wish to design a product, they should be given the opportunity for more of the same kind of or different experiences. If the individual feels handicapped with the media, steps should be taken to find out if this is caused by lack of desire for or fear of expression, or by a feeling of insecurity with that particular media. If these individual differences are not taken into account, there can be no move toward coherent, meaningful experience.

1. Discuss environmental sounds for a few moments:
   How does a bumblebee sound like a fire engine? (Synectics)
   What does getting up in the morning sound like?
2. Ask each person to say his name and complete the sentence "If I were a sound I would be the sound of a (car engine; brook; a quiet beach at night; jello, when you stick in your thumb and pull it out again).
3. Ask each person to close his eyes and pretend he is with his sound. "Get in touch with the feelings that sound gives you." Talk about these if there is time and a quiet, supportive atmosphere. Help bring out the implications of sounds:

   SMALL BOY: My sound is a car motor and it's loud and I'm going fast—br-r-r-r-r!!
   TEACHER: Is that fun? (*To establish mood.*)
   BOY: Yes
   TEACHER: Are you going any place or riding around to see how fast you can go?
   BOY: To see how fast—it's a really noisy motor too—everyone is looking to see what the noise is.
   TEACHER: (*To satisfy the "approval-seeking" need.*) Show us! (*He does and conversation can flow.*)
   TEACHER: What if your motor breaks down, how do you feel? (*Answer.*) Can you repair it?

   The purpose of these questions is to expand the awareness of the sound and find the feelings attached to it and to help the individual focus on the sound experience rather than extraneous motivations.

4. Introduce a few selected instruments (triangles, tambourines, drums, cymbals, etc.) and ask each person to tell about his sound briefly with one instrument. Discuss the feeling–tone again, not the imitation of the sound. (This should not be the first introduction to instruments. Children should have had plenty of time before to explore each instrument.)
5. Ask each person to select a few instruments. Then have each play his own sound while he leads. The "pieces" can be taped for playback. The composer may want to dance to his "piece." The discussion which follows should at first be limited to the "composer's" satisfaction or dissatisfaction with the music.

Children will do this many times before they begin to notice lack of direction or form.

The best music in this situation usually comes from keeping very close to the original idea. When amateurs begin to abstract, they begin to use stereotyped rhythms and lose a sense of form. When a very good piece is done, everyone will know it, and that is the time to discuss the reason it is good—the coherency of the experience.

This experience can take many directions: toward focus on self-discovery through the sound analogy; toward extracting feelings—tones of environmental sound; toward discovering the nature of musical or any aesthetic form; etc. This decision of direction should come from students and teachers working together. The teacher can suggest various alternatives in focus to individuals for their own continued experience.

THE VARIOUS ME's—*Lyman B. Brainerd*

This is an exercise designed to accomplish the following goals:
1. To provide a setting which will give participants the opportunity to deal consciously with the complexities of "masked" vs. "genuine" behavior in their dealings with themselves and others.
2. To provide new insights in each participant by a combination of experience, reflection, and feedback.

The success of this exercise depends to some extent on the openness, trust, and warmth already built up within the group. (Although it also works to foster these feelings.) It's therefore important to do something at the outset such as a warm-up that will help renew these feelings. An interesting warm-up consists of dividing the group in half, giving each group a bottle of hand lotion, having them put it on their hands, and then slippery, slidey mulching their hands together. The entire process is non-verbal and, for a time, with eyes closed. The idea is that this "thing" will loosen people up, give a sense of intimacy, and new and pleasurable shared experience.

There is something in the ritual effect of this that can contribute to a sense of solidarity in some groups. A warm-up is useful. There are a number of techniques already developed that could also work, including the metaphor game, the blind walk, falling backward, and dyad communication games.

Description

The facilitator takes about 15 minutes to give the following instructions: "Room one will be the 'mask room,' you may go there if and when you are wearing a mask." "Room two will be the 'transition room,' a place where you may try to get rid of your mask." "Room three will be the 'real me room.' Go there when you want to be the real you, and thinking you are prepared to be real."

"You may, of course, move around between rooms, the ground rule being that you must at any time be in the room which represents where you think you are at at that time. Be as honest as you can be about that judgment. There are no values put on being in any particular room. None is considered any better than another. There will be signs in each of the rooms to remind you of where you are supposed to be and full length mirrors in the transition and real me rooms in case you want to use them to check on yourself. From time to time I will stop the proceedings to give new instructions. Are there any questions? All right then, you may begin."

Now allow the students to have 30 minutes to mill around freely in the various rooms.

Stop everyone and have them silently reflect for 5 minutes on their experiences and feelings during the last 30 minutes. From time to time ask questions to guide reflections. These questions can be drawn from your observations about what has been going on and attempts to empathize with the participants. Some suggestions: "how did you feel when you were told to begin?" "Were you threatened?" "What kind of negotiations did you conduct with yourself?" "Which room were you most comfortable in?" "Least?" "How do you know when you are being the 'real me'?" "Can you be it alone?" "What kinds of things do you talk about when you are the 'real me'?" "Did you find you wanted/needed other people?" "Did you try to do it alone?" "What would you do differently now?" Begin again.

Allow free milling for 10 minutes more.

Now allow milling, but non-verbal, for 10 minutes with no talking.

Bring everyone together. Again provide a silent reflection period, with new and fewer questions for five minutes. "Were you more comfortable verbally or non-verbally?" "What, if anything, was any different for you since our first reflection period?" and other general questions brought up by your observations.

General discussion and feedback—remaining time.

Observations:

1. About six people were in the "real me" room after some four minutes.

2. Four of them grouped closely together and carried on a conversation most of which was "what I feel about you," a little of which was "what I feel about me."

3. The other two in the "real me" room seemed to alternate between internal reflection and an attempt to become a part of the larger group.

4. For most of the time the others stayed in the transition room. They seemed quite ill at ease there. They carried out desultory conversation, self-conscious joking, walked about quite a bit, often peered into the "real me" room.

5. One person remained in the same place in the transition room during the entire verbal part, talking very little, seeming most uncomfortable. She never really said what she was feeling during this time.

6. By the time of the first reflection period a very intense conversation was being carried on by the four in the "real me" room.

7. The "mask room" was used very seldom, and then only by one or two for short periods.

8. People seemed to be more at ease after the first reflection period.

9. During the non-verbal part the person who had remained so passive in the "transition room" moved to the "real me" room.

10. Also during the non-verbal part a number of participants evidenced anger at me, the facilitator, for my non-participation. None of this had come out during the verbal part.

11. A few people used the mirrors.

12. The general discussion and feedback session afterward flowed, for the most part, easily and unselfconsciously. People seemed anxious to talk about some of the things that went on inside them and in their interrelationships with others.

13. There also seemed to be a great desire among some of the participants to continue the conversations begun in the various rooms.

14. This seems to have been a good experience for nearly all of the participants.

15. There was some feeling that the beginning was threatening, but nearly all were able to loosen up quite quickly.

16. The "real me" room was viewed as a "freeing" place.

17. No one seemed to know quite what to do in the "mask room."
    This accounted for its neglect far more than any low value
    that might be imputed to "wearing one's mask."
18. Some felt that the questions during the reflection period were
    useful, others that they were superfluous and disruptive to the
    process of personal reflection.
19. There was quite a lot of feedback shared among participants
    during the reflection period.
20. Most expressed the wish that there could have been more time
    given to the experience.

Conclusions

I feel that the technique is a good one and showed many signs of
achieving its goals in the time available. I would guess that it would
require two–three hours to get some results for everyone. It would
have been better with more people, probably 16–20, so that there
could be more participants in each room and so that people could
break down into groups of two or three instead of the kind of "in-
group" situation that prevailed in the "real me" room.

I really can only make some wild guesses about whether people were really "at" where they said they were "at" (if anyone can
really know in the first place) and in fact that kind of judgment is
really not relevant to the meaning of the experience so long as the
participants were able to make some judgments of this kind about
themselves and then use these judgments to get to some new insights about their "genuineness" and "phoniness" in any given
situation, the reasons for it, and what they can do to achieve more
genuine relationships with themselves and those around them.

PRISM-ISM—*Janet Brecher*

> . . . I faced the gigantic mirror on the wall.
>
> I saw myself for a brief instant as my usual self. . . . But I had
> scarcely had time to recognize myself before the reflection fell to
> pieces. A second, a third, a tenth, a twentieth figure sprang from it
> till the whole gigantic mirror was full of nothing but Harrys or
> bits of him, each of which I saw only for the instant of recog-
> nition.

An important part of self acceptance, I believe, is the realization that an individual, like a prism, may consist of many interacting parts or "facets." In the described lesson in "Affective

Education," I tried to show that a change of environment or perspective might possibly introduce a person to new combinations of facets or sides of himself; I also hoped to demonstrate that it is possible for one to feel several, perhaps conflicting, emotions towards the same object, action, or person. (Just as it is possible to derive selfish pleasure from a charitable deed, so too is it possible to feel love while also feeling hate.)

I tried to apply my prism model to the individual, his sense perceptions and his environment.

My first exercise might possibly be used for children in a ghetto school. To arouse curiosity within the members of our group and also to allow them to work within a familiar "environment," I asked everyone to bring "something UGLY" to class. Using rolled colored paper and rubber bands, we "made cameras." Then, I suggested that each person focus upon a small part of their "ugly" object or try to find some type of beauty. If a change in intensity, texture or lighting did not help, I suggested that individuals use the aid of another person's eyes or perspective to do the exercise. At the time, it was objected that after consideration certain people still did not want to find their objects (e.g. a picture of the Chicago convention) to be beautiful; I realize now that if the exercise is tried and a person does feel this way, I would not want to alter his vision. Perhaps, though, awareness that some objects can inspire different reactions might help in other situations.

Second, using a seemingly dissonant recording, *Requiem* by Charles Ives, I tried to suggest that the combination of five instruments, like the visual aids, might be perceived in a different manner. By sharing with us another of her "facets," her ability to play the flute, one of the group members played just the music of one of the five instruments. (So far, our class has helped us to feel towards one another through our exchanging ideas and some talents; imagine how many other facets may be brought out by allowing for a wider range of "environments.") In breaking down the music, we found that it contained certain "inner harmony." If we could react to each of the instruments as well as to the whole piece, a multitude of feelings might be aroused.

When I first spoke of "ugly objects" both to my friends as well as to the group, I was amused to find that a number of persons immediately responded, "I'll be the ugly object, myself." While this might seem humorous to adults, I think that many children do tend to categorize their physical appearances or their emotions as "ugly." The following techniques, therefore, deal with the concept of "self." Elbows, I have found, seem to be the most universally ugly, but the least personal parts of people's physical selves. With the use of magnifying mirrors, we examined the lines, textures and shades of our elbows closely. Perhaps children might learn to relate this exercise to other physical features. At the same time, maybe, they might discover that no single part of them, no matter how conspicuous it seems, need determine one's feelings towards his appearance.

To tie this theme in with a literary work, I asked a member of the class to read aloud from Jonathan Swift's *Gulliver's Travels*. In the selection, Gulliver is repulsed by the breasts of female giants. He finds that just as his size had influenced him to regard the complexions of tiny Liliputian women as perfect, so too did the change in his perspective cause him to despise the pores and blemishes of the larger ladies.

The possibility that even man's thoughts and feelings might be a complex of facets was expressed in the imagery from Herman Hesse's *Steppenwolf* which introduced my "lesson plan." To help people to better identify with or at least be sympathetic to this idea, we used another exercise.

I created a list of various situations which might bring out different reactions or feelings or motives in an individual. For each situation, I asked the participants to imagine that an invisible "third person," a "bug on the wall," might observe them for the first time at that moment only. On a scrap of colored paper (used to make the exercise less composition-like and less inhibiting), each person jotted down a word or two which might describe the observer's insight into him at that moment. Afterwards, I asked that everyone view the total list and note positive and negative reactions. The objection that "this is not me" was a valid one and it made it possible for me to explain my own "prism theory of people." Since a person is composed of so many facets, he cannot be "jotted down on paper." Nor can a limited number of situations reveal his infinite-sided prism. Ideally, love would be a feeling which allowed and encouraged many and new facets to be manifested without altering the overall emotion. Hate, with the help of this model, might be recognized as being temporal and spacial and not necessarily everpresent.

(Before we had discussed the final exercise and objections to it we heard a dramatic reading from the novel *Steppenwolf* where the protagonist begins to discover that his "self" is not simply composed of a 'detestable animal nature' and a higher spiritual one, but rather of infinite fragments of an ever growing "whole.")

BLACK-WHITE COMMUNICATIONS THROUGH SOUND AND SOUL

In this exercise Bill Hasson, one of the black members of our group, gave a moving "affective" performance which has application to the predominately white, middle-class surburban school. The performance communicated many things to the group. One of the messages which came across vividly was an understanding of the bitterness and frustration that black people feel, oppressed as they have been by this society.

We all gathered in a darkened candlelit room. Bill Hasson arrived in dashiki to the rhythm of a tambourine beat. He then proceeded to use a variety of multi-media to "blow our minds." To the soul beat of music he first showed a rapidly changing series of slides showing a beautiful, long-haired white girl with miniskirt walking hand in hand with a black man down the sidewalk. In a second series of slides the same slides were expanded to show background containing white people staring, frowning, and pointing with both open and concealed disapproval. The next phase of this experience involved the reading of a powerful poem which uses the word "nigger" in about fifty different ways (e.g., "lazy nigger, house nigger, yard nigger, mean nigger, black-ass nigger, etc.) chanted by Bill Hasson with strong inflection and emotion. This was followed by improvisation using every conceivable sort of "soul sound." This phased into the music from *Hair* and the touching of each other's hair. At the end of this experience, words would have been irrelevant. The group sat in stunned silence more aware than they had been before of the deep feelings and emotions that the black man feels about his oppression. Bill Hasson's description of this experience follows:

For purposes of invention, it is helpful to employ as many devices as possible. In my case I chose sound, both spoken and recorded, with the audience at certain points participating with their own ideas. This can be done by setting the mood with objectionable and non-objectionable materials. You can involve slides, music and poems separately or all three simultaneously. Once the experience has started hopefully you can have as much attention and involvement as possible, so the selection of materials and the thought that goes into the selection of those materials is very important. An example would be the taking of an issue or concept either original or contrived which would marshall the attention of your participants, then proceeding to allow the materials to form an impression. From the beginning to end if possible, try not to force upon the group your own "ego trip" and allow them to have full participation.

Juxtapositions are very important. Not everyone in the group may be operating on the same level at the same time so the variety of materials that you use are significant. Hopefully something in the experience would have been appealing to each of the participants. In my presentation I felt that the reading of the poem called, "Nigger—or The Nice Colored Man" was a good shock exposure for the non-participation that the preceding event had produced. This event was a sentimental song about freedom and a series of slides of an integrated couple (black male—white female) walking down the streets of New York and showing the offended expressions of the faces of their observers. Once there are various selections of materials for the audience to groove on, you can see the development of choice on the part of the observers and participation taking place within the experience.

Next the introduction of abstract (normally irritable) dissonant music that can be enjoyed once the listener realizes that he can react in ways other than just listening and trying to understand or interpret its parts. What I did was to play some of the new jazz music of Archie Shepp. In this music the artist gives a feeling of his total self through various instrumental sounds in the hope that the listener will exert similar responses in relation to his own capacities. This evocation by the listener may be vicarious, but I feel that the relationships developed out of this shared common experience legitimized and enhanced the abstraction of the music and the artist. In between selections either silence or sounds can be used to retain the mood.

There was incense burning to involve the sense of smell. The ultimate participation of the senses should be achieved if possible. Also at this point I called on the possibilities of individual use of time for people to conjure up their own creation either in thought or action. There were many free thoughts floating around.

Then followed the selection, "Hair," performed on tape by a group of "hippie" actors. It was sung and the words described the different types of hair. This gave the audience an opportunity to experiment with each other's hair. This solidified the group in many ways. In particular was the transfer of feelings from one person to the other. This afforded the individuals a chance to make physical contact outside of themselves—a kind of reciprocal imposition that was supposed to have positive connotations.

Then I played more so-called abstract and dissonant music from a tape and participated with other instruments including a piano. Even though I have had no formal training in piano I felt that the sounds that I produced were congruous with the experience. In such an experience all participants can join in. In fact, you can have an experience where people make sounds or noises with their bodies or with instruments they have brought or made. Anyway, my feeling is that the most flexible abstractions are those which give the most alternatives. There are many more angles and levels which can be ascribed to the meanings of those abstractions that you perceive.

By this time the group should have had a total experience and the exhaustion should be worth it. Now you can either take an assessment of what happened or simply let the experience go at that.

AN EXERCISE IN NON-VERBAL COMMUNICATION—
Bob Mackin

Part I

The purpose of the initial exercise described below is to show how commonplace our use of non-verbal communication is in expressing ideas, giving directions, etc. The group leader enters the room and, without speaking, passes out a paper to all members of the group (Note: Parts 1, 2, and 3 are all presented non-verbally). Directions on this sheet explain what will occur in Part 1 and give a brief introduction to the lesson:

Most of our lasting perceptions of people are based upon what they say—i.e., their verbal communications. What would happen if we could only express ourselves non-verbally—through gestures, facial expressions and the like? Or are we already experts in non-verbal communication but not totally aware of it?

In this lesson I would like us to consider the way we perceive others and the way we communicate non-verbally.

To test our ability to understand non-verbal communications, I would like to express some ideas, and instruct you to do certain things. As I communicate with you each time, jot down on your paper what you think I am trying to 'say.'

I then attempted to express the following ideas non-verbally by expressively acting them out:

1. I can't hear you
2. Come here
3. You, out!
4. Look around us
5. Hitchhiking
6. I'm cold
7. Quiet, ssh!
8. Thinking to myself
9. I'm tired
10. My arm is sore

Part II

Upon completion of Part I, the leader passes out the following instructions and then waits for the group to complete the exercise.

The "Metaphor Game"

Now I'd like to play a game to help discover what your perceptions are of me (try to imagine that this was the first time you had ever seen me).

Imagine that I have been transformed into something in each of the following categories. What would these four things be:

Animal   *Food*   *Color*   *Furniture*

My rationale for this part is founded upon the following belief: most of our lasting perceptions of people are based upon what they say verbally. When verbal "information" is not available, however, we must base our perceptions upon that information which is most immediately available, namely non-verbal "communications" —appearance, gestures, facial expressions and the like. Part II is an effort to determine how these two types of perceptions may vary, if at all. By playing the "metaphor game" prior to having the leader speak (ideally this lesson would be presented as the introductory group or class session), but after observing the leader for a short period, the group will be basing its perceptions on non-verbal feedback.

These results would then be compared with the perceptions of the group a few days later (again using the "metaphor game"), after normal verbal interaction had been established.

The reason for this part would be discussed with the group following the non-verbal exercises.

Part III

After completing Part II, the leader passes out the following instructions to each member of the group and then expresses a variety of feelings and emotions non-verbally.

Now instead of merely expressing "ideas" to you non-verbally, I would like to try to express certain feelings and emotions. Again, as I proceed, I would like you to list what you perceive these expressions mean.

I attempted to express the following feelings and emotions non-verbally:

1. Disgust, frustration, let-down
2. Anxiety, upset, nervous
3. Fear
4. Love
5. Anger, rage
6. Surprise
7. Hope, expectancy
8. Depression, sorrow, unhappiness
9. Dreaming, reminiscence
10. Disdain
11. Condescending
12. Discomfort
13. Stubbornness

Whereas the communications in Part I are rather simple, overt expressions, often directed to a second party, the communications of Part III express feelings and emotions which are more internalized—more automatically and unconsciously conveyed. They are not ordinarily conceived with a second party (a "receiver") in mind, and therefore might be expected to be more difficult to perceive.

This difficulty did not show itself to any great extent primarily because, whether or not we are aware of it, these expressions are an integral part of most everyone's non-verbal "vocabulary" and are pretty much universal in nature.

Part IV

The leader discusses with the group his basic rationale for the lesson—the universality of non-verbal communications and the frequent, often unconscious use of it. By rejecting verbal communication, non-verbal communication becomes vividly apparent, almost overpoweringly introduced into the conscious. (As an example, consider sitting with a small group in a circle and maintaining silence for 10 minutes. Notice how aware you become, particularly, of facial expressions—communicating self-consciousness, edginess, confidence, and other feelings.)

Comparisons are made as to how the various expressions were perceived by members of the group. In the actual presentation, agreement was extremely good. It was interesting to note in a few instances the relative agreement upon a perceived feeling which I had not intended to convey, thus indicating the extent to which the presentation depends upon the effectiveness of the presenter.

My objective extends beyond merely developing an awareness of non-verbal communications. However, I am concerned also with helping kids individually to look at and define their "self" in a nonthreatening way. These exercises can be used to give youngsters feedback about themselves—to answer questions like "Who am I?" "Do other kids feel the same things I do?" "Do I perceive things in the same way as others?" These are questions which children often ask themselves but which prove too threatening to ask of their peers.

By comparing the perceptions of the class in these exercises, kids will discover that most of them do see things in the same way—they do perceive feelings and emotions as others do. In short, they are similar to others of their age. These exercises often can become a first step in destroying the superficial barriers that restrain kids from identifying the "self."

Part V

The leader gives the following instruction:

> Close your eyes and think for a moment about the worst thing you have ever done in your life—the thing that you would most like to forget about. How did you feel after you did it? Jot down two or three words which describe how you felt.

Thereafter the leader asks the group members to share their feelings.

I found, as I had hoped, that feelings were markedly similar—guilt, depression, etc. This simple exercise, again, is used to show

how much people are alike and to give this additional feedback to members of the group. It seems to further increase a person's confidence that his "self" is much like that of other "selves."

I later presented the first three parts of this lesson to a class of senior high school students in Hartford, and then compared perceptions and discussed the lesson. Previously described as apathetic and unresponsive, the students became highly involved and reacted very positively. Most felt that it was not only fun, but an interesting learning experience.

I had entered the class quite apprehensively, realizing that I would have trouble speaking to them verbally if they responded hostilely to the exercises, refused to cooperate, or the like. Fortunately (being apathetic, I guess) they accepted it, and reacted almost identically to the session with graduate students—there was little if any talking as everyone seemed to get caught up in the non-verbal atmosphere. At one point, when a girl entered the almost perfectly silent room about ten minutes late, someone hushed her and said, "He can't speak to you, now."

The class perceived the non-verbal communications in a way comparable to the graduate group, also. There seemed to be large scale agreement.

One of the strange feelings that I had at the start of the session was the insecurity of being without a verbal shield to hide any nervousness or to ward off any hostility. I really felt nervous. I was also very conscious of being "stared at"—of having people concentrating upon my non-verbal communications, and consequently my physical being, rather than upon my voice. Fortunately, these feelings passed after a short time and I was able to enjoy myself. I think the class had fun, too.

THE AFFECTIVE DOMAIN—*David Sadker*

In the late 1940's, a group of educators, including Benjamin Bloom, David Krathwohl, and Bertram Masia met in Boston to develop coherent direction in education. This attempt to clarify goals led to the development of three domains: Cognitive, Affective, and Psychomotor.

It was just over a decade ago that a group, under the guidance of David Krathwohl, constructed the *Affective Domain* (Handbook II of the *Taxonomy of Educational Objectives*). Although this work was a milestone in Humanistic Education, it has received little practical application in the public schools. Perhaps one reason for this lack of implementation is the dearth of knowledge regarding the taxonomies themselves. Practical application of the taxonomies in classroom situations presents still another problem. It is our intent to deal with these two shortcomings. My wife and I devised a program to implement the affective domain of the taxonomy in the classroom. Before dealing with the practical classroom application that my wife presented, a short description of the taxonomy is in order.

The taxonomy is a classification system which demands the inclusion of lower categories in higher categories. The cognitive domain is concerned with intellectual operations, the psychomotor with physical coordination, and the affective with the formation of values, termed by Myrdal "valuations." The following definitions will clarify the affective domain.[3]

1.0 Receiving or Attending—This primary level is concerned with an individual's reaction to stimuli. This first step, almost cognitive in nature, is concerned with awareness of and attention to one's environment.

2.0 Responding—Once one attends to a stimulus, the next level of the taxonomy is response. The repertoire of response ranges from acquiescence to willingness to satisfaction. In other words, the individual is not just perceiving a phenomenon, but is doing something with or about it.

3.0 Valuing—This means that a thing has worth. Valuing is a product not only of a person's own assessment, but is much more a social product that has been slowly internalized or accepted. Behavior at this level has become a belief or an attitude. The range at this 3.0 level includes acceptance of a value, preference for a value, and finally a commitment to a value.

4.0 Organization—As values are internalized, situations occur which are relevant to more than one value. Thus, it becomes necessary to organize a value system with a priority of values. This is a gradual process. The two subcategories are conceptualization of a value and the organization of a value system.

5.0 Characterization by a Value or Value Complex—At this level, the organization is complete and consistent. Behavior is "natural" and consistent. This level includes a person's being character-

---

[3] David R. Krathwohl, Benjamin S. Bloom, and Bertram B. Masia, *Taxonomy of Educational Objectives Handbook II: Affective Domain* (New York: David McKay Co., Inc.: 1956), p. 176–185.

ized by certain tendencies, and having total philosophy or world view.

Krathwohl offers some examples of objectives at the various levels of the affective domain:

1.1 Develops awareness of aesthetic factors in art
1.2 Attends when others speak.
1.3 Listens to music with discrimination as to mood and meaning.
2.1 Obeys playground regulations.
2.2 Acceptance of responsibility for his own health.
2.3 Finds pleasure in reading for recreation.
3.1 Continuing desire to develop the ability to speak and write effectively.
3.2 Assumes responsibility for drawing reticent members of a group into conversation.
3.3 Devotion to those ideals which are at the foundation of a democracy.

My wife Myra utilized three levels of the taxonomy [see below]. She made the students aware (1.0) of outsiders. She had them venture opinions concerning them, as well as partake in role playing and other appropriate learning opportunities. This is at the responding level (2.0). Finally, Myra asked the students to re-examine their original comments concerning hippies. This process suggests the beginning of value formations (3.0). Obviously, such a value program demands much time as a coherent part of a curriculum. But the presentation which follows suggests the practical manner in which the taxonomy can be utilized in a classroom.

CHANGING VALUES—*Myra Sadker*

While it is obviously worthwhile for schools to develop cognitive skills, one might question their policy of devoting such enormous amounts of time and effort to reaching objectives in the cognitive domain. Another vital area of the child's development is too often neglected—that of affect, of emotion. Schools, too often, deny their responsibility in the development of appreciations, interests, attitudes, and values. These are formed in children every day of the school year—incidentally. Incidentally, children learn to love or hate literature—or school. Incidentally, they learn to value tolerance—or bigotry. Since this hapahazard formation of values occurs daily, would it be wise for the school to begin the development of values in a systematic, planned, and organized fashion?

Dr. Jack Fraenkel answered this question in an article, "Value Education in the Social Studies," which appeared in *Phi Delta Kappan*. In this article, Fraenkel comments, "It is important to consider whether we intend deliberately to influence their value development in directions we consider desirable. I contend that the systematic design of appropriate teaching strategies to bring about desired values is crucially important."[2]

If one believes, as does Dr. Fraenkel, that values should be taught systematically in the schools, he must then solve the problem of how to go about teaching them. Studies have shown that existent methodology in the teaching of values is ineffective. Current practice generally involves either a moralistic telling or an exposure of children to the "right" atmosphere. Not enough use is made of techniques which directly and intensely involve students. Following is a description of a lesson which attempts to substitute sociodrama and frank discussion for didacticism and exhortation in an attempt to begin value change in a class of thirty 6th graders in the Marks Meadow Laboratory School at Amherst, Massachusetts. The objective of this lesson was that the children should become more willing to accept people different from themselves.

I began the lesson by presenting the students with the following situation:

Imagine that you are riding in your car with your parents and you see a boy and a girl hitching a ride. Both the boy and the girl have long hair, the boy has a beard, and neither one is wearing any shoes. Would you write down on your paper in a sentence or two what thoughts pass through your mind as you drive past these two hippies.

Of the thirty students in the class, twenty-six responded very negatively. Following are some representative replies.

1. What a couple of weirdos. They look stupid.
2. They look terrible. Their hair looks like a rat's nest.
3. Long haired nuts with dumb looking clothes and beards.
4. How dirty! Which is the boy? I don't want to pick up that blob of dirt.

---

2 Jack Fraenkel, "Value Education in the Social Studies" *Phi Delta Kappan* I, no. 8 (April, 1969), 457–461.

5. I would let them walk. I wouldn't want them to be seen in my car. They look so foolish. And if you did let them ride, they would probably try to make you crack up, by either clubbing you or keep distracting you so you will get hurt.

The only three sympathetic or neutral comments were the following:

1. Gee, I wish I could be like that. I'd love to go barefoot, and what cool haircuts . . . On second thought . . .
2. I think how some people pass them by just because their thoughts are different than ours. And because they dress differently, and because they don't take a bath every night. But that's not true. Some hippies are clean, wear shoes, and take a bath every night. But they are still hippies because of their thoughts.
3. Where are they going? What makes them think that they can be nonconformists by conforming in ways like not wearing shoes?

When I asked the class for words or phrases which described hippies, the following list was compiled on the board:

Weird
Stupid
Lazy
Filthy
Poor in thoughts and education

Only one member of the class objected and claimed that hippies were rebelling against things that were bad in American society. During the following discussion, I led the class to the generalization that most hippies were outsiders, outcasts from the mainstreams of American society.

I next asked the class to get into groups of five. I told them that to qualify a group must have exactly five members, no more and no less. Immediately there was an anxious scramble to get into groups. Friends sought out friends. Quickly six groups of five were formed. I then told the class that a group with five members would no longer qualify. The new rule of eligibility was that a group had to have only four members. The groups responded in a variety of ways. Some rejected members by going through a "one potato, two potato" process. In other groups, a volunteer left. In a few groups, one member was callously removed when a selfappointed leader said, "O.K. We four are together. You're out," and the other members would acquiesce.

Interviews immediately following this group selection process produced some interesting responses. To the question, "How did you feel when I asked you to get into groups?" the most common response was, "I hoped I could get into a group with my friends." To the question," When I told you that you had to reduce your group from five to four, how did you feel?" the most common response was, "I hope I'm not the one who gets kicked out." To those who managed to survive the cut in group size from five to four, I asked, "How did you feel when you found that you were still in the group?" "Safe" and "happy" were the two most frequent answers. I finally asked those who were rejected how they felt about it. Some were quite defensive and gave replies such as the following, "I didn't care. I didn't like that group anyway. I was just about to volunteer to leave when they told me to go." Some, however, were more frank in their responses: "I felt left out." "I wondered what was wrong with me. Why did they send me out?"

After this discussion, the students put on a short sociodrama. The scene was as follows: A group of boys was walking to school, and another boy, new in the neighborhood, attempted to join them. The task of the group was to politely get rid of the intruder. A girl played the part of the boy's inner thoughts or alter ego, and, throughout the role play, expressed what the outsider was really feeling. For example, when the new boy said aloud, "Why are you in such a rush?" the girl interpreted his real feelings as, "Why don't they want me? What's wrong with me?"

Short discussion after the sociodrama showed that most of the class agreed that outsiders felt "left out," "rejected," "depressed," and "unhappy." I then asked the class to reread their reactions to hippies to see if there were any changes or additions they wished to make. I was careful to be casual about these instructions and to emphasize that whether or not they made changes or additions was completely up to them. Some members of the class didn't change their first reactions. Some students, however, did make some additions, all of them more sympathetic toward hippies. Following are some of these students' original reactions and their later modifications.

First thoughts: "Boy, what hippies! I wouldn't pick them up for anything." *Second thoughts:* "Maybe I will pick them up. They could be really good kids after all."

First thoughts: "I'm not so sure I'd like to give them a ride. How can they wear such clothes and grow their hair so long?" *Second thoughts:* "People can believe different things if they want to. Hippies just believe that growing their hair and wearing such clothes expresses their feelings."

First thoughts: "I think they are usually dirty and taking part in riots." *Second thoughts:* "I don't have anything against hippies. You have to get in someone else's shoes to really understand him."

The students read their answers aloud, and we discussed why some changed their reactions and some didn't. When the lesson was over, and the class had left, one boy handed me the following note: "The reason that at first they thought that hippies were bad is because their parents think so. But after they thought differently."

This lesson may possibly have produced a beginning in the area of developing the value that one should be accepting of people who appear to be different than he is. If such lessons were taught in an organized fashion from kindergarten through college, in all areas of the curriculum, perhaps it would be possible to systematically develop desirable values.

AFFECTIVE LEARNING EXERCISES AND GAMES— *Shimshon Zeevi*[4]

This center is characterized as a "leisure-time agency," "group-work agency," "informal educational agency," "character building agency" and "Jewish Culture Agency." Like over 300 Jewish community centers throughout the country, the staff concentrates its efforts on helping men and women of all ages to grow and mature at their own rate of development through self-selected activities and associations.

The basic premise of the methodology used in working with the groups at the Center is the acceptance of the proposition that activities which provide affective experiences allow for greater cogni-

---

[4] Mr. Zeevi is Assistant Executive Director of the Jewish Community Center, Springfield, Mass. He developed this section with the help of full-time staff members.

tive learning. This is also a major premise of humanistic education. Humanistic education was first introduced in a class and at staff meetings and individual conferences in order to highlight the value of incorporating the teaching of cognitive material with feeling responses in small groups. The emphasis was placed on the development of a few exercises covering different leadership and group situations.

Even though these exercises were developed for application in small group situations they can be applied to larger groups and used as part of a human relations unit.

ACTIONS AND REACTIONS IN NATURE

This exercise is for experiencing and learning about relationships (or the lack of relationships) between items in nature. It is also an exercise in creativity. Each member of the group selects a name representing an item in nature: wind, mountain, sun, snow, ice, sand, river, etc. and is asked to "be" it. (*Note:* If there is a large number of children, two or three can select the same item.)

Ask the children to pair off and work out a skit, pantomime, dance, etc., which will express the relationship between the items they represent. Ask the pair to find a comfortable place in the room and start working. They are to return to a central place when they finish. After the children complete their task, each pair presents its "act" to the others. A discussion may follow each presentation.

Once the first part is completed, tell the children to form groups of threes. They may select new items, or use the same ones they had before. They are now to "work out" the relationships between the three items in form of a dance, a skit, etc. After this is completed, the teams present their "thing" to the group. A discussion may follow. (*Note:* The children may pair off in such a way that there is no direct, noticeable, "action–reaction" pattern in the items they selected. The leader should not intervene, for each pair of items allows for a different level of learning.)

For example: the "wind" pairs off with the "mountain." The wind does not *blow* the mountain, but the mountain can *slow* the wind.

The leader's direct involvement with each pair or group depends on the age of the children, or their abilities as observed by the leader.

This exercise was developed during a supervisory conference for a leader working with a drama club. The group (4–6 grade boys and girls) planned to work on a play: "Who is Strongest?" (Adapted from a folk tale by Jean Feather.) The main theme of the play is the nature of the relationships between "things." One of the sessions was taped. The following is an excerpt from the tape:

The Ice and the Sun

> ICE: I am the strongest thing in the world . . . e . . . e . . . except for the. . . . Go away . . . You're going to melt me . . .
> SUN: My job is to melt you through . . .
> ICE: No! No! get away from here! ! get away . . . you are melting me! . . . you melting m . . m . . me . . .

The Wind and the Tree

> TREE: I am the strongest thing in the world, boy.
> WIND: No you're not . . . (the "wind" started to blow, the "tree" bent.)

On one occasion, the pair "confused" the roles. The following discussion took place:

The Fire and the Tree

> FIRE: NO! NO! NO!
> TREE: What NO?
> FIRE: I don't like you . . .
> TREE: SO?

Other children started to intervene:

> MEMBER A: Are you the tree?
> FIRE: NO, I am the Fire.
> MEMBER B: (talks to the Tree): Then you should be afraid of her . . .
> TREE: That's what I told her, but she did not want to . . .
> FIRE: I am not afraid of her . . .

There was a great deal of interaction among the children. They were intrigued by the challenge. A few could not "act out" different roles than those they assume generally.

We all see and react to different things in our own particular way, based on our previous experiences. This exercise can also be used to highlight individual perceptual awareness. For example: One can deal through this exercise with the relationships between senses and thought processes, inanimate and animate objects, etc.

This exercise can also be used in school after the completion of a social studies unit which was concerned with different geographical areas. How would children feel in Switzerland when relating items in nature? etc.

PROGRAMMING THROUGH PERSONAL INVOLVEMENT

The second exercise is to allow the students to experience the process of planning a program. It teaches how to plan a program based on personal experiences.

A group or a committee meets to plan a program. Ask the members to sit as comfortably as possible and think about a program or activity in which they were involved and to which they felt committed. After about 1 minute, ask them to close their eyes and continue to think about the program. Ask them to imagine that they are standing in the middle of a large field. Now say: "Look at the left side of the field. Think about the program. . . . Think about what it was that made you like the program. . . . Try to identify it. . . . Call it a name and place it on the left side. . . . Think about as many items as you can remember. . . ." After 5–10 minutes (the leader can judge the amount of time needed by the movements of the members) say: "Now look at your right. . . . Place on the right side all the things you did not like about the program."

When this part is over: Give each member a piece of paper. Ask them to tear the paper to pieces. Ask them to write on each piece of paper one item relating to the positive aspects of the program. Once they finish, each member reads his list. Write each item on the blackboard. *Note:* There is no need to write the same item twice.

This procedure is repeated for the "negative" items. Once everything is written down, the discussion starts. The discussion focuses on the most important aspects in the various programs, and the most "negative" aspects which should not be repeated.

Once the group reaches a consensus about the items, the group identifies the program they are interested in planning. The planning now includes all the items which were selected.

In experimenting with this exercise, we found that once people get used to this *unorthodox* way of looking at a program, there was a general sense of enthusiasm for the planned program. The discussion about "positives" and "negatives," as introduced by the participants, allowed for an intensive involvement in the process on part of each member. Various generalizations were introduced by the leader and, unlike other experiences, they seemed to have been incorporated well in the final processes of the decision making activity.

This specific group planned a dance. Through the exercise the members were able to cover almost every aspect of planning for the dance. This included: promotion, budget, creation of an atmosphere, etc.

This exercise has application for group planning for itself, a class planning a trip. The children can discuss the things they like to see happen in the trip. They participate in the process. This will encourage them to also take on various responsibilities.

It also has application for a committee planning a program for others. In this case, the members of the committee discuss first their own preferences and then project based on the interests of others. In this discussion, members of the committee learn to differentiate between their personal interests and needs, which may or may not be of interest to others.

This exercise can be used also as a "before and after" exercise in studying a social studies unit in school. What was most important about the country? The people? Geography? Industries? etc.

This exercise can lead to a discussion of preconceived ideas about a place, program, etc. Because of the nature of the experiment, it is suggested that one could get better results with children 13 or older.

BUT I CAN'T BE ME . . .

The purpose of this next exercise is to give experience feeling the "loss" of free choice in conformity, learning about consequences of "blind conformity," and learning to "give" up personal desires in a group activity.

Tell the members of the group to walk in the room. They can walk wherever they want to. After a few minutes, ask the members to pair off. The couples, standing anywhere in the room, are asked to tie their inner legs together. They are now told to walk wherever they want. After a few minutes, ask the couples to form teams of four. They stand in line and tie their inner legs. In this formation, only those at the beginning and end of the line have one free leg.

Now ask the groups to walk wherever they want to. If needed, you can try the same exercise with groups of 8.

Events:

As expected, the members of the group became increasingly frustrated. They found it difficult to adjust and wherever more than one natural leader emerged in the group there was an open conflict. The exercise was tried with a group of fifteen 5–6 grade boys. There was a great deal of shoving and verbal arguments. One of the boys summed up this experiment by saying: "But I can't be me. . . . I can't walk. . . . I can't go where I want to. . . ." Another boy remarked: "When we are together we cannot do whatever we wish. . . . We have to talk to the others. . . ."

This exercise is designed to bring about two opposing yet related issues in group activity. When people join groups, they learn, among other things, to "give up" some of their own needs and desires in order to be accepted by others in the group. Members learn to compromise, adjust and discuss in order to achieve a comfortable degree of functioning in a group. This exercise allows for discussion on the need to engage in communicating with others as opposed to "doing what you want to do" when others do not feel like it. At the same time, the issue of doing because "He told me to. . . ." is being highlighted and the item of "loss of individuality" can be discussed openly by the members of the group.

It is an acceptable form of interaction. As a result of participating in this exercise, the leader may notice other forms of "interaction." Played with young children, one would observe pushing, shoving, yelling, etc. If this becomes a priority in the process, the leader may discuss this issue—then repeat the exercise.

ON BEING LOST

This exercise gives the participants the opportunity to experience the feelings of being lost.

The participants are blindfolded. Forming a line, they hold each other's shoulder. The leader takes them for a walk. The purpose of the walk is to bring the participants to a larger room in a way that they will not be able to identify it. In order to achieve this goal, the leader takes them in circles, in and out of rooms. Once they reach the larger room, the participants are separated and left in different places. He asks the children to find their way around without making a sound. After about 10–15 minutes, the leader brings the children together, forms a line and takes them to their room. Once in the room, and the children see each other again, a discussion focuses on how they felt during the exercise.

Trying this with a small group of children in the neighborhood, I noticed two children (9 year olds) that became rather frightened. Others were confused and somewhat scared. A great sigh of relief was on the face of two children who "found each other." Prior to playing this "game," we talked about what happens when someone is lost. "Like the astronauts, or at night, etc."

Possible applications for this exercise include the following:

1. A science club about to embark on a program dealing with issues of space.
2. A group of children reads a story, or are about to study a book, in which someone is "lost" in the desert, etc.
3. Teenagers very frequently discuss their peers. Many times they talk about someone who seems to be "lost." They talk about "being alone in a crowd," etc. This exercise may highlight for all concerned the feelings and various meanings of "being lost."

ON BEING NEEDED—HUMAN ANAGRAMS

The purpose of this exercise is to experience the feelings of being needed by others in achieving a goal. Learning that not being needed by others in achieving a goal does not necessarily mean being rejected by others. It is also useful for observing role-behavior of group members.

The leader prepares pins and pieces of paper. On each piece of paper he writes one letter. Each member of the group receives one letter which he pins on his chest. The letters are visible to all. It is important that the letters include enough vowels and consonants to form a number of words. The leader asks the members to form many words with the letters available to them, within a given time limit.

The game is played twice. The first time, members of the groups are asked not to talk during the game. The second time the game is played, the members may talk to each other. The discussion following the game picks up on the issue of performing a task and the meaning of being needed or not needed.

This exercise was performed by me with six children participating (three boys and three girls, 10 and 11 years old).

I prepared six letters: S, N, R, E, I, A. For a few seconds after we started there was confusion. Then they started to form words.

One of the boys took the leadership and started to arrange the
words. Since they did not talk, he motioned to others where to
stand. At times he pushed someone or moved the other to a different position. One boy was moving very slowly. By now, one of the
girls took over the leadership. She started to push the "slow" boy.
Another boy joined her. The "slow" boy started to withdraw from
the group. He didn't like being shoved. The others needed him, and
intervened. From that point on, one of the girls did not allow the
others to push the "slow" boy. He seemed to enjoy the game and
became a little more active.

I rearranged the letters for the second part of the game, during
which the children were allowed to talk. There was a great deal of
yelling. An interesting thing happened during this part of the
game. One of the boys, who was pushing and shoving others during the first part of the game, was being rejected by the others.
I noticed this when the group started to form words which did not
include his letter. He felt it too. I could see it on his face. However, in order to make the maximum number of words, the group
needed him and later started to involve him too.

The discussion which followed included a remark which he
made: "Ok. You taught me a lesson. . . . I am sorry. . . ."

Played with elementary school children, this exercise can be
used as a "diagnostic tool" by the leader. The experiment, as discussed above, shows rather clearly that various modes of behavior
by members of the group are made visible and can be dealt with
either through the group or individually by the leader.

Additionally the leader may lead a discussion with the children
about how their roles and behaviors affect others in the group. The
focus here is on the feelings as expressed by various members of
the group.

This exercise can be used also as part of a leadership training
program. The trainees participate in the exercise and then discuss
their own roles. Through this, the discussion moves to a look at
various roles people play in groups, and the meaning of roles to
people.

READ THE LETTER AGAIN

The purpose of this exercise is to experience meaning through
different voice inflections, and for evaluating alternatives to understanding.

People react in various ways to comments they hear, or letters they read. One may observe that often negative reaction to a comment comes as a result of "negative hearing" or, in other words, a result of a projection of a negative intent. This exercise aims to explore this phenomena through the introduction of alternatives to this "projected hearing."

The members form groups of five. They read a letter, or parts of a play, which deals with interaction between people. Members of each group read the material with different tones of voice. The others try to identify the meanings of the expressions and discuss these meanings. The discussion focuses on "why do we hear what we want to hear?" and "Is it possible that the other person did not mean it this way?" For example:

MOTHER: John, come home, supper is ready.
JOHN: One minute, Mother, I have to finish something.
MOTHER: Hurry up the food will be cold.
JOHN: Ok. I am coming.

(John comes home late at night.)

FATHER: Where have you been?
JOHN: With the boys.
FATHER: Where?
JOHN: All over the place.
FATHER: What did you do?
JOHN: Nothing.

Members of each group may try to write their own script. This exercise can be used in preparation for participation in a play.

THE TRIP

The purpose of this exercise is to experience involvement and relaxation with music. Participants sit where they please in the room. The leader puts music on and says: "Now sit as comfortably as you can. . . . What I would like you to do now is close your eyes and listen to the music. . . . Just listen to the music. . . . Close your eyes. . . . Relax. . . . Listen to the music. . . . Let the music take you with it. . . . Just "GO" with the music. . . ."

The leader keeps the music on for 10 to 15 minutes (or longer, depending on the situation). The members discuss their reactions and feelings to the exercise.

In experimenting with this exercise I found that there seems to be a relationship between the person's ability to relax and being able to "be with" this exercise.

This exercise might serve as an introductory activity to programs on music appreciation. The perception of feelings and awareness of music which are incorporated in this exercise may be followed by others aimed at intensifying awareness of music.

LET'S DRAW A PERSON

The purpose of this exercise is to experience the uniqueness of individuals in a group.

The group is divided into teams of six members. Each team is given an assignment to draw a composite picture of a person. The members are instructed to draw a person whose characteristics are those of the members of the group, i.e., they may decide to draw the head of Member A, nose of Member B, shoulders of Member C, etc.

The group has to decide whose characteristics they will draw before starting the picture. When selecting the eyes or lips of a person to represent the group, one is selecting much more than just eyes or lips. Feelings and attitudes are also involved in the decision and they become important aspects of the discussion.

This exercise could serve also as part of a sociology unit dealing with uniqueness of peoples around the world. Additionally this exercise may be used to highlight the area of intergroup relations, by pinpointing similarities and differences, as well as the meaning of these similarities and differences. Quite often the group becomes very supportive of the various members and parts of their anatomy which they had thought little of.

THE SELF—*Barbara Skibiski, Karen Lundy, and Connie Eshbach*

What follows is a unit of exercises to promote an increased awareness of self as well as a feeling of freedom through the contrasting of rigid and less rigid exercises.

Physical exercising involves the total physical being and too often is done without self awareness. In this experience, we gave the group two types of exercises. With the males in the forward line outside on the lawn, the group performed the traditional toe-touching and jumping jacks by direction of the leader. Next, having moved anywhere they desired, they were brought to attention, and then the group members regained total body movement under the guidance of the leader by gradually mobilizing parts of their body from head to foot. Then the participants were asked to go inside and finger paint how they felt while exercising. Discussion followed.

Next the group, while listening to music, drew with finger-paints and crayons, respectively. The former necessitates the hand being the tool of creation while the latter makes the implementation for creation. Discussion followed during which the group members brought out how their feelings for the music had been reflected in the fingerpaintings and crayons.

In the next exercise two groups (5 members each) in a circle were directed to listen and discover what feelings or emotions were aroused by a selected musical piece. With paper and crayon they were asked to express the aroused emotions and/or feelings. Having given them only 20 seconds to draw, the leader instructed them to stop, pass their papers to the person on their left, and continue. Repeated, five composite drawings resulted which reflected the various moods and individuality of the members. Discussion followed during which the students discussed their feelings.

Physical contact between persons can bridge the dividing barrier of physical autonomy so prevalent in this society. Hopefully, such contacts can lead to satisfaction and joint creativity or at least to a desire for accomplishment or understanding or bridging the barriers which separate individuals.

In this exercise, dyads were formed in two circles of 4 and 6 members respectively. With crayon and paper and by joining and using nearest hands, each individual dyad was instructed to draw a cooperative drawing while listening to selected music. Upon completion of the music, mutually-decided dyads were formed until the allotted time ended. Discussion followed during which the dominance or submissiveness of the various members was brought out.

The final section of the unit began with the entire group sitting in a tight circle with their eyes closed. Each person was handed a piece of material which he was to feel thoroughly and then pass to the person on his left. Each piece of material was of a different texture.

When all the different pieces had been felt by every member of the group, they were placed within the center of the circle and everyone opened his eyes. The group then discussed what they had just done; the feelings they had gotten from feeling different textures with their eyes closed, the colors they had expected different things to be, etc.

The next step consisted of asking each person to select one texture (or more, if they wished) which either held some special meaning for them or was in some way reflective of their self. Then, using this as their focal point, they were asked to create a "collage of self"—a self map or portrait—from a collection of collage materials which had been provided (pins, bows, paste, ribbons, magazines for cutting, paint, metal scraps, combs, excelsior, etc.). As before, when everyone was finished, they discussed what they had each created. Each person became somewhat transparent in his collage and fascinating strengths and insights were shared with the group as they explained their collages.

We had hoped to produce a unit of exercises which would promote an increased awareness of self as well as a feeling of freedom. Through contrasting rigid and less rigid exercises and types of art, we hoped to arrive at this feeling of freedom and awareness.

The feedback seemed to indicate that the presentation was a success. Adoption of this unit or parts of it to the classroom is feasible provided an atmosphere of trust exists.

Some of the self portraits contained vivid revealing portrayals of personality traits and deep feelings of the participants. In the discussion that followed the making of collage self-portraits, a strong feeling of group concern and intimacy developed.

In a letter from Barbara Skibiski written to me a few months after she took over as a teacher for a class of 31 fifth graders she said:

> I almost wrote to you last month after my first deliberate use of the affective education techniques we developed in your class, but I hesitated as I couldn't really believe their tremendous success.
>
> We played the metaphor game using names of animals ("My name is _____ and I am a _____") which was a good warm up and lots of fun. We also played a self awareness game ("close your eyes and notice where your feet are, etc."). They liked the exercises even to the extent of telling the school principal who entered my class in the middle of a session. My greatest success so far has been achieved through "the drawing together exercise" (two people hold one marking

pen together and make a cooperative drawing of what they feel about selections of music). My kids went wild! They were great! I had never seen them so happy!

Unfortunately as with most good ideas in education barriers exist which limit their use in teaching. The first is time. Our school is on double session so academic subjects have been scheduled to the minute. The second is that I am so new to the academic subject matter that I am hesitant to integrate humanistic approaches with it.

A friend wrote me from the university that she was in on one of the classes where you were a guest "humanistic education leader." She called it "one of the most wonderful experiences" of her life. There's still hope that we can humanize our schools! Please let me know of new developments. . . .

CONCENTRATION, IMAGINATION AND COMMUNICATION—*Barbara Woodbury*

The aim of this exercise is to improve or initiate student ability to explore moods, emotional reactions, and develop consciousness of different reactions to the same stimuli. An important aspect of this exercise is to request communication of the resultant experience.

The teacher should have prepared on tape three or four different mood-provoking pieces of music. Turn off all lights. Try to eliminate as many outside distractions as possible. Have the students sit as far as possible from anyone and close their eyes.

The directions were to futurize, fantasize, or reflect as the music takes you. They were directed to pay special attention to the place they went, the situation, the feel, the smells, the people, and as much as possible their reaction to the situation. After each three-minute selection, they were allowed a few minutes to recover and jot down any pertinent notes to remind them later of that particular trip. They were then asked to break into two groups and share their trips.

The first piece of music I play is the prayer sequence from *Madame Butterfly*. The reactions are usually quite diverse and imaginative: a funeral procession, French paintings, a south seas caravan, a sunset on a mountain, and one poor soul saw himself dying in a boat that kept going over wave after wave. The telling is a lot more complex than this brief description would lead one to believe. The second piece I play is "Chase" from the Beatles' *Help*. This also provokes some unique trips: a carnival, a blowfish blowing up and out in time to the music, a belly dancer, a stomach receiving a coke, potato chips, and other assorted hors d'oeuvres, a Santa Claus that ended up in a Morrocan souk that led into a dark and lonely room, and "pure, unmitigated sex." This is usually the most successful piece of music. The third piece is Mahler's Fourth Symphony, and the romantically inclined females enjoy the music, but on one occasion it invoked in one person the memory of an old teacher playing "Country Garden" and telling the high school class merely to imagine they were in an English country garden. He was turned off by the idea. The last piece is "Good Morning, Starshine" from *Hair*. A juke box in a teeny bopper hamburger joint was as far as this went.

Music per se in creative exercises seems to me to be of unquestioned value. However, I think that the necessity to communicate the experience is almost as important as the experience itself. The poems, Haiku, short stories, or dances that result from this experience are surprising.

A HUMANISTIC EDUCATION EXPERIENCE

What follows is a description of a humanistic education experience which was a composite of various techniques gleaned from my students, associates and readings. I presented the experience to a class of "difficult" fifth graders in the Marks Meadow Laboratory School in Amherst, Massachusetts. The class contained many exceptionally bright children and had an imaginative male teacher who had built excellent rapport with the students in spite of the steady stream of interns, researchers, psychologists and people like me who had paraded through the classroom to expose the children to some innovation. The session was a 2–½ hour period with one hour before lunch and an hour and one-half after lunch. Perhaps the most significant thing for me is the important learning experience I achieved in gaining control of the class after lunch. Before lunch, with the exception of the initial non-verbal exercise I gave the children, the morning was a most frustrating and unpleasant experience for me. Things were fine until I broke the class up into dyads to experiment with several communication exercises. It was then that chaos broke out and I began to be treated as just another "substitute." Though some interesting things were going on, mainly among the girls, I was so completely distracted by the rowdiness of others that I found myself shouting directions and still not being heard. Thank God, the lunch break came! This gave me a much needed chance to reconsolidate my thinking and come up with a new approach.

After lunch, I began by saying to the class that the morning's experience had been extremely unpleasant for me and that I didn't like to shout, and that I was very uncomfortable with all the rowdiness which interfered with what we were trying to do. I added that I thought some of the children also had an unpleasant experience because of this. I explained that "noise" wasn't bad as such, but when I had to give directions with noise, it was uncomfortable for me as well as for those who wanted to hear. (I did not tell them they were bad, but rather that I couldn't work with the rowdiness.) I asked for suggestions on how this situation could be improved They immediately began to suggest ways to guide us toward a more rewarding experience. I was amazed as they began to evolve rules for their own behavior which I wrote on the blackboard! The afternoon was a complete delight though we ran out of time and had to end prematurely. After class at least eight students came up and asked if we could do more next week.

Brian Anderson, the skilled teacher of the class, suggests several other effective guidelines he uses with the class. First, before doing something he always asks himself the question. "Can a student perform this task instead of me?" If the answer is "yes" he lets a student do it. I taped this experience on video tape which can be distracting at times. The tape and interest might have been better if I had let a student instead of me take the microphone (an incumbrance I wish I didn't have in this experience) around to get student responses. Another good suggestion Brian Anderson makes is to minimize directions and instructions to students and get them involved in the exercise as soon as possible.

The purpose of this exercise is to get in closer touch or to practice communicating feelings with others using less conventional ways such as non-verbal means, touch, and finding new ways to come into contact. The exercise helps us to realize how much of ourselves we have been cutting off and suggests that we can bring ourselves more fully to life with our friends and associates.

The learning facilitator introduces a series of exercises which demonstrates new or less used ways of communicating, and which gets the students to explore their feelings with themselves and others. The exercises as listed below are planned for a two and one-half hour block of time. They may be used at almost any grade level. The preferable setting would be a large room without desks with a circle of chairs. It is helpful if the teacher, teaching assistants, and aides who may be present, also participate in the experience. Each student should have a name card on his shirt. A brief introduction should be presented emphasizing how little we use all of our communication capability and how in the time which follows the class will explore some new ways of coming into contact with others, ourselves, and our feelings since what we learn and become depends in large measure on how we feel about ourselves, our class mates, teachers, etc.

Finding new ways to come into contact

First ask the students to pair off with anyone in the class. Find a comfortable place to sit, and sit down, first, back to back and communicate with each other only by talking. (Allow this to proceed for about three minutes.)

Now have the students in each pair sit face to face and communicate only visually, without talking or touching, for three more minutes.

Now have the students close eyes and communicate without speaking again, but this time through touching hands. Ask them to say hello through their hands, to get acquainted, take a walk, have a fight, make up, dance, and say goodby. This should last about three minutes.

Finally, have the students explore their partners' faces with their hands, again keeping eyes closed and not speaking for a moment or two, getting in touch with the texture and various parts of their partners' face.

Now break and have the partners discuss in dyads how effective the various means of communication were and how they felt while engaging in them (give them about five minutes for this feedback session).

Now ask the students to close their eyes and think of another name that they have been called at one time or another by their parents or friends. "Get in touch with the feelings you had about this name, the circumstances when it was used, and whether or not you liked it." Now ask each student to share the name with his partner or "new friend." Each student should then close his eyes, visualize the circumstance of being called the name, and his partner should whisper the name in his ear as though he were being called it in an attempt to evoke the feelings associated with the name.

After both partners have had a chance to whisper the name and fantasize about it, break, and allow three or four minutes of feedback discussion. (This exercise should take about ten minutes.)

Now have the students think of names which they would like to be called if they could have any name they want. They can do this in open discussion with their partners discussing why they like the name. They should then write the name on the back of their name card and turn it around so the new name shows. The students are then told that for the rest of the morning they will have a chance to experiment and use their new name to see how it feels. (On a later day an interesting open class discussion can be held about how people liked their own and others' new names, and additional opportunities can be developed to use new names if the class desires.)

Now, have one partner close his eyes and the other partner lead him around the room wherever he pleases with no speaking, in an attempt to give the "blind" partner the maximum amount of sensory experiences possible. (After three minutes break for feedback and discussion between partners.)

Now ask each person to introduce his partner by telling something special about him. This should be done back in the circle in front of the entire class. Each statement should be just a short sentence. This exercise should take about fifteen minutes.

Questions About the Self

In this exercise the teacher can either pass out a mimeographed list of questions with space for answers under each, or write the questions on the board. Each student writes a short answer to each question followed by open discussion. (Allow about ten minutes to answer the questions with about another fifteen minutes for discussion. The discussion on this can be continued on later days.)

1. What would be the situation if you refused to get out of bed this morning?
2. What if you said "no" instead of "yes" much more often?

3. What would be the situation if you were four inches taller?
4. What would be the situation if you were a girl instead of a boy?
5. What would be the situation if you were black instead of white?
6. What if you were 16 for the rest of your life?
7. If you were an animal what would you be?
8. If you were a color what would it be?
9. If your parents were hippies what would be your situation?
10. If you could tell the group the one thing you like most about yourself what would it be?

The "yes and no" subselves

In this exercise the group is told that you would like volunteers to present something to the class. After a few moments of conflict about whether or not to volunteer, the learning facilitator says, "I do not really want the volunteers now, but I would like you to focus on the experience you have just had, the experience of trying to decide whether or not to volunteer. Imagine two people inside your head—one telling you to volunteer, one not to. Picture a conversation between the two arguing until one wins. After the discussion have the two meet non-verbally and see what happens. Close your eyes for two or three minutes and imagine this encounter. I will tell you when to open your eyes." (Allow the class a few minutes to fantasize.) Now have the students report the way the two subselves looked, sounded, how big they were, what they said, where they were, their physical position, and who won. (This exercise takes about fifteen minutes.)

The Wardrobe of the Self

Ask the students to relax, close their eyes. "Concentrate on yourself as you really are. Let your mind give to your consciousness some words that describe you. Get in touch with the words and see if they really describe you. When you are satisfied the words really describe you, open your eyes but remain quiet and do not look around." (Pass out paper and pencils. Instruct the students to tear the paper into 8 pieces. It doesn't matter if the pieces are even as they will throw them away in a few minutes.) "On each piece of paper write one of the words that describe you.

(You are the only one who will see them, so be honest.) Arrange the papers in order, placing the one you are happiest about on top and the one you are least happy about on the bottom. Now keep your eyes on the papers. Take each in order and spend some time with it. Try it on like you would clothes in your closet. Then do with each what you want. Put it back in your wardrobe, tear it up (you do not like it), throw it away (it used to fit but does not anymore, or it's not your style, etc.), or whatever you want.

To bring this session to a conclusion have each student write down on a paper two things he learned about himself during the day. These can be presented in an open discussion if time permits. At a later date, if desirable, each student can write a paper on these two things.

Here are some examples of responses to this last exercise written by the fifth graders: "I found I'm not satisfied with myself. I want to be something more than I am now." "I like to work with small groups better than large ones cause I can get my way better." "I'm not a very good actor doing things different from the way I really am." "There are many ways of communicating, some better than talking." "I'm very smart." "I really like people." "You can have fun in school while learning."

The last point made the entire lesson a success as far as I was concerned. It's true. Learning can be fun.

This chapter has been based upon my work with a group of fifteen students who, together, experienced the various humanistic education techniques described in Chapter 4. The units presented in this chapter were planned by the students to achieve certain classroom goals using the repertoire of humanistic techniques they had learned. The classroom applications were experienced by my entire class and then tested in school classrooms. The descriptions presented in this chapter included an exercise using a short film and role-playing to experience "Feeling About the Cause of Our Actions;" using improvised sound and music to promote aesthetic experience; an exercise involving three rooms—a "real me room," a "mask room," and a "transition room" through which the students wandered and acted appropriately; "Prism-ism," an exercise bringing out the many facets of a person; a multi-media black–white communication facilitation exercise; a non-verbal exercise and "Metaphor Game;" a unit on changing values; a series of affective learning exercises and games; a self-awareness exercise using physical exercise, music, drawing, and finger painting; a "Concentration, Imagination and Communication Exercise" using reaction to different stimuli such as music, art, and a "collage of the self;" and a humanistic communication experience used in a fifth grade classroom.

These are examples of humanistic exercises developed by students themselves in a humanistic university course (or more appropriately, "noncourse") and tested out by the students in classrooms during their student teaching experience.

part **IV**

Training Humanistic Teachers and Managers

Introduction to Part IV

*The goal of education must be to develop a society in which peo-
ple can live more comfortably with change than with rigidity. . . .
But such a goal implies, in turn, that educators themselves must
be open and flexible, effectively involved in the processes of
change. . . . Develop a climate in the system in which the focus is
not upon teaching, but on the facilitation of self-directed learning.*
Carl Rogers

In this part of the book we will examine ways of approaching
the vital problem of training humanistic teachers and administrators. After all, this is the crux of the problem. We must look to the
institutions where our teachers and administrators are being trained
if we are to make any impact at all. Chapter 6 will give us a peek
at a model approach for both pre-service and in-service training
geared toward increasing a teacher's potential for working in a
humanistic classroom.

Chapter 7 will deal with the problem of humanistic management,
applying the work of such managerial psychologists as Douglas Mc-
Gregor, Chris Argyris, and Rensis Likert to educational management or administration.

6

Training Human Teachers

The possibilities that occur as one works in a T-group with teachers and thinks about typical meetings and encounters seem utopian, and they may be. Think how relaxing it would be to get an honest and open exchange of views, to be able to trust the advice of a colleague who feels like a colleague, not a servitor, or an oppressed one, or a sycophant.

—A Long Island School Superintendent—

Now we get to the crux of the problem—our schools of education. This is where the problem must be solved, if at all. It's an impossible task to reach and change individual teachers all over the country without first changing the teacher training institutions where these teachers are receiving their pre-service and in-service training. Unfortunately, a generalization can be made about our schools of education around the country: They are in a sorry state. In most cases they are rigid bastions against change. They're a decade or more behind the times, and on many campuses the more imaginative students wouldn't waste their time in the schools of education.

There are a few exceptions, and this chapter will focus on one of those and the factors that create an excitingly different climate—hence, attracting and producing an excitingly different caliber of teachers.

Unfortunately in education, where it is so desperately needed, there is no really efficient dissemination system to broadcast innovations or developments. There are several research oriented systems such as ERIC (run by the U.S. Office of Education); however, this information is about researchers and read almost exclusively by researchers rather than by teachers, administrators, parents, or school board members. Many noteworthy developments, and a few important breakthroughs in education, are taking place around the country, but few schools of education are exposed to these models.

Those that are either clam up in their shells of intellectual conservatism, or hear about them through third– or fourth–hand hearsay. What is needed is a national education dissemination system that would tap into each of the 19,000 school districts around the country, tying them together in a communications network. If one of the large film companies, for instance, would be interested in making a serious investment in education, it seems that it would have the potential to make some real progress in this area.

For instance, such a company, already having the large investment in facilities and equipment, could produce, every other week on a subscription basis, a top caliber 16 mm. film. This film could be accompanied by appropriate printed supplementary material which could be mailed every other week to each of the subscribing school districts in the country. Federal funds could be used or legislated, perhaps, for each school district to subscribe to this service. Each superintendent or principal could set up two hours every other week for in-service training when all teachers would gather to view the film and discuss it. Each film could feature some innovation being tried in a school or school of education. Supplementing the teachers in the film could be such narrators as Robert Vaughan, Bill Cosby, Gregory Peck and other actors who have already demonstrated their desire to make a contribution to education (of course these skilled actors would already be under contract with the large film company). In this way dramatic skill and film expertise could be married to the knowledge of educators in a most productive way. The American Film Institute made a modest but important start in joining film makers with educators in a 1968 summer institute at Santa Barbara funded by the Education Profession's Development Act of the U.S. Office of Education. However, in the dissemination area, much potential remains to be tapped.

On a small but quite effective scale, Dwight Allen has made a start in distributing film lectures about some of the innovations in which he has pioneered, such as micro-teaching and differentiated staffing. It is on this model for innovation that the remainder of this discussion on humanistic teacher training will focus.

As mentioned in Chapter 3, a unique environment and climate has been created in the School of Education at the University of Massachusetts. There are over fifty new faculty members on the staff and only seven tenured faculty. With this kind of odds, change is possible even in a school of education. There are over one hundred fifty new doctoral candidates, most of whom do not fit the description of the average "education major." Several were recruited in jail, several have been ghetto gang leaders or members, most have had several years of experience teaching or running programs for the disadvantaged.

Carl Rogers names the following three criteria for selection of graduate students as the ones he would use in a revolutionary program of graduate education:

1. Intelligence
2. High degree of empathetic understanding
3. High degree of spontaneous curiosity and originality

Doctoral students at the University of Massachusetts School of Education meet these criteria. The climate is a most fertile one. New ideas are nurtured, encouraged—even celebrated. New ideas, after all, are delicate. They can be killed by a frown, a laugh, a sneer, or a vacant look. At the same time we must treat them like we treat baby fish when stocking them. We throw out hundreds, and only the best survive. This school is a greenhouse for innovative ideas tempered by the actual past classroom experiences of the faculty and students.

Another key factor in the fertility of the climate is the fact that it is very student-centered. Students enjoy equal status in almost all ways with faculty. The first year of the new school was declared a "planning year." The entire faculty and graduate student body flew on a chartered jet to a retreat in Colorado to "brainstorm" a fresh start in teacher education. They jointly decided to scrap all the old required courses and begin with a new start—a *Tabula Raza*. They organized around planning committees with such names as Aesthetics, Humanistic Education, Urban Education, and the Learning Theater. Students didn't have to take courses but rather received academic credit for their work on the committees planning the new, more relevant school. If, for some reason, people lost interest in one committee they left and went to something that did interest them. If too many deserted, the committee would disband as being irrelevant.

Needless to say, one had to have a high tolerance for ambiguity to enjoy this fluid, free-wheeling environment. Those who didn't, experienced frustration. Additionally, there was great resistance from certain other departments in the university who accused Dwight Allen of lowering the academic standards. The fact is that it is rare for a school of education to attract psychology, government, and history students away from their departments, and these departments do not welcome this attraction. There were some enlightening and revealing battles in the Faculty Senate during the first year when the school of education presented its final package of "learning experiences," all to be administered on a "pass-fail" system. Chapter 2 touched on this and Chapter 4 mentioned some other innovative aspects such as the portfolio of significant learning experiences which each graduate student accumulates during his enrollment in lieu of the useless transcript of grades.

In short, however, the most important thing is the fertile climate of openness and freedom which has been created. All communications, faculty and student ratings, and recommendations are open to the entire educational community—the body consisting of faculty, administration, and students—which votes on all procedures and programs.

Juxtaposition is the rule rather than the exception. Among the faculty are hard researchers, historians, musicians, artists, businessmen, psychologists, and even teachers. Overlapping and conflicting ideas and programs are allowed to progress for a time. People are encouraged to tackle a problem from different directions. Though such an environment is not without its administrative headaches, it is the kind of environment which spawns humanistic teachers and managers.

In addition to the initial retreat in Colorado, the School of Education has instituted a series of ongoing small group retreats in which mixtures of old and new faculty and students embark upon three-day "idea and contemplation sessions" to recharge their batteries and refresh their minds. The following ideas about teaching which were generated at one of these retreats characterize the kind of fresh thinking upon which this institution is gearing its revolution in teacher training.

DEGREE TRAINING—PRESENT AND FUTURE

ASSUMPTIONS UNDERLYING CURRENT APPROACH TO DEGREE TRAINING
—*Dave and Judy Evans*

Stability of Knowledge: Knowledge consists of the accumulated efforts of the centuries and is basically a stable body which retains its validity over the years. New knowledge is gradually added to this body with an occasional rare internal rumbling as some basic structural element is shifted slightly.

Rate of Change: The rate of change of knowledge and the creation of new knowledge is quite small in comparison to what is known. Professionals can assimilate the increments by relatively small and periodic effort.

Source of Knowledge: In general, training institutions are considered to have a near monopoly on knowledge; they are the repositories and the principal creators of new knowledge, hence they are uniquely qualified to train people by transmitting this knowledge.

Oral Tradition: Training institutions are lineal descendents of structures designed under the limitations of an oral tradition. Learning and certification are still based primarily on becoming fully oral in one's subject, i.e., independent of other sources.

Acquiring Expertise: Expertise in any field can only be acquired by a process of sequential acquisition of material closely paralleling the historical development of knowledge in that field. (One can only get to the top of a ladder by starting at the bottom and touching each rung on the way up; and as a corollary, there are no positions independent of ladders.)

The Professor: His basic role is to "profess," i.e., to transmit the knowledge which he has accumulated with so much effort during training. This is a natural outgrowth of the assumption that knowledge is basically a stable entity. The major barriers to certification are criteria based on the ability to demonstrate mastery of his body of knowledge.

Creation of Knowledge: The university and the professors have the role of presenting new knowledge, although the institutional characteristics of the university make this a goal to which more verbal than behavioral effort is devoted. The researcher is thoroughly trained in the traditional set of his discipline and then attempts small steps forward within the framework of that subject. Research methods are as thoroughly and narrowly learned as the content and, as a consequence, limited to those techniques which have produced the current knowledge.

Job Demands: Skills and knowledge required of persons holding jobs are essentially constant with only small changes occurring over time. Changes can be easily handled by periodic additions of content. Satisfactory performance depends primarily on the continued ability to do what has been taught in training.

DIFFICULTIES WITH THESE ASSUMPTIONS IN TODAY'S WORLD

Growth Rate of Knowledge: Growth in the amount and quality of knowledge can no longer be viewed as gradual accretions to a relatively stable corpus. In some fields, the amount of knowledge is *doubling every decade,* and the rate is increasing. STOP and think seriously what the educational implications of this single fact are.

Obsolescence of "Facts": The new knowledge is less and less characterizable as more of the same. Rather it is frequently different in ways which invalidate or seriously limit what were previously considered facts—even in the hard sciences. Consider the fact that the most common chemical substance, water, has recently been discovered by incredulous scientists to occur in a polymer form with radically different properties—a fact totally at variance with all our knowledge of water. Much content thus has a rapidly shortening "half-life" during which it is valid.

Structure of Knowledge: Not only is the knowledge often obsolescent, but the entire framework in which it was learned is probably radically different. Likewise, the techniques learned even ten years ago for creating knowledge are frequently inappropriate or even useless in light of the current structure of many fields.

Mean Distance from Education: With an average working life of forty years after completing formal education, the typical professional spends his working period an average of twenty years removed from his education. Thus for any group of professionals, they are on the average twenty years away from the end of their training.

Explosion of Information Sources: There has been a revolution in the number and type of information sources which when coupled with fantastically improved information storage and retrieval systems, and when coupled with modern communications systems, has effectively destroyed any claim to monopoly of the possession, communication or creation of knowledge for universities.

The Professor: In almost any class at any level, one can find at least one student who knows more about the subject under discussion than the teacher. In graduate school this is more often the rule than the exception. Graduate faculty are quite routinely kept current today by learning from their graduate students.

Job Demands: Similarly, the rate of change in skills and knowledge required by jobs has gone from a very small rate to one of complete turnover every decade or so in some technical jobs. Moreover, the rate of creation of totally new jobs is considerable and accompanied by the obsolescence of many other jobs. A single block of content-oriented education followed by periodic updating is no longer adequate.

PROPOSALS FOR A NEW APPROACH

Content Versus Process: The typical ratio of 80% content and 20% process in the learning experience should be reversed. Major emphasis should be placed on strategies, techniques, procedures, evaluation methods and feelings. Current content should become secondary in view of its limited lifetime. Doctoral candidates would thus focus on acquiring learning strategies, techniques for becoming informed, and ways of testing and creating new knowledge. Content would serve as laboratory material on which to practice the new process skills.

The Concept of "Informant": This should be expanded to mean any source of information and learning techniques. Thus books, libraries, computers, people, children, and environments would all be informants. The task of graduate study would be to teach the maximal use of informants for self-teaching. Problems selecting the best informant for the situation, of designing optimum strategies for using the informant, and of consolidating the input received from an informant would become the substance of graduate study.

Acquiring Expertise: Conscious effort should be devoted to the design and perfection of alternate approaches to the task of becoming an informed and functioning expert in a subject. Emphasis should be placed on efficiency, speed, depth of understanding, and ability to use the expertise in a new situation. The traditional, sequential, heuristic pattern should be regarded as a minimal strategy to be used when all else fails.

Certification and Granting of Degrees: Degrees should be awarded for process proficiency in field of study. Performance criteria should be based on demonstrated ability with efficient and effective strategies, on ability to propose and carry out strategies for creating new knowledge in the area, and demonstrated proficiency as a result of applying these techniques in selected exemplary content areas of the subject. In the last analysis, content emphasis of today should be replaced by process emphasis since that is the only thing which will be useful in the future.

Automatic Expiration of Degrees: For those involved in educational enterprises (at a very minimum), terminal degrees would expire unless renewed within a specified time period—say 5 years for the doctorate. Renewal would be based on a set of performance criteria similar to those used for the original award, but updated to include new process and content generated in the interim. Criteria to be set and revised by a board, all of whose degrees must be current. Major universities would form a consortium, all of whom could revalidate a degree granted at any member institution.

Permanent Portfolio: Professionals would keep permanent portfolios keyed to the type of performance criteria relevant to the degree. Revalidation would be based in part on evidence of continued ability to use "informants" and to acquire expertise in newly developed fields. The portfolio would also be used to demonstrate currency in the latest developments in process, much as in the old days it was required to show knowledge of the latest content development.

Professor's Role: One of facilitator, experimentator with process, joint creator of new knowledge, and occasional transmittor of critical pieces of content required by a student. Resources of the institution to be viewed as both students and staff jointly. It would be expected and encouraged that *every* member of the community would be an informant on some subject as well as having highly developed process skills. It is natural and desirable that members seek out other members as informants, independent of status hierarchies.

University Becomes Coterminus with Life: The university has no unique claim either to storage or creation of knowledge. At best it would have a unique claim to being an ideal location to facilitate the acquisition of process skills and perfection of them. Also, it would function to insure minimal professional standards for degree holders in the society.

Job Demands: Since the training emphasis would be on process, the job would be viewed as a permanent involvement in vocational training to approach the task at hand. The requirement of updating degrees to insure maximum currency on the part of degree holders would make them more valuable to employers. More important, though, would be the updating of facilities. Updating produces a totally different attitude toward education. The degree is seen as an initial step rather than a terminal one. The degree would certify a high level of process skills, not the quantity of content digested.

This brand of free unencumbered thinking seems to be a vital ingredient in an institution (or more appropriately, a "counter-institution") that expects to have any chance of success in moving teacher training off the "dead center" stable position it has rested on for the past twenty years.

So much for the general climate at the School of Education, University of Massachusetts. What about a specific program geared to developing humanistic teachers?

A PROGRAM FOR HUMANISTIC
TEACHER EDUCATION

Chapters 3 and 4 touched lightly on some of the work of Gerald Weinstein and his Center for Humanistic Education. More specifically, because of a school of education's acceptability to the educational school system around it (this is not to suggest that the conservative Massachusetts school systems are swallowing all of Dwight Allen's innovations without a case of indigestion), a school of education, or a center as part of one, can facilitate the direct implementation of humanistic education in schools more effectively than can independent affective agencies such as Esalen. However, some aspects of the development of affective education can and should continue to be carried on by these independent organizations outside the University. Yet the Center for Humanistic Education, because it is housed in an already uniquely innovative school of education, is a natural base from which to implement the needs of the humanistic education movement. In turn, it will support and utilize as resources agencies such as Esalen and the

Center for Studies of the Person which remain on the cutting edge of the humanistic psychology and humanistic education movement, as well as encouraging other departments and schools of education interested in carrying out work in humanistic education. The center at the University of Massachusetts probably will become a model from which to design other centers for humanistic education throughout the country.

The University of Massachusetts Center for Humanistic Education[1] is engaged in the following activities:

Development of humanistic education theory.

Development of techniques, units, curriculum guides, lesson plans, as well as a variety of curriculum development modes.

Invention of new functional affective approaches.

Collecting and cataloguing of humanistic education strategies from all sources and developing ways to disseminate these.

Testing of procedures in school districts, laboratory schools, and university settings.

Research and evaluation.

Marketing—developing a variety of marketing packages for school districts with varying needs and problems.

Develop curriculum for humanistic education oriented teacher training. (This would include on-campus experiences and in-service training program models.)

These may be divided among five major categories: 1. Curriculum Development, 2. Training of Personnel, 3. Implementation, 4. Evaluation, and 5. Information Gathering and Dissemination.

CURRICULUM DEVELOPMENT

A substantial portion of the resources during the initial planning period are being devoted to planning for the development of

---

[1] The following materials concerning the University of Massachusetts Center for Humanistic Education have been adopted largely from a plan developed by Gerald Weinstein and George Brown for the creation of Humanistic Education Centers—one at the University of Massachusetts and one at the University of California, Santa Barbara.

curriculum in humanistic education. At the present time, the Center has identified nine potential dimensions of curriculum development:

1. The Center collects existing work in curriculum by making contact with those already using it in the field.

2. They maintain contact with Esalen, Bethel, and other such groups to examine affective techniques which might be integrated with cognitive learning.

3. They locate what they call "improvisational" teachers and university instructors–teachers who are able to develop new curricula "on the run." Plans are made for observers to be sent into their classrooms to record their techniques. And meetings and workshops are planned for participation of these teachers.

4. Program Center staff member teams anticipate the development of new programs on the basis of the perceived needs of divergent sample schools and districts. These include ghetto, suburban, and rural schools. Staff are available to college and university academic departments who are interested in working in this area.

5. The Center explores the possibilities of having students in the classroom create their own programs.

6. The Center also sponsors meetings through support for released time and retreats during which, for example, the English Department of a high school could have time to create new programs.

7. Successful teachers will be brought to the Center on sabbaticals or in graduate study to develop programs.

8. The Center also works to develop structured articulated sequences of curriculum material embodying humanistic techniques. This necessitates teams of elementary and secondary teachers generating their own programs within an overall public school framework. University level instructors are involved.

9. The Center encourages programs concerned with the invention of new affective techniques which would be appropriate in a formal educational context.

TRAINING OF PERSONNEL

Of high priority is the planning of programs for the training of trainers. A variety of sources are utilized from teachers and doctoral students as well as from housewives and retired executives.

For the training of teachers, varying criteria are being explored to assess which teachers are most appropriate for which kinds of humanistic education programs and which trainers can be used with them. There is an effort to begin with good teachers who are already very successful in their status quo, teachers who are most ready to move into the affective domains, and train them first. However, other training programs are being planned for those less ready.

The following are some examples of varying *training modes* that are being planned for in the Center—there are many others. One way to develop the curriculum for teacher training is to have teachers innovate teacher-training curriculum. Teachers who have been teaching for a number of years will be brought back to the Center to work with faculty on this. Another example is to take the notion of micro-teaching, which has been aimed at conventional teaching episodes, and transfer its use to the affective domain and humanistic approaches. Use of video taped feedback allows teachers to experiment with new behaviors. Much more of this will be structured. The center is looking also for the kinds of training that will help teachers expand their repertoire within emerging or branching kinds of teaching. Another training mode is the improvisational theater. Professional actors will be used in the training process working with teachers or improvisational techniques. This will help teachers expand their repertoire of roles.

In summary, along with programs for training trainers the Center is planning to develop two major types of experimental teacher-training programs: 1. those which move affective approaches into conventional programs by in-service education of experienced teachers, and 2. those which create new models for training new teachers for new school programs.

MARKETING AND IMPLEMENTATION

The Center is concerned also with strategies for introducing the new programs into the schools and assuring that these programs are effectively pursued once accepted by schools or individual teachers. They call these two concerns *marketing* and *implementation*.

Marketing

The Center is planning a type of building block technique, persuading a limited number of schools to incorporate humanistic techniques and then using the effectiveness of these models to "sell" the programs to other schools. They also plan to develop humanistic learning "marathon packages" as another means of introducing the programs. These three- to four-hour, multi-media presentations will include a teacher who has used humanistic techniques successfully in the classroom; video tapes showing an actual classroom experience; training tapes and other tangible materials; a package of lesson plans; and also an audience participation "lesson" in which those in the audience can personally experience one of the humanistic approaches. Other "marketing" methods such as brochures, films, speeches, seminars, and workshops will eventually be part of the Center's effort to incorporate humanistic programs into the school curricula.

A specialized part of the Center's overall marketing strategy will deal with confronting suspicions and uncertainties about the implications of a humanistic approach to learning. There is talk, for example, that some consider these programs "left wing." The Center will investigate these attitudes and attempt to dispel such doubts where possible.

As the demand for local control of schools increases, an important dimension of implementation will be the maintenance of communication with the community. This raises the possible necessity of developing program models for either special groups in the community such as parents or a massive overall community humanistic education program.

Implementation

Since the humanistic approach to learning is very different from the way most teachers have been taught to teach and the ways they have been teaching, great care must be taken to assure that these teachers receive excellent training. As mentioned, the Center is developing a series of workshops, institutes, seminars, and other types of in-service training to assure high quality training, and it is continually modifying these approaches with increasing excellence as a goal.

However, two crucial challenges will be to overcome those pressures in school situations which work to force the school back to its original state. This kind of resistance to innovation, discussed in earlier chapters, which works without regard to the merits of any new program, has been responsible for the general lack of innovation in schools. More often than not, genuine innovation is transformed by these pressures back into the "same old thing" with a new name. Therefore, the Center is planning for a number of teams who will work with teachers, administrators, and all areas of the school environment to assure that programs are effectively implemented. Members of these teams will have skills in community liaison, general curriculum development, humanistic curriculum development, administration, finance, and human relations. They will be able to help schools with problems in all areas and will do so; even so, their primary mission will be to sustain a fertile environment for the continuation of humanistic programs accompanied by a high quality of teaching. These teams will not visit the schools on a "one-shot" basis, but will maintain contact with the situation to assure that the integrity of the humanistic program is maintained. These teams will also provide valuable feedback to the center on the status of its programs in the field.

The School of Education at the University of Massachusetts also has a Center for the Study of Educational Innovations, one of whose major functions is to implement the integration of innovation into the schools.

EVALUATION

Evaluation procedures are being planned for each curriculum attempt or unit for training effectiveness and also for the overall Center. The initial evaluation effort in the program will be to make a first step toward generating data from which various analyses can be made.

Each curricular attempt (unit, topic, experience) would be considered separately for evaluation purposes. It might be necessary to develop new instruments and measures to be used to evaluate certain affective behaviorial outcomes. Attention, of course, would also be paid to cognitive learning through the use of available measures.

To evaluate the outcome of an entire humanistic education curriculum, a conventional experimental situation is envisioned in various school settings. Experimental and control groups would be pretested. During a school year the experimental group would experience a humanistic curriculum, and control groups the conventional curriculum. Post-testing would be accomplished through the use of the above-mentioned instruments.

INFORMATION GATHERING

A fifth function of the Center, which serves the other four functions, is the collecting, cataloguing, and dispensing of data relevant to all aspects of humanistic learning. Information collected includes humanistic education strategies from all sources, research findings relevant to humanistic education, relevant books and journals, tapes and videotapes, micro-film, newspaper articles, personnel data, and data on research techniques.

So there exists a model in the University of Massachusetts Center for Humanistic Education all ready for launching, ready for others to view, select, and choose from. Moreover, the most significant thing about the setting is the fertile climate from which humanistically oriented teachers will probably grow, even if the Center for Humanistic Education were not present.

It would be very promising if within a few years there were several large humanistic education summer workshops where teachers could go to experience a few weeks enlightenment such as the teachers at Esalen did with George Brown under the Esalen–Ford project (described in *Human Teaching for Human Learning*, Mc-Graw-Hill Book Co., 1970). This, coupled with several good pre-service schools of education training human teachers such as the University of Massachusetts will be doing, could advance us far in changing and revitalizing education in this country today.

This chapter touched on the poor quality of the schools of education in this country where our teachers are being trained. We focused in some detail on an existing model for innovation at the University of Massachusetts School of Education where the entire process of graduate education is being revamped and a revolution in teacher training is taking place. Some assumptions underlying our current approach to degree training, the fallacies in these assumptions, and proposals for a new approach were brought out. Finally, the plan for a center which would train humanistic educators, develop and evaluate curricula, and gather and disseminate information was presented.

It is hoped that the bold steps being taken by a very few innovators in the country can serve as models for the multitude of outdated schools of education around the country.

Moreover, it is my hope that we can begin to develop some schools of education which emphasize that the *process* of teaching is just as important as the *content* being taught; that the emotional "peak experiences" of children in the classroom should be treasured as the most relevant of learning experiences; that a "learning facilitator," sharing in a learning experience with a group of student-colleagues, is a much more relevant and effective person in the classroom than is the teacher with "status authority" lecturing down at the class, dispersing her superior knowledge.

When a teacher finally discovers, as I did just a few years ago, that you don't have to have all the answers, that it is more beautiful and enjoyable to be a naturally human being in the classroom than it is to wear your "perfection" mask, a transformation takes place. I spent most of my first thirty years of life, in overachiever fashion, trying to be perfect, trying to have all the answers, or at least playing that role. Teaching is a whole new, beautiful scene when you can be human with your vulnerabilities and strengths bringing all your resources, including the students in the class, to the experience.

Somehow we must build a model school of education which will help provide teachers with the power that discovering and loving one's self gives—the power to take off their teacher roles and become human beings, sharing in learning experiences with colleagues.

7

Humanistic Educational Management

Better courses, better curricula, better coverage, better teaching machines will never resolve our dilemma in a basic way. Only persons acting like persons in their relationships with their students can even begin to make a dent on this most urgent problem of modern education.

Carl Rogers

If our schools and our educational systems are managed by less than human managers, we cannot expect our teachers to be humanistic in their orientation. Accordingly, emphasis on people-oriented management must begin at the top echelons and flow down if it is to have any positive effect on teachers.

An interesting study was done by the managerial psychologist, Rensis Likert of the University of Michigan's Institute for Social Research. Likert, in a study of the management of 5,000 corporations throughout the country, focused on those managers found to be either extremely high producing or exceptionally low producing. He eliminated from his study managers who were of average or questionable productivity. He then isolated those personality traits or characteristics which were common to the high producing managers as contrasted with those which were common to the low producing managers. This effort is one of the few empirical studies done in this area. The traits which Likert found to be common to high and low producing managers were the following:[1]

Low Producers	High Producers
1. Production oriented (people considered tools to get the job done).	1. People oriented (people considered to be unique individuals).

[1] Rensis Likert, *New Patterns of Management* (New York: McGraw-Hill Book Co., 1961).

Low Producers	*High Producers*
2. Little two-way personal communication (relatively inaccessible to workers).	2. Good two-way personal communication (is accessible to workers).
3. Autocratic	3. Allows subordinates to participate in decisions.
4. Poor delegator	4. Good delegator
5. Punitive	5. Relatively non-punitive
6. Identifies with only his superiors or only his subordinates.	6. Identifies and relates with *both* his superiors and his subordinates.
7. Fails to plan ahead.	7. Plans ahead effectively.
8. Holds frequent formal meetings.	8. Holds few formal meetings (not necessary since communications are effective).
9. In time of crisis, pitches in with workers, thereby relinquishing his role as a supervisor.	9. In time of crisis, maintains supervisory role.
10. Workers in his unit feel little pride toward their work groups.	10. Workers in his unit feel strong pride toward their work groups.
11. Workers feel their boss is ineffective in his relations with top management.	11. Workers feel their manager has good communication with top management and can effectively represent their interests.

Even without showing empirically (as Likert has done for industry) that the characteristics of high producing managers have 100 per cent relevancy for educational administrators, many of us through participation in and observation of real life leadership situations, have gained enough substantial reinforcement of Likert's findings to accept them personally as being valid for most leadership situations—including those in our school systems and the universities.

Take a minute and evaluate your favorite school superintendent or administrator against the list. How does he stack up? How about the worst administrator you know? Now check yourself as objectively as you can. Are you on the "high producer" or "low producer" side of the list? Certainly it must be remembered that few, if any, high producers have all the characteristics on Likert's list of high producing managers. They will probably have several of the high producer traits which they emphasize and use to great advantage.

While serving in the U.S. Office of Education, it became clearer to me every day that many of the management practices of the middle managers there closely approximated those of Likert's "low producers."

In the civil service bureaucracy (and also in educational bureaucracies!), the feeling seems to prevail that civil servants shouldn't be expected to be motivated—that if they have personal problems or career advancement problems they should go to the personnel office instead of to their particular superior who is supposed to play an impersonal, objective role rather than to develop a personal caring relationship with his subordinates. It seemed to me that even the bureaucracy could become an enjoyable place to pursue one's career if it could become more "people-oriented." Of course, making the bureaucracy people-oriented goes against the grain of bureaucratic theory, which stipulates that the bureaucracy protects itself and the public it serves by being very impersonal and objective.

It seemed obvious to me that each leader of each unit should assume responsibility for his team of subordinates, their motivation, career development, morale, and goals. I felt that if this were done more frequently, morale would rise and along with it motivation and productivity. It seemed to me that in an organization such as the Office of Education, where most of the employees are highly educated, Likert's findings should be even more relevant.

I prepared a memo to the Commissioner of Education and other top management people presenting Likert's findings and proposing that each manager make a self-evaluation of how he measured up on the high producer or low producer traits. I even prepared a little self-evaluation form which had the traits of the high and low producers scrambled and somewhat disguised as to values. I suggested that each supervisor might wish to rate himself and then give the evaluation form to his subordinate supervisors who could rate themselves. This, I suggested, could be followed by a "leadership discussion" hour during which the supervisor and his subordinate supervisors could discuss their ratings and each subordinates' view of how he stood on the high and low producer traits. The subordinate supervisors could then, in turn, and in their own way, hold similar discussions with their subordinates. I soon found out how naive I was. I received a barrage of extremely defensive memos (with copies sent to the Commissioner) telling how I just didn't understand what a great job the managers in the office were doing under very difficult circumstances with personnel shortages, dynamic increases in workloads, etc., etc. I was tactfully informed that after I had served in the organization for a longer time I would realize that they had made great strides from the place they were five years before. However, a few enlightened bureau chiefs, the Deputy Commissioner, and the Commissioner finally became interested enough to begin a few trial management development retreats. Eventually the Commissioner instituted a retreat for the top ten executives run quarterly with the assistance of Chris Argyris from Yale. Some fantastic "hidden agendas" began to surface, and these top executives began to slice through the communication barriers that their masks had become. Most of them actually began to care about each other. Another very promising outcome was that a new institutional cooperative approach to problems began to emerge. These top managers began to view themselves as something of a "board of governors" who together had *joint* responsibility for the Office of Education's programs rather than only their own specialized program interests.

Organizations like universities or school systems are also somewhat unique in that they contain a large proportion of highly educated people. In such organizations one might find the traits characteristic of the high producing managers to be even more relevant than in the average organization. Peter F. Drucker made a pertinent point when he stated that in an organization of highly educated people, "we will have to learn to organize, not a system of authority and responsibility or a system of command, but an information and decisions system—a system of judgment, knowledge, and expectations." Such people can "only be motivated." They must *want* to contribute. The supervision that we give to the manual worker simply cannot be applied effectively to people who have to contribute their knowledge, conceptional skill, imagination, and judgment.

The conventional bureaucratic philosophy, so often practiced in our school systems of management by "direction and control," is inadequate in motivating today's employee, whether teacher or mechanic. The physiological and safety needs on which the traditional management approach relies are, in these modern times, reasonably satisfied and, accordingly, unimportant motivations of behavior. "Direction and control" are somewhat useless in motivating people whose important needs are of the higher social and egoistic variety, such as needs for self-esteem, recognition, independence, achievement, knowledge, status, and self-fulfillment. Chapter 2 reviewed how Abraham Maslow's hierarchy of needs progresses with a higher order of need emerging and motivating behavior only after the lower order is reasonably well satisfied. The characteristics which Likert has found to be common to "high producing managers" are conducive to creating the kind of atmosphere in which social, ego, and self-fulfillment needs can begin to be satisfied.

Douglas McGregor and Chris Argyris also have management philosophies which parallel Maslow's philosophy. In McGregor's classic book *The Human Side of Enterprise* he postulates his "Theory X" and "Theory Y" idea. Theory X management is almost identical to Likert's low producer style of management. It is based on the assumption that workers do not like responsibility or work and, hence, must be manipulated. They are apathetic, resist managements' goals, must be rewarded and punished and persuaded with "carrots and sticks" to accomplish the organization's goals. In educational settings, you've seen many Theory X administrator's, faculty, and students. They use money or other incentives such as grades as the carrots and sticks. Students and teachers, however, quickly either learn how to sabotage the Theory X person or how to take advantage of him, which only reinforces and strengthens his belief in the Theory X management philosophy.

Theory Y, on the other hand, assumes that people like responsibility when they can be self-directed, and that motivation for work or learning is natural and inherent in all people. Under Theory Y management humanistic education could flourish. Trust and confidence would develop. Student centered or directed learning could result. The administrator would see his task as creating the maximum opportunities possible for teachers or students to realize their potential.

McGregor feels that under both Theory X or Theory Y management everyone is still governed and motivated by unmet needs. Under Theory X managers, the emphasis is still on the already-met bodily, social, and security needs. However, under Theory Y, there is the opportunity to meet some of the higher order of ego and self-actualization needs. He feels that the organization should be managed in such a way that people can satisfy their own needs best while working toward organization objectives. In this way, self-motivation is built in. Certainly, this is the epitome of humanistic education and management. Chris Argyris also says that the methods used by modern management are inconsistent with the needs of the modern-day worker. Once again, he is saying, as have Likert, McGregor, and Maslow, that an individual will not be motivated to work for that which does not meet his most pressing needs. Today in these times of prosperity, most people's pressing needs are the higher ego or self actualization needs. The organization must learn how to integrate opportunities for satisfying those needs into the workday responsibility, rather than outside the job through higher pay, greater fringe benefits, longer vacations, and all the other relatively less important things organizations keep offering their ego-starved employees.

The application of these ideas to the educational setting is quite apparent. Students need more than the "carrots and sticks" of grades. Teachers, though they badly need higher pay, really need more from their administrators. They need the opportunity to satisfy their ego needs in the school system. Likert's list of high producing traits in administrators could provide teachers with that freedom and opportunity.

How are such people-oriented managers developed? Are they born leaders? Can they be trained? I could list and describe dozens of effective techniques such as sensitivity training, lectures on management theory, simulation, use of process observers, the case study method, role playing, management games, or Matrix. As effective as these techniques are, however, they will accomplish very little if the on-the-job managerial climate is not a fertile one.

Most good managers are developed on the job. They must have the freedom to develop, and that means they need a managerial climate which provides fertile opportunities for growth. This in turn means that their supervisors or superintendents must be enlightened enough—that is on the high producer side of Likert's chart—to allow their subordinates the freedom to grow. Douglas McGregor has termed this approach to executive development the "agricultural" approach, analogous to agriculture because:

> It is concerned with "growing" talent rather than manufacturing it. The fundamental idea behind such an approach is that the individual will grow into what he is capable of becoming, provided we can create the proper conditions for that growth. Such an approach involves . . . more emphasis on controlling the climate and fertility of the soil, and methods of cultivation.[2]

The most significant aspect of this philosophy is that it approaches the development of managerial skills, not so much as a program but:

> . . . as a state of mind, a way of life. It presupposes acceptance of the principle that developing one's subordinates is a fundamental responsibility in any management job. It requires particularly the convictions and encouragement of top management, but is dependent as well on the whole-hearted participation of all . . . echelons . . .[3]

This approach to developing executives or teachers cannot be reduced to one plan. There are as many plans as there are teachers or faculty in the organization. Each person is directly responsible for his own self-development and for providing challenges and opportunities to foster the self-development of his subordinates. This can become a reality only if the manager creates a managerial climate that is conducive to growth. If the managerial climate is conducive to growth then ". . . individual manager's throughout the whole organization will be involved in a process of self-development leading to the realization of their potentialities."[4]

It is apparent that the degree of success which any management development will have is significantly affected by the pervasive intangible known as the managerial climate:

---

[2] Douglas McGregor, *The Human Side of Enterprise* (New York: McGraw-Hill Book Company, 1960), p. 197.

[3] Lawrence A. Appley, "Forward," in Harwood F. Merrill and Elizabeth Marting (eds.), *Developing Executive Skills* (New York: American Management Association, 1958), p. 11.

[4] McGregor, *op. cit.*, p. 197.

"By the right climate . . . we of course mean that way of doing business which emphasizes the development and growth of men at all levels through delegation, training, coaching, and communication."[5] "In general, the managerial climate is the working environment created by policy and practices, organizational structure, and general philosophy. It is the way the majority of management is thinking and acting."[6]

". . . The major responsibility for creating a proper climate falls upon the top executive, . . . [because] . . . every institution reflects the personality and character of the boss."[7] Certainly, if the superintendent is concerned with creating a fertile managerial climate, his principals will become concerned with it also.

For example, if the district superintendent tends to hold most of the decision making for himself, the structure of the organization will tend to become more centralized. Such a structure seriously limits the opportunity for executive growth. Peter Drucker has stated that maximum decentralization of the organizational structure will:

> . . . always improve performance. It will make it possible for good men, hitherto stifled, to do a good job effectively. It will make better performers out of many mediocre men by raising their sights and demands on them. It will identify the poor performers and make possible their replacement by better men.[8]

Certainly, in a decentralized organization, an individual must take greater responsibility for his own actions and behavior. But he will receive rewards in the form of ego and self-actualization satisfaction causing him to seek more responsibility and to grow in the process.

Teachers, principals, and superintendents at all levels should be able to make decisions without the fear that a mistake is fatal. Wil-

5 DE Balch, "The Problems of Company Climate," Merrill and Martug (eds.), op. cit., p. 66.

6 Harold C. Lyon, Jr., "An evaluation of Executive Development in Industry and the Military" (unpublished thesis, 1965, George Washington University, Washington D. C.), p. 68.

7 Frederick C. Crawford, "Creating the proper climate," in Bursh (ed.), *How to Increase Executive Effectiveness* (Cambridge: Harvard University Press, 1954), p. 9.

8 Peter F. Drucker, *The Practice of Management* (New York: Harper and Row, Publishers, 1954), p. 226.

liam B. Given has pointed out that giving young administrators the "freedom to fail . . . is a vital way of spreading responsibility within the organization . . . . Freedom to venture and take calculated risks mean nothing if failure is always punished."[9]

Given's wise philosophy of "freedom to fail" really says that the best investment we can make in a young teacher or administrator is to allow him enough freedom to get a few substantial failures under his belt, and still survive. How many principals or superintendents allow their new teachers this "freedom to fail?"

A study of most of the practitioners in the field brings us always back one way or another to Likert's people-oriented high producer management characteristics. They work in industry. The author's personal experience in the military taught him that, even in the military, the traits Likert found common to the high producer have application! As a young army first lieutenant, I was given command of what must have been the worst airborne rifle company in the 101st Airborne Division. The previous commander had run the company by fear of punishment (low producer traits). Court martials were the rule rather than the exception. The unit had failed its annual army training tests, its annual general inspections, its Strategic Army Corps Readiness Tests, etc., etc.

The first day I took over I removed all the little signs—"off limits during duty hours"—which were nailed up on the doors of every relaxing or comfortable room in the barracks such as the pool room and the lounge. I had the first sergeant call the entire group of 220 men together and I informed them that this was *their* company, *their* community for better or worse, and that it could be as good as they wanted to make it. I told them I knew that they had the potential to be the best in the division and that I wanted us to realize that potential. I suggested that I would make arrangements for anyone who didn't want to see the unit begin to go places to transfer to another unit. I said that three months from then we would *know* and *feel* we were good. In six months, we would be the best in the battle group, and in a year we would be the best in the division. I began, with my lieutenants, an immediate open-door policy whereby anyone with a problem could see his supervisor and

---

[9] William B. Given, Jr. *Bottom-Up Management* (New York: Hayer and Brothers, 1949), p. 6.

know that an effort would be made to help him. I also began a weekly leadership talk with all my sergeants, during which I expressed the view that they were the most important men in the army. Each squad leader, after all, had direct responsibility for his eleven men—responsibility for their motivation, morale, education, development, personal problems, etc. Each would have to be motivated in a different way by his squad leader. Some would have to have their pride appealed to; others might require a combat boot in the rear end. It was a joy to see these tough old combat veterans begin to use other more positive methods of leadership than the usual kick in the ass so often practiced by them in the past. I was amazed at the effect these talks had on these soldiers who began to think of themselves as the elite professional leaders they really were. In three months we had scored an "excellent rating" on an annual equipment inspection that the unit had failed the previous year. Seven months later we had scored higher than any of the other companies in the battle group on our annual combat training tests. A year later there was no doubt in anyone's mind, with men from everywhere trying to transfer into our company, that we were the best in the division. Likert's traits, which I hadn't heard of at that time, were the norm in the company and, I believe, the reason for the transformation. My experiences in the educational world suggest that Likert's traits might be equally valid among "high producing" educators as well.

In short, the best humanistic administrator development program is a "way of life" development program, with the fundamental responsibility on the shoulders of every administrator to provide subordinates with the opportunity to grow. There is evidence that Rensis Likert's "high producing" manager traits have validity for educators as well as business executives. As important as this people-oriented philosophy is, its corollary is equally important. The organization needs a fertile managerial climate, without which humanistic growth will probably be virtually non-existent.

This chapter has dealt with the problem of training humanistic managers for education. Certainly, if we expect our teachers to become humanistic, we must train "people-oriented" managers and administrators, beginning at the top echelons and on down, who will encourage and support teachers in their efforts to change their classrooms through the integration of feelings. This chapter applied the work of such managerial psychologists as Douglas McGregor, Chris Argyris, and Rensis Likert to educational management. Additionally, my personal managerial experiences in the military, the university, and the federal government were applied to educational management. It was concluded that without a fertile managerial climate—something that must be fostered by the everyday leadership of top administrators—humanistic growth probably will not flourish within the teachers or within the classroom.

8

Evaluating the Results of Humanistic
Education

If those of us who have a deep gut conviction that it is not only beneficial but vital to integrate feelings with cognitive content are ever to make our point with the hard researchers of the educational world, we must gather data. It is extremely difficult to evaluate the results of humanistic education experiments. How does one evaluate the joy that comes from self-awareness or the feeling of warmth and intimacy that rises like mercury in a thermometer in a class which has just described what they have seen while wearing the "strong point glasses" described in Chapter 4?

One researcher suggested to me that we should teach the *Red Badge of Courage* to two groups—one conventionally and one humanistically—then test both groups on the content of the book and compare results. The problem is obvious. The question is: are we teaching the *Red Badge of Courage* so that students will learn the content—i.e., that the hero deserted the 137th Regiment at 12:22 p.m. on the 21st of March—or are there more lofty reasons such as wanting him to better understand the concept of courage, fear, and cowardice, or a little of both? If we're interested in content, the suggested test might be a valid measure and the humanistic group might not do so well. If we're interested in the concepts or a combination of the concepts and the content, I'll bet on the humanistic group.

But how do you measure an understanding of courage, fear, and cowardice? Someone will suggest that if we are interested in something other than content, perhaps we should chuck the *Red Badge of Courage* entirely and just use a purely humanistic curriculum of the self. So this is the kind of problem we get into when trying to evaluate the affective experiences. However, this doesn't take the burden of proof from our shoulders. If we believe, then we must continue to search for evidence showing that we are right.

There are beginning to arrive on the scene a few useful and valid measures of attitudes and feelings. One that I have been interested in is the Rokeach Measure of Dogmatism. Not knowing just how to approach the problem of evaluation of the affective, I felt that, rather than theorize, the least I could do would be to gather some test data. Accordingly, in my courses in humanistic education and in several other group types of experiences and courses, I administered the Rokeach test, both before and after the experiences. The idea was that if the humanistic education experience had been a productive one, individuals, perhaps, would score significantly better on the post tests in flexibility. The plan was to later compare these results with the results of other control groups not having the affective experience to see whether or not there is a general trend for most students in the University of Massachusetts, School of Education environment, where I did the testing, to achieve similar results even without the humanistic experience. Recognizing that this is based on an insufficient sample and that there are other contaminates, I present the following results of a rather unsophisticated attempt at testing, mainly in the pure interest of gathering some data.

The individuals whom I tested on the Rokeach averaged 121.03 on the pre-humanistic experience test. (*The lower the score the more flexible the person on the Rokeach.*) In the post-humanistic tests, they averaged 110.81 or quite a bit more flexible. These were all individuals in the University of Massachusetts, School of Education which, as I have described, is an untypically humanistic environment. It is interesting, in this regard, to compare these students' scores with norms of people from other walks of life:

English Colleges (national)	152.80
Ohio State University students	142.00
Veterans Administration Domiciles	183.20
University of Massachusetts School of Education students: (Post test)	110.81

This would seem to suggest that the humanistic environment at the University of Massachusetts, School of Education (according to the Rokeach Test) is either making individuals more flexible and less dogmatic or that it initially is attracting that kind of individual.[1]

---

[1] However, as interesting as these data appear, in performing a correlated "T Test" to 99 useable pre- and post-Rokeach Tests, the T value was .503 (196 DF) which indicates that the difference is really not significant.

It would be interesting to do more work with this measure and with the University of Massachusetts School of Education where there is such a concentration of humanistic experiences open to the students. For example, work should be done to test a large sample of individuals upon arrival before exposure to determine if, in fact, the experience is what is making them more flexible or if the environment is simply attracting flexible people. I expect a combination of the two is occurring. However, both of those things are good—attracting flexible people and causing them to become more flexible—and more testing is in order.

These results are based on insufficient samples and there are various contaminants such as the entire fertile climate and environment at the University of Massachusetts. Accordingly, it is premature to say objectively that these results are more than suggestive of the positive effects of humanistic education experiences. There is a great need for many more sophisticated attempts to evaluate humanistic education experiences if what so many of us feel is true is ever to be proven intellectually to the educational community, and it is important that this be done.

The ROKEACH TEST[2] follows: take it and see how you stand up in flexibility against the norms presented above:

ROKEACH TEST

The following is a study of what the general public thinks and feels about a number of important social and personal questions. The best answer to each statement below is your personal opinion. We have tried to cover many different and opposing points of view; you may find yourself agreeing strongly with some of the statements, disagreeing just as strongly with others; and perhaps uncertain about others; whether you agree or disagree with any statement, you can be sure that many people feel the same as you do.

Mark each statement in the left margin according to how much you agree or disagree with it. Please mark every one.

Write +1, +2, +3, +5, +6, or +7, depending on how you
    feel in each case. (Note: There is no "+4")

---

[2] Dogmatism Scale, Form E, from *The Open and Closed Mind* by Milton Rokeach, © 1960 by Basic Books, Inc., Publishers, New York. Reprinted here with permission of the publisher.

+5: I AGREE A   +3: I DISAGREE A
     LITTLE   LITTLE
+6: I AGREE ON THE   +2: I DISAGREE ON
     WHOLE   THE WHOLE
+7: I AGREE VERY   +1: I DISAGREE VERY
     MUCH   MUCH

_____ 1. The United States and Russia have just about nothing in common.

_____ 2. The highest form of government is a democracy and the highest form of democracy is a government run by those who are most intelligent.

_____ 3. Even though freedom of speech for all groups is a worthwhile goal, it is unfortunately necessary to restrict the freedom of certain political groups.

_____ 4. It is only natural that a person would have a much better acquaintance with ideas he believes in than ideas he opposes.

_____ 5. Man on his own is a helpless and miserable creature.

_____ 6. Fundamentally, the world we live in is a pretty lonesome place.

_____ 7. Most people just don't give a "damn" for others.

_____ 8. I'd like it if I could find someone who would tell me how to solve my personal problems.

_____ 9. It is only natural for a person to be rather fearful of the future.

_____10. There is so much to be done and so little time to do it in.

_____11. Once I get wound up in a heated discussion I just can't stop.

_____12. In a discussion I often find it necessary to repeat myself several times to make sure I am being understood.

_____13. In a heated discussion I generally become so absorbed in what I am going to say that I forget to listen to what the others are saying.

_____14. It is better to be a dead hero than to be a live coward.

_____15. While I don't like to admit this even to myself, my secret ambition is to become a great man, like Einstein, Beethoven, Shakespeare.

_____16. The main thing in life is for a person to want to do something important.

_____17. If given the chance I would do something of great benefit to the world.

_____18. In the history of mankind there have probably been just a handful of really great thinkers.

_____19. There are a number of people I have come to hate because of the things they stand for.

_____20. A man who does not believe in some great cause has really not lived.

_____21. It is only when a person devotes himself to an ideal or cause that life becomes meaningful.

_____22. Of all the different philosophies which exist in this world there is probably only one which is correct.

_____23. A person who gets enthusiastic about too many causes is likely to be a pretty "wishy-washy" sort of person.

_____24. To compromise with our political opponents is dangerous because it usually leads to the betrayal of our own side.

_____25. When it comes to differences of opinion in religion we must be careful not to compromise with those who believe differently from the way we do.

_____26. In times like these, a person must be pretty selfish if he considers primarily his own happiness.

_____27. The worst crime a person could commit is to attack publicly the people who believe in the same thing he does.

_____28. In times like these it is often necessary to be more on guard against ideas put out by people or groups in one's own camp than by those in the opposing camp.

_____29. A group which tolerates too much differences of opinion among its own members cannot exist for long.

_____30. There are two kinds of people in this world: those who are for the truth and those who are against the truth.

_____31. My blood boils whenever a person stubbornly refuses to admit he's wrong.

_____32. A person who thinks primarily of his own happiness is beneath contempt.

_____33. Most of the ideas which get printed nowadays aren't worth the paper they are printed on.

_____34. In this complicated world of ours the only way we can know what's going on is to rely on leaders or experts who can be trusted.

_____35. It is often desirable to reserve judgment about what's going on until one has had a chance to hear opinions of those one respects.

_____36. In the long run the best way to live is to pick friends and associates whose tastes and beliefs are the same as one's own.

_____37. The present is all too often full of unhappiness. It is only the future that counts.

_____38. If a man is to accomplish his mission in life it is sometimes necessary to gamble "all or nothing at all."

_____39. Unfortunately, a good many people with whom I have discussed important social and moral problems don't really understand what's going on.

_____40. Most people just don't know what's good for them.

Now add up your score and compare your score with the national norms given on page 264 to see how flexible you may or may not be. Remember, the lower your score the more flexible you are.

EVALUATION OF A HUMANISTIC HIGH SCHOOL

A fascinating example of a humanistic school where some interesting evaluation is being performed is the Community High School Project, Berkeley, California. Jay Manley and Peter Kleinbard, the school's co-founders, have worked with Dr. Jeanne Block of the University of California, Institute for Human Development, to define a list of specific behavior objectives against which to measure the progress of the school. All aspects of the Berkeley Community High School evaluation involve two groups of students: those in the experimental project compared with a control group of others not in the project. Since this project is not only an ongoing and changing model humanistic program, but also a model evaluation effort, I will present in some detail Jay Manley's description of the program from his "Director's Report" (1969) one year after the start of the experiment.

The initial goal of the Community High School was to create a model for re-structuring Berkeley High School into small, personal units which would create for its students a sense of community, personal commitment, and a sense of personal autonomy, self-direction and power.

Perhaps most significant has been our discovery that the concepts of community and autonomy are exceedingly complex. They constitute a finely woven fabric of many layers, threads of many textures, interwoven and interrelated at every level. As we recall our thoughts on these concepts just one year ago, we are bemused by our own naïveté. We have created several major structures in the last year in our effort to achieve these twin goals, and essentially we have not found a structure that serves the goals effectively. Therefore we now approach the spring semester with an entirely new organizational scheme. Again we hope that this approach may be the "one." Simultaneously, we know that the project is a work in progress and that we will continue to make major changes as the experiment continues.

Initially, we established the following basic objectives for our project and its students:

CREATION OF A MODEL

1. "We will create a school-within-a-school, small and controlled enough to allow us to experiment with a variety of approaches to the problems of the larger school, yet large enough and heterogeneous so that it will serve as an applicable prototype for the larger school."

Certainly our heterogeneous student body of 240 students (120 tenth graders and 120 eleventh graders) is such an environment. The structural changes we have made suggest that we are small and controlled enough to experiment with a variety of approaches to educational problems. At the same time, the rapidity of change within our school causes anxiety and frustration for administrators in the larger school. Because we are so tied to the existing departments and structures within the larger school (course content, course offerings, etc., must be negotiated with department chairmen and curriculum associates), changing course content, for example, involves long and time-consuming discussion which often counterposes the philosophies of the existing department with those of Community High School which do not vary significantly from the existing pattern. The more radical the proposed departure, the more difficult it is to achieve permission to vary from prescribed departmental policy. And yet we are finding that the rather mild alternatives we proposed to the problems of Community High School initially are providing only mild relief to those problems. Increasingly, we realize we are going to have to make more major departures from prescribed patterns in order to solve the deep and serious problems that plague the school.

We propose a system whereby we fully inform all responsible parties of what our curriculum policies are and the rationale for them, but that the primary authority to establish those policies rests with our staff.

The second aspect of Community High School as a model rests with its applicability in a larger context. We can point to certain positive activity which is surely attributable to Community High School.

a. The appearance of groups of teachers on our campus who are planning future schools-within-the-school, utilizing some aspects of Community High School, but with different focuses and points of view.

b. The development of "schools-within-the-school" at two junior high schools and an elementary school. Our staff has consulted with teachers from those schools and, hopefully, have been helpful.

c. Significant attention to our program in several forthcoming publications: Terry Borton's *Reach, Touch and Teach* (published by McGraw-Hill); *Teaching Strategies* and Classroom Realities, edited by Mildred McCloskey and Ruth Mandlebaum (published by Prentice-Hall); and the Spring 1970 edition of the *Harvard Educational Review.*

d. The continual flow of teachers, administrators and visitors from all over the country who view us almost daily.

While this has been a year of administrative reorganization at Berkeley High School, and a year of considerable tensions and difficulties for the total campus, there is too much at stake in the project for it not to be viewed in depth and evaluated fully. We are certainly not encouraging haphazard or rushed evaluation. But we want administrators to get involved with us, to learn what we are about, and to help us resolve the problems that beset the small school, and, consequently, the large school.

Finally, as a staff, we have not been altogether successful in trying to interpret our program to the administration and the school as a whole. For many teachers and administrators, Community High School represents a threat to academic excellence, to teacher control of students, to teacher autonomy, to departmental consistency in course content, etc. While we have distributed newsletters, operated workshops, encouraged visitations, and met with individual departments, the average teacher or administrator is too busy with the ongoing program to take the time to carefully observe Community High School. The result is a certain amount of gossip and hearsay, perhaps inevitable, which produces distrust, competition and adversary relationships. We are proposing more regular meetings with the administrators and departments, specifically teacher-directed newsletters, personalized invitations to visit, in the hope that these means may help.

A PROTOTYPE FOR INTEGRATION:

2. "We will create a prototype for genuine integration through a program that not only tolerates, but depends on heterogeneity."

Predictably, this has been an exceedingly difficult objective. However, we can report certain positive progress:

a. Integration within a given classroom has been very successful. By using a variety of materials, small group work and tutorials we have managed to get students working well together. The non-graded aspect of the program has been a very positive force for inter-student cooperation.
b. The arts classes, in which virtually all Community High School students are engaged, generally have provided important opportunities for students to work together cooperatively.
c. The total operation of the school (its use of the "one man one vote" principle to decide all issues) seems to offer an important opportunity for all students to work together in the daily creation of our community.
d. In the spring semester our English and History classes were grouped heterogeneously. This fall we moved to a situation in which classes were developed around expressed student interest, e.g. "The City," "Social Change" or "The Renaissance." Simultaneously, we incorporated a small Black Studies pro-

gram. The net effect on integration tended (though certainly not completely) to segregate students. The heterogeneous grouping last spring tended to limit student choice and individualism of instruction. The interest-centered classes this fall tended to support social and racial separation. In the spring of this year we envision a plan which will maintain the advantages of both plans, hopefully, with fewer disadvantages. However, it should be noted that in any program in which students have the power to decide what and how they will learn, absolute and numerical integration is not possible.

FLEXIBILITY

3. "We will create a situation that depends on flexible use of time, skill, talent and personnel."

Generally, we have used time more flexibly than in the regular school. Our classes do not meet every day and they generally last more than the characteristic 40 minutes per day. When we have a pressing community need (e.g. planning the schedule for the next semester), we can cancel classes for a community meeting. This last semester we have had one "non-scheduled" day each week during which special activities and events are set up.

However, we have not used the skills and talents of our personnel very flexibly. And we have barely begun to tap the enormous talents of our students themselves. We are now developing plans for the spring which structure the school around clusters of people rather than around subject areas. This "tribal" form will depend very much on students teaching other students. We are building a skill file on every student in the project. We also have a skill file on parents which is most impressive.

Here it is important to discuss another important area of growth: our relationship with Community High School parents. We hold regular meetings with parents to discuss problems of the school, educational theories and philosophies. These have been extremely well attended (generally we have about 150 parents) and the discussions are lively and useful. This has been an important instrument in interpreting our program, explaining our objectives and methods, and making personal contact with the parents. We intend to continue these meetings, and we intend to begin to use parents as teacher aides and resources for which there is strong enthusiasm from the parents.

RELATIONSHIPS BETWEEN TEACHERS AND STUDENTS

4. "We will re-define the relationship of student to teacher and student to student as we strive to create a community within the school."

This is perhaps the area in which we have achieved the most gratifying results. There can be no question that the relationships between our students and our teachers is a completely different sort of thing than that which generally occurs in the regular school. Because we plan and create the school together, we all have a stake in the school. When something goes wrong the teacher or administrator is not the villian or the oppressor. It is *our* problem, together, to be solved together. This is a significant development. Because of continual tutorial and conference meetings between student and teacher, a closeness and personal relationship is present. The teacher does a great deal of personal counseling. The teacher also gets constant feed-back on what is happening to the student, in the class and in the school.

Students are also involved in the hiring of our teaching staff, evalution of teachers and evaluation of themselves. A friction between Community High School and the regular school develops here. Because students are present and participating at virtually all meetings (only the staff "encounter group" is closed to students), there must be a very candid sort of discussion of what is happening in the school, problems with the administrations, etc. Because students may participate in this candid and open manner, they sometimes forget that this is not the mode of operation in the regular school. For example, a student in Community High School may (and often will) tell a teacher how disappointed he is in the way a teacher is teaching, or has dealt with a student, or has handled a problem. Such candor is not so often solicited in the regular school. Consequently, we are forced to teach our students a kind of double standard for relating to staff in the two environments.

We are also concerned with the relationship of student to student. A year ago we wrote "The student will be encouraged to help his fellow students when he is able, to seek help from others when he is in need." We have found this a difficult objective to achieve. We hope that one of the fundamental aspects of next semester's "tribal form" will be students teaching other students. The concept is built into the plan.

CURRICULUM

5. "Curriculum will emerge from the combined efforts of students and teacher."

We have progressed well in deepening this objective. At the beginning of this last semester students and staff developed the classes they wished to have offered. Instead of a program of English III, U. S. History I and P.E. 100, a student might take "Utopias," an interdisciplinary English and History class studying ideal communities past, present and projected, Black Studies Projects, and Aikido (Japanese self-defense) and Yoga. However, we found that once planned, the teacher generally took over the teaching in the class. In the spring, we hope the organization around human resources rather than subject area will cause the student to direct his own education.

ARTS COURSES

6. "The curriculum will depend uniquely on the arts courses to synthesize the student's experiences."

We have found important success in this area. Students have been able to develop interdisciplinary studies using the arts as means to learning English and history. For example, one student did a series of woodcuts representing scenes from "The Canterbury Tales," another a photographic essay on athletics, another a Black drama project for history. Because the staff meets together, it is possible to build on a student's talents and strengths in overcoming his weaknesses. That is, an English teacher having difficulty in reaching a student will know from staff discussion that the student is deep into music and may be able to find a way for the student to tie together his musical and English studies.

On the other hand, we were unrealistic in our belief that the arts classes would touch all students. We are, therefore, extending Community High School into the areas of math, science and manual arts in order to provide for those students not arts-and-humanities oriented. We hope that our extensive skill files will make major volunteer help available to us and that such help will open infinite opportunities for our students. We have a parent who wants to teach sewing, another soul-food cooking, another Yiddish. There is tremendous variety and talent available.

BASIC SKILLS

7. "We will help students to improve such basic skills as reading and writing, especially those who are far below grade level."

Our evaluation would indicate that we are doing this with some success. But we still feel the inadequacy of a single English teacher for 27 students (our basic class size). We anticipate that the use of volunteers on a large scale in the spring will provide intensive personal help to students with severe reading and writing deficiences.

UNITY AND COHERENCE

8. "Because the coherent structure of the disciplines will cause the student to handle similar problems in many different ways, we will see improvement in concept manipulation and in the relating of ideas."

Again our formal evaluation indicated progress here. But we are generally disappointed in our development of inter-disciplinary studies. We have found ourselves terribly accustomed to dealing with "our subject areas" and this is a habit hard to break. With the reorganization in the spring, we will force ourselves to center our activities around students and their interests, and the studies will evolve from there. Additionally, we will be better able to tap the talents of our teachers, beyond their subject area competency.

DECISION MAKING

9. "We will explore ways to help the student realize and explore all alternatives to every problem as he strives to reach decisions."

Our evaluation reports progress in this area. This is mostly due to personal, one-to-one conference and tutorial time between student and teacher in which the contract for learning is negotiated and re-negotiated.

It is aided by the teacher meetings in which teachers talk to each other about the same students in an effort to diagnose problems and help students establish direction for themselves. I am not sure that the staff is a particularly effective model in respect to decision making. Working closely together, we have discovered how difficult genuine cooperation is, how essential but hard it is to submit one's own personal desires to the needs of the total program. Our staff-student meetings are often characterized by long and agonizing debate in which staff, just as much as students, are learning the processes of decision making and group communication. Our staff "encounter group" has been an important vehicle for resolving staff tensions, disagreements, and misunderstandings.

STUDENT AUTONOMY

10. "Because the student will find his education guided by his own ideas and motivations, he will find a general increase in his autonomy —that measure of self-confidence which enables people to make well-reasoned, individualistic decisions."

Again our evaluation reports positive growth. An interesting and predictable outcome of this growth is the increased demand from students for more and more control over what happens to them. We regard this as a sign of significant vitality and development.

On the other hand, we have many students who lack the self-confidence to exercise control over their own actions. We have not done enough to try to teach ways of using time and resources effectively. This problem is the more disturbing because an unbalanced proportion of these students is Black. The lack of a full-time Black teacher on our staff aggravates this problem.

Again, we see well-meaning, liberal, white teachers attempting to predict what is good for Black students. At least one full-time Black teacher, able to attend all planning and counseling meetings, would help this situation. (*Note:* Because our full-time teachers in English and History must be drawn from the existing departments at the high school, we have been unable to hire full-time Black staff members. Presently, we have three part-time Black teachers— one has certification, two do not—out of a total of twelve teachers. One of these twelve is Chicano, none are Oriental—another imbalance we would like to correct.)

We have received some excellent advice and help from Black parents which has been most useful. Nonetheless, one of our most pressing problems is to find ways of teaching the students who are not yet capable of guiding themselves and to help them begin to take a role in determining their own destinies.

SELF IMAGE

11. "We hope to develop the self-image of those who are insecure and to provide students with many opportunities and mirrors to help to view and to realize themselves."

Once again, our formal evaluation shows significant growth in this area. Our policies with regard to student evaluation (constant verbal discussion, written teacher evaluations, and written student responses) seems to have caused our students to look at themselves more objectively and more honestly. It is not an uncommon response for a student to admit that he has not gotten down to work, or that he has failed to accomplish work, but he will often write "... I just don't seem to be able to get myself to do it." Again, this indicates that we, as a staff, have to provide more direction for students to "learn how to learn."

On the other hand, sometimes our problem is to convince the student that he has, in fact, grown and learned. We have viewed dramatic and significant change in many of our students, yet often the student will not recognize it himself. For most students, there is a period of real adjustment in the project. The old securities are missing: workbook assignments, point system evaluations, enforced work, etc. The student asks, sometimes in frustration, "What do you want me to do?" And he is constantly asked in return, "What do *you* want to do? What is worth your time and effort? What can you commit yourself to?" It is a painful process, but most of our students seem to be growing through it. Our staff need is to find more ways to guide them through it so they do not flounder and drown.

STUDENT ATTENDANCE

12. "If the student feels genuinely involved and effective, the student's attendance record will show improvement."

The evaluation shows no appreciable difference in attendance between students in Community High School and Berkeley High School. But that measure is drawn from Period 2 before Community High School is in session. Because in Community High School no disciplinary pressures are exerted for non-attendance, students are, in fact, more free to cut classes. We are gratified that in most cases our cutting rate is not excessive. The most reliable students will use the freedom to cut occasionally, and that seems most understandable. As a district, we might well consider "personal business leave" for students.

But again, we must reflect on a core of students who seem unable to take any part in directing their own education and who seemingly get lost. We know we are not creating new school dropouts. And we know that some students who were drop-outs or potential drop-outs before have come to find new meaning in their Community High School education. But there are also a number of pre-Community High School drop-outs who are still drop-outs in Community High School. We make use of telephone contact with students and their parents and home visits when that seems useful. But we, as the regular school staff, have a serious, unresolved problem.

We still find that many of our students wish to graduate early, feeling that while Community High School is more beneficial than the regular school, it still leaves much to be desired. We will not be satisfied until the number of early graduates decreases. At the same time the distractions and resources of Berkeley are a powerful and seductive force pulling away from the school. We hope to try to use some of those resources in the spring.

CONDUCT AND DISCIPLINE

13. "We hope that involvement and motivation will produce improved conduct."

This is another area in which we have encountered real success. We have virtually no discipline problems such as fighting, vandalism, or hostility to teachers. No teacher has needed to write a disciplinary referral to the dean since the school began.

However, we do have the problem of cutting which we mentioned earlier. And in areas like our student lounge we have problems of littering which indicate a lack of concern for others in the community by some of our students. And, in trying to create an open and trusting environment, we have attracted a significant number of non-Community High School students who find it easier to steal purses from our classroom areas, vandalize property, and steal from our student's mail boxes. As one distraught student put it, "We set out to create an open atmosphere. Most of the time I just feel exposed." The problem is compounded by the primary teaching area we use which is the Community Theatre exhibit galleries. These are long hallways with innumerable doors, making security a very difficult matter. A student goes out a door; someone on the outside props it open. It is a continual problem to our students and staff.[3]

These behavioral objectives, presented above in narrative form were translated, where possible, into operational techniques by Dr. Jeanne Block for assessing the extent to which the program's ob-

---

[3] Jay Manley, "Director's Report—Community High School," 1969.

jectives were successful. Block (1969) summarizes the evaluation process as follows:

> The evaluation of the Community High School project at Berkeley High School was concerned with the kind of change in both cognitive skills and knowledge and affective attitudes in our students after one semester in the program. To measure cognitive changes, tests of reading achievement (TAP) and problem-solving capacities (the Gottschaldt Hidden Figures Test) were administered. To evaluate affective changes, tests measuring the students' self-image and self-concept (the Adjective Q–sort Self Description) and the level of ego maturity (the Loevinger Sentence Completion Test) were administered at the beginning of the community High School project in February and readministered at the end of the first semester in June.
>
> Students in the Community High School were assigned randomly to the CHS group of the Control group of non-CHS students so that the Control and CHS groups would be proportionate to the 10th grade as a whole in sex, race and academic track. Comparisons at the time of the initial testing proved the equivalence between the Control and CHS groups in intelligence and reading achievement.
>
> Note: There was found, however, a reliable tendency for male students in the Control group to score higher on the Gottschaldt Hidden Figures test and for female students to score at significantly higher levels of ego maturity. These differences were attributed to the differential attrition in testing wherein students in the lower tracks of the Control group more often failed to appear for the test sessions than was true of lower track students in the CHS program. This selective factor was responsible for higher test scores for the Control group at the outset of the study.
>
> The statistical analysis used to compare the amount of change over the four-month period from pre-testing to final evaluation allows for such existing differences as were found between groups at the time of pre-testing and provides a direct and powerful test of the amount of *change* shown by individual students over the four-month period.
>
> *Results:* The results of the evaluation, summarized below, show that the students in Community High School program showed significantly greater improvement in reading achievement, problem-

solving abilities, and level of ego maturity than did students in the Control group. The self-image and concept of the CHS students also indicated personal growth consistent with the findings cited below. Finally, evaluations of Berkeley High School completed by parents of CHS students were significantly more positive than the parental evaluations completed by the Control Group.

The research design for this evaluation made use of an appropriate control group, non-biasing sampling strategies, objective test scores, and rigorous statistical procedures. The consistency and significance of the findings allows us to conclude that students in the Community High School showed reliable positive changes consistent with the goals of the CHS staff. The extent to which the operation of the well-documented "Hawthorne Effect" has contributed to the significant changes found cannot be assessed without follow-up evaluation to establish the stability of performance increments over a longer time span.[4]

TEST	CHS			CONTROL			Eval. of T Test Change	Level of Signifi- cance
	Pre-	Post-	Change	Pre-	Post-	Change		
IQ	110.10	—	--	110.35	—	—	—	—
TAP Reading Achievement	34.30	31.42	−2.89	37.44	31.24	−6.20	2.47	<.02
Gottschaldt Hidden Figures	42.53	50.41	+7.88	54.00	55.92	+1.92	2.38	<.02
Ego Maturity	3.99	4.59	+ .60	4.66	4.69	+ .03	2.21	<.02

In a news letter to parents, CHS staff member Peter Kleinbard wrote:

In every area tested, Community High School students showed significantly greater growth than students in the regular program at the high school. In the profiles, C.H.S. students saw themselves as more self-controlled, more considerate, more perceptive, and more responsive than they had at the beginning of the year. Students in the regular program described themselves as more adventurous, more playful, and more competitive.

Clearly, tests such as these cannot be the sole means to judge the value of the program. Like all aspects of the evaluation, they are

---

[4] Jeanne Block, "Report on the Evaluation of the Community High School Program at Berkeley High School—February to June 1969." Unpublished mimeographed report, 1969.

being used primarily as a means to help guide revision of the program.

Another aspect of the evaluation was a questionnaire to parents. C.H.S. parents noted that their children liked school better, seemed to be learning more, and had more contact with their teachers than they had experienced before entering C.H.S. Our parents also expressed more worry about whether their children were receiving enough "basics," and about whether their children were doing enough work.

Another perspective from which it is important to view the program, is that of its effect on the staff and the school district as a whole. Here, too, the results appear extremely positive. The eight staff members of the project took a total of only two days sick leave last semester. In three other schools of the district, the existence of our project attracted teachers to try similar cluster schools and to consult with the staff on how to do this. Predictably, there are also many teachers in the district who have strong reservations about the Community High School.

I should like to mention the student essays and comments which are one of the most influential aspects of the evaluation. Generally, students expressed pleasure with the warmth of the staff, the lack of external pressure, and the freedom. Quite a few thought we had not succeeded in creating a close community. And some worried that the program was not adequately preparing them for college. I should like to quote from one statement by Linda Robinson:

> When I first came to C.H.S., I didn't do anything because you and Susan [Mrs. Susan Bement, CHS history teacher] kept saying, "Do what you want to do." I couldn't do what I wanted to do because I didn't know what I wanted to do. All my life I've been told *what* to do.
>
> So I finally decided to do a report on the Black Panthers which I still haven't done. Although I will do it on the day I turn this paper in.
>
> I know you must be wondering what I have been doing all this time.
>
> Well, at the beginning I would either cut or just stay home. You wouldn't believe some of the excuses I gave the attendance lady. Anyway, I got tired of cutting so I started coming to school; then something happened. For once in my life since grammar school I began to like school. Before, in the ninth grade all I wanted from school was to learn, but I wasn't learn-

ing. That made me begin to hate it. And now I was learning and almost a new person. I started reading books, a little writing to myself, and most of all, thinking. I thought about all the things I was not told to think about or question, such as God, for instance, and things that were just locked up in mind, the problems of Black and White. I was taught things and I myself taught some of the things I'd learned to others. It's been a whole new experience on my part.

I no longer waste my time. It's too precious. I write on my play or study what I'm writing.

I no longer lay around watching TV. I think pictures instead of watching pictures. I don't make the excuse, "There's nothing to do," we ourselves create the "nothing to do." [5]

After one year of this experiment, the staff of the Community High School remained flexible enough to revise procedures to better meet the goals they set initially. They did not change the goals, but recognized that the process of education which leads toward such goals is a dynamic, changing one. They began the second year of their experiment with these new strategies in mind. Consider the following proposal by Brice Todd, one of the CHS teachers:

A PROPOSAL FOR REVISING THE COMMUNITY HIGH SCHOOL

A. *Some guiding thoughts behind the revised plan.*

1. Some factors common to the learning environment that this plan tries to avoid.
   a. A dehumanized atmosphere.
   b. Fragmented use of time and space (rigid structuring).
   c. Excessive routine and monotony.
   d. Coercion of students and teachers into relationships that they do not work out among themselves.
2. Some factors not currently common to the learning environment that this plan tries to include.
   a. Priority is placed upon more involved human relationships through smaller, longer lasting groups.

---

[5] Peter Kleinbard, "Newsletter," Berkeley Community High School, September 30, 1969.

    b. Greater short term flexibility in use of time and space.

    c. Students are encouraged to make many choices thus developing greater self-reliance.

    d. Greater student involvement in the process of his education.

B. *Some guiding thoughts expressed as goals for CHS*

1. To develop greater autonomy (self-reliance, self-actualization, inner-direction) for every CHS student.

2. To develop more awareness of others through involvement in an intense community experience.

3. To develop greater short term flexibility to enable students to fulfill their ever changing learning needs.

4. To help students learn how to learn so that they can continue to learn and change effectively in an ever more rapidly changing culture.

5. To provide an environment in which students can learn the skills and knowledge necessary to the achievement of their current goals.

6. To integrate all "subjects" and "skills" into a single learning process that does not distinguish between learning and life or between one subject area and another.

7. To develop an environment where students can learn from their mistakes rather than be punished for them.

C. *Initial organization*

1. This next year CHS will divide into several moduals (tribes) centered around full-time staff members who may combine in units of 1, 2, or 3 members. The ratio of 40 students to each full-time staff member will be maintained. Each student will choose the tribe (modual) to which he wishes to attach himself. This division could also be accomplished by random selection.

2. Part-time staff, volunteer adults from the community, and student teachers will be attached to each group as they are needed.

3. CHS will be in operation from 8:30 to 3:00 each day and each student will be encouraged to function as much as possible within the CHS scene.

4. Students and staff must be free to meet together each morning from 10:35 to 11:30 for the purpose of planning the

operation of their group. Individual and community projects may develop from these meetings.

5. A central executive council will approve distribution of funds. Each 40 person unit will send two representatives to the executive council.

D. *Staff functions and responsibilities*

1. To continuously push (persuade, help, manipulate) students to learn the skills, knowledge, and values that they need.
2. To codify the talents of the members of the group and to coordinate the passing of these skills from those with a talent to those who want (need) that talent.
3. To keep students continuously aware of their goals and the consequences of any actions that may seem contrary to the effective accomplishment of those goals.
4. To record the goals, accomplishments, personal evaluations, and staff evaluations of each student in a cumulative file.
5. To reach out and tie students and other adults into CHS, partially by asking them to help us wherever their known talents can be useful.
6. To continuously demonstrate the skills and values we verbalize.
7. To guide students to other learning experiences outside the tribe that will help each student to achieve his goals.
8. To participate regularly in the weekly encounter group.

E. *Functions of a master teacher (tribal chief)*

1. Primarily to facilitate inter-personal relationships among all people involved in his group.
2. Secondarily to carry out the above mentioned functions of any staff member.

F. *Student functions and responsibilities*

1. To clarify and record his immediate learning (life) goals.
2. To grow (learn) toward those goals in ways that are relevant to him. While each student should have great choice as to what he wants to learn and how he wants to learn it, he should not have the option to do nothing.
3. To help the community to grow in a way that is of value to him.

4. To attend tribal (modual) meetings each day.
5. To fulfill the requirements for graduation from BHS.

G. *Transfer between tribes*

1. The permanent transfer of people from one tribe to another is not encouraged since among the basic assumptions made in developing this plan is the idea that people should learn to work out their relationships where they are. In other words, to change one's group is often used as a way to cop out from an important learning experience.
2. However, sometimes change from one tribe to another may be desirable for any number of reasons.
3. Therefore, a person may change from one tribe to another:
   a. at the beginning of any semester without restriction.
   b. during a semester by receiving permission to leave from his tribe and by receiving permission to join from his new tribe.

H. *Credit and grades*

1. Credit can be given on the basis of time involved and/or work done based on a contract (commitment) negotiated between student and teacher.
2. Grades can also be negotiated between student and teacher.

I. *Matters needing immediate action to facilitate this kind of operation*

1. Arrange for students to learn foreign languages, science, math, business skills, and so forth in CHS, elsewhere in BHS, or in the greater community with the assurance that he will receive credit for his accomplishment no matter where or how it is learned.
2. Approach responsible officials at California and San Francisco State asking them to accept any student who graduates from CHS in good standing regardless of course titles entered on his transcripts.
3. Students, parents, and school administration must be educated to understand what we are doing and why.
4. Aggressively negotiate better arrangements for CHS with the Board of Education, District Administration, and BHS administration

5. Arrange for more effective evaluation of each staff member utilizing students, community members including parents and other staff members. The emphasis on such evaluation should be on growth for the staff.[6]

In his "Director's Report," Jay Manley sums up their progress this way:

We find ourselves a year after beginning with many of our original problems incompletely solved. However, we have made inroads in every area of concern. As a staff we have learned a tremendous amount from our experiences. Within our staff we are far from unified in educational philosophy. But we are together in our desire to find means of making education a personal process, a self-developing process, a dignifying process, a humanizing process. The divisions within our staff create frustrations at times, but provide the staff with balance and some degree of objectivity. And what staff is not without its divisions and differences of point of view? The significant matter is that we have raised the major questions of education today, we talk about them daily among ourselves and our students, and we are trying many approaches to solve them. The Community High School is very much alive and vital. Our experiences should be valuable to the future direction of secondary education in Berkeley.

Carl Rogers has also made a significant contribution in presenting some evaluation evidence to support his convincing humanistic education philosophy:

First of all, in the field of psychotherapy, Barrett-Lennard (1962)[7] developed an instrument whereby he could measure these attitudinal qualities: genuineness . . . , prizing . . . , empathy. . . . those clients who eventually showed more therapeutic change as measured by various instruments, perceived *more* of these qualities in their relationship with the therapist than did those who eventually showed less change.

So we may say, cautiously, and with qualifications . . . that if, in therapy, the client perceives his therapist as real . . . one who prizes, and emphatically understands him, self-learning and therapeutic change are facilitated.

---

[6] Brice Todd, "Appendix III, A Proposal for Revising CHS by February 1970," from an unpublished mimeographed letter to parents, 1970.

[7] Barrett-Lennard, "Dimensions of therapist response as causal factors in therapeutic change." *Psychological Monograph*, 1962, 76 (Whole No. 562).

Now another thread of evidence, this time related more closely to education. Emmerling (1961)[8] found that when high school teachers were asked to identify the problems they regarded as most urgent, they could be divided into two groups. Those who regarded their most serious problems, for example, as "helping children think for themselves and be independent"; . . . "helping students express individual needs and interests,"fell into what he called the "open" or "positively oriented" group. When Barrett-Lennard's Relationship Inventory was administered to the students of these teachers, it was found that they were perceived as significantly more real, more acceptant, more empathetic than the other group of teachers whom I shall now describe.

The second group of teachers were those who tended to see their most urgent problems in negative terms, and in terms of student deficiencies and inabilities: "trying to teach children who don't even have the ability to follow directions;" "teaching children who lack a desire to learn;" . . . "getting children to listen." . . . when the students of these teachers filled out the Relationship Inventory they saw their teachers as exhibiting relatively little genuineness, acceptance, trust, or empathetic understanding.

Hence, we may say that the teacher whose orientation is toward releasing the student's potential, exhibits a high degree of these attitudinal qualities which facilitate learning. The teacher whose orientation is toward shortcomings of his students exhibits much less of these qualities.

A small pilot study by Bills (1961, 1966)[9] extends the significance of these findings. A group of . . . teachers were selected, . . . (half) of them rated as adequate and effective by their superiors, and also showing this more positive orientation to their problems. . . . The students of these teachers were then asked to fill out the Barrett-Lennard Relationship Inventory, giving their perception of their teacher's relationship to them.

The more effective teachers were rated higher in every attitude measured by the Inventory: they were seen as more real, as having a higher . . . regard for their students, were less conditional or judgmental in their attitudes, showed more empathetic understanding.[10]

A more comprehensive study, by Macdonald and Zaret,[11] studied the recorded interactions of . . . teachers with their students. When teacher behavior tended to be "open"—clarifying, stimulat-

---

[8] F. F. Emmerling, "A study of the relationships between personality characteristics of classroom teachers and pupil perceptions." (Unpublished Doctoral dissertation, Auburn University, Auburn, Alabama, 1961.)

[9] Personal correspondence from R. E. Bills 1961, 1966.

[10] Rogers, *op. cit.*, 117.

[11] J. B. Macdonald and Esther Zaret, "A study of openness in classroom interactions." (Unpublished manuscript, Marquette University, 1966.)

ing, accepting, facilitating—the student responses tended to be "productive"—discovering, exploring, experimenting, deriving implications. When teacher behaviors tended to be "closed"—judging, directing, reproving, ignoring, probing, or priming—the student responses tend to be "reproductive"—parroting, guessing, acquiescing, reproducing facts, reasoning from given or remembered data. . . . It would appear that teachers who are interested in process, and facilitative in their interactions, produce self-initiated and creative responses in their students. Teachers who are interested in evaluation of students produce passive, memorized, "eager to please" responses from their students.[12]

Carl Rogers goes on to present some evidence that the student actually learns more where these attitudes are present. Finally, he presents rich testimonial evidence from students and teachers that when these three attitudes—realness, trust, and empathetic understanding—are exhibited by the teacher, learning is facilitated.

Another fascinating humanistic education experiment that bears close watching involves the entire Louisville, Kentucky, School System. The superintendent, Newman Walker, has a large grant from the U.S. Office of Education which he is using as a leverage for humanizing the system. Before a school can receive its share of the funds, it must come up with a comprehensive plan for change and humanistic reform of its school. So far, 14 of the 44 schools in the district have implemented plans for reform. Sixteen hundred school board members, administrators, and teachers have been through six months of "encounter" work. Interesting data are being gathered. One early statistic shows 92 per cent more vandalism in the schools that have not undergone reform when compared with schools that are participating in the reform program. This appears to be one of the largest and most comprehensive humanistic education experiments conducted to date.

Sophisticated evaluation efforts of humanistic education projects are rare. Usually the results are academically indecisive in spite of the conviction of the teacher and students involved that they are succeeding. Norman Newberg and Nat Vaughn are in the midst of doing some promising work with in-depth interviews after having spent several years trying unsuccessfully to devise and test

---

[12] Rogers, *op. cit.*, p. 118.

more objective measures. Al Alschuler and Dale Lake from Albany have made a significant contribution in this area. Dick Schmuck of the University of Oregon, and Matthew Miles from Teachers College at Columbia, and Gerald Weinstein of the University of Massachusetts are doing some interesting pioneering work in evaluation of affective experiences. However, there are very few breakthroughs, and much work needs to be done.

Perhaps one of the problems is that humanistic education work is so joy producing that few people who really get into it want to back away from it long enough (and it takes years) to do the disciplined evaluation work so badly needed.

At the present time, Humanistic Education is a movement, rather than a discipline. It lacks a sound theoretical base, and there is little research to prove, disprove, or improve the efficacy of its techniques. Those of us who are presently working in the field are anxious to see it legitimized. We have suggested that university programs in education and psychology should attempt to discipline the movement by bringing to it their inclinations to theory and their competence in research. If the movement is not able to move in this direction, it will have only a minimal effect on the educational system.

If our education system is to become more humanized, those having a stake in the movement—and this should include faculty, teachers and parents—must begin to devise evaluation and research that will establish empirical evidence of the effectiveness of humanistic education. In other words, we have much "affective" evidence of the success of these humanistic approaches to education. We must now integrate these feelings with some cognitive evidence if the affective is ever to take its place as at least an equal with the cognitive component in the classroom.

Epilogue

It's not easy to reach someone through a book. Sometimes it's difficult to reach them even when you're face to face, speaking in person. It's often much easier to communicate non-verbally or by touching. Some of the non-verbal exercises presented in this book make it clear that words often get in the way of what we would like to say. So for me to expect that I have really been heard using the media of print is to hope for too much. What I do hope for is that somehow you have captured through this book some of the joy that permeates the classroom in which feelings are dealt with rather than suppressed and ignored; some of the excitement that the students and teachers who have shared their experiences have felt; and some of the newly found "realness" in me which has helped me to come closer to some of the experiences I have described.

Where have we been in this book? I would hope that some of you have been "in" and "out" of the book taking out with you some ideas to build on or use in your own classrooms, coming back in to get your imagination tickled again, and then going out to try other things. That's what this book was written for. It's meant to be a fuse, a catalyst or stimulator, a launching pad for your ideas.

In the first part of the book I tried to make the point that we are faced with some serious problems in education today. We have an educational system dominated largely by one-dimensional teachers and faculty— half-men whose intellectual capacities may be highly developed, but whose affective capacity is often severely stunted. These educators have functioned to foster almost purely intellectual learning in the classroom. The nurturing of the emotional side of the student—love, empathy, awareness, and fantasy—either has been neglected or left to chance.

Additionally, the first chapter looked into the notion widely held by teachers and parents that learning should involve hard, unpleasant work in order for one to earn his place in middle-class society. It's the idea that you work hard now, and that later—always later—rewards will be yours. Our society seems to be "hung up" on waiting. "Wait 'til you're twenty-one; wait 'til graduation; wait 'til you're in love; wait 'til you're married; wait 'til you've saved enough; wait 'til retirement." All this waiting and your life is over; you've waited 'til you're in the grave. Life slips by so quickly. If you lie down in the grass at night and look up at the stars and think how many millions of years old they are, you can quickly realize—it becomes shockingly apparent that in comparison to them—your lifetime on earth is only a spark of time—a flash! How important it is not to numb yourself and miss what's happening! How vital it is to be able to feel! "The times they are a changin'," sings Bob Dylan. Many young people are no longer numbing themselves until they're middleaged and potbellied to try to enjoy living only to find that they're too numb to feel.

In the first parts of this book we looked at some of these problems from the viewpoints of students from whom we, as teachers, have much to learn. They make the point that learning need not be unpleasant and that students need not aspire to the same goals their parents or teachers had. Young people today are, for the most part, much more in touch with their feelings than were youngsters of the past few generations. Many of the problems in our classrooms and on our campus stem not from overt rejection by students but from the fact that teachers and faculty deny feelings or refuse to integrate them with the intellectual content of the classroom.

In Chapter 2, we explored what it is that makes many teachers and faculty members so willing—in fact, so determined—to avoid their students' as well as their own feelings, and, hence, become intellectual half-men. One of the possible answers we looked into was that prospective teachers in our graduate education systems may be conditioned into certain insecurities from the process of having to jump over a continuous series of artificial hurdles in their training. We took a look at the insecure personality traits of the typical faculty member who we found to be an inwardly focusing individual with basic personal insecurities. On the one hand, he had feelings of superiority about intellectual matters stemming, perhaps, from easily won cognitive victories in the classroom; on the other hand, he had basic feelings of inferiority, maladjustment, and hostility to that which is emotional or nonbookish.

Again, we tried to empathize by looking at the problem through the eyes of a student who presented his view of the importance of integrating the intellectual with the affective to produce a more humanistic education.

Finally, Chapter 2 explored the notion that a faculty member or teacher who wears what I call "status authority," standing at the podium as "Doctor or Professor So-and-so" lecturing at his class, will probably not be very relevant to his students. On the other hand, the faculty member or teacher who is able to earn what I call "natural authority," authority gained from sharing with his students the resources he has— himself, his friends, his knowledge, his experience, and his feelings— will find that being relevant comes naturally. Natural authority is gained from sharing a relevant learning experience—an experience in which the students and the teacher become colleagues, learning from each other.

Chapter 3 samples some of the pioneering efforts in humanistic education of such notables as Maslow, Lowen, Rogers, and Perls, as well as some of the great work being carried out by a handful of courageous, though perhaps less well-known, educators. It was apparent from this look that the approaches being developed are varied, and in spite of the fact that the movement contains some great names in psychology and education today, it consists primarily of an unorganized aggregate of highly individualistic innovators.

In Chapter 4 we surveyed some of the humanistic education techniques being developed and used by teachers in various levels of classrooms throughout the country. We took a look at group training—the T–Group, sensitivity training, the encounter group, micro-labs, and marathons. We looked in some detail at a university level course of study, "Education of the Self," which uses the student himself as content. We also looked at some other exercises such as "Geography of the Self," the "One-way Feeling Glasses," a "University–Student Crisis" role-playing exercise, the varied activities of the Learning Theater, and took a glimpse at Gestalt Awareness Techniques. Some of the problems which arise when educators indiscriminately use the first "affective" or group approach they find as a panacea for the ills of their schools, were brought out.

In Chapter 5 we again went back to the students—a group of fifteen who, with me, experienced the various humanistic education techniques described in Chapter 4. The units presented in Chapter 5 were planned by the students to achieve certain classroom goals using the repertoire of humanistic techniques they had learned. The classroom applications were experienced first by my entire class, and then most were tried in school classrooms.

Chapter 6 touched on the poor quality of the schools of education in this country where our teachers are being trained. We focused in some detail on an existing model for innovation, the University of Massachusetts School of Education, where the entire process of graduate education is being revamped and a revolution in teacher training is taking place.

Chapter 7 dealt with the problem of training humanist managers for education, and applied the work of such managerial psychologists as Douglas McGregor, Chris Argyris, and Rensis Likert to educational management. Additionally, my personal managerial experiences in the military, the university, and the federal government were examined and applied to educational management. Without a fertile managerial climate —something that must be fostered by the everyday leadership of top administrators—humanistic growth probably will not flourish within the teachers or within the classroom.

In Chapter 8, we took a brief look at some attempts to gather data about the effectiveness of humanistic education experiences. It was interesting to note that a sample of students from several different classes had post-experience scores indicating more flexibility in attitudes after humanistic experiences than indicated by their pre-experience test scores. We took a detailed look at the Berkeley Community High School and the positive evaluation being done there.

This is a very very meager beginning in evaluation. We have a long way to go. If our educational system is to become more humanized, those of us having a stake in the movement (and this should include faculty, teachers, and parents) must begin to devise evaluation and research that will establish empirical evidence of the effectiveness of humanistic education. In other words, we now have much "affective" evidence of the success of these humanistic approaches to education. We must integrate these feelings with cognitive evidence if the affective is ever to take its place as, at least, an equal with the cognitive component in the classroom.

So much for where we have been in this book. Where do you go from here? That's up to you. I know where I want to go, and it's toward more "realness"—realness in the classroom and in my life. I want my students, friends and associates to know when they talk to me or approach me that they will get a "real" or a straight response. That's not an easy goal to achieve. I don't think that real trust can exist between two people—be they student and teacher or husband and wife—until they show what they really feel to each other. So it's vital, first of all, to learn how to feel—to be able to be in touch with what you are feeling here and now. But what you do is up to you. I like the way Carl Rogers expresses it:

> I have come to think that one of the most satisfying experiences I know and also one of the most growth-promoting experiences for the other person is just fully to appreciate this individual in the same way that I appreciate a sunset. People are just as wonderful as sunsets if I can just let them be. In fact, perhaps the reason we can truly appreciate a sunset is that we cannot control it. When I look at a sunset as I did the other evening, I don't find myself saying, "Soften the orange a little on the right hand corner, and put on a bit more purple along the base, and use a little more pink in the cloud color." I don't do that. I don't *try* to control a sunset. I watch it with awe as it unfolds. I like myself best when I can experience my staff member, my son, my daughter, in this same way, appreciating the unfolding of a life . . . A person who is loved appreciatively, not possessively, blooms, and develops his own unique self. The person who loves non-possessively is himself enriched.[1]

It takes great personal strength to allow another human with whom you are close to "be," or even to allow your students to grow in their own individuality. In addition to the inner strength required for allowing humans to "be," it takes a great deal of courage to step out on a new frontier—especially a frontier characterized by conservatism and resistance to change, as is the field of education. Fortunately, the reader who has decided to take the step advocated by this book—that is, taking some of these ideas and actually experiencing and trying them—will not be alone. For years a handful of others have been smuggling feelings into the classroom through the affective underground. A small group of other courageous pioneers are now openly practicing humanistic teaching in their classrooms in a variety of different ways. Some are integrating feelings into their conventional academic curriculum so as to make it more relevant and meaningful. An English teacher teaching the *Lord of the Flies* breaks the class down into groups of five and asks each group to get rid of one member. They then discuss how it felt to be rejected and have a vivid feeling for how Piggy felt in *Lord of the Flies* when he was ostracized from the group.

---

[1] Rogers, *op. cit.*, p. 236.

Another group of humanistic educators is pushing for an entire humanistic curriculum or block of instruction where students would get in
touch with their feelings of identity, power, and connectedness.[2] This
would make the humanistic curriculum, or a curriculum of the self, a
separate block of instruction with it's own autonomy just as any other
discipline.

There are as many ways of being a humanistic educator as there are
human beings. So if you have become a believer, let your humanistic
educational efforts reflect your own unique individuality and ideas. If
this book has stimulated you to experience and feel some of the things
presented, and you appreciate the warmth of the humanistic classroom
and decide that you don't want to return to the emptiness of the purely
intellectual classroom, please don't stop there. Go on to build your own
techniques and ideas. And most important, get others to experience what
you have discovered. If we are going to change education and breathe
life into the classrooms of our country, thousands of teachers must take
it upon themselves to spread to other teachers the word, the feeling,
and that joy that comes from "learning to feel and feeling to learn."

---

[2] Weinstein and Fantini, *op. cit.*

A Bibliography on Humanistic
Education and Associated Subjects[1]

I. *Articles and Books*

Allen, M. S., *Morphological Creativity*. Englewood Cliffs, N.J., Prentice-Hall, Inc., 1962.

Allinsmith, Wesley, and George W. Goethals, *The Role of Schools in Mental Health*. New York, Basic Books, Inc., 1962.

Allport, G., *Pattern and Growth in Personality*. New York: Holt, Rinehart and Winston, 1961. Chapter 12, "The Mature Personality."

Alschuler, Alfred S., "The Achievement Motivation Development Project: A Summary and Review." Harvard Research and Development Center, Harvard Graduate School of Education, 1967 (available through Publications Office, Longfellow Hall, Appian Way, Cambridge, Mass. 02138).

————, *Psychological Education*. Mimeographed chapters of a book available from Peabody House, 13 Kirkland Street, Cambridge, Mass., 02138.

Anderson, R. C., "Can First Graders Learn an Advanced Problem-Solving Skill?" *Journal of Educational Psychology* 56 (6) (1965): 283–294.

American Association for Curriculum Development, "Perceiving, Behaving, Becoming: A New Focus for Education" (collected convention proceedings). Copies available from the National Education Association, 1201 Sixteenth St., N.W., Washington, D.C., 20036.

American Psychologist 21 (6) June, 1966. Whole issue devoted to Community Mental Health issues, practices, and possibilities. Note: Smith, B., "Explorations in Competence: A Study of Peace Corps Teachers in Ghana," pp. 555–567.

Argyris, C., *Personality and Organization*. New York: Harper & Row, Publishers, 1957.

————, T–groups for organizational effectiveness. *Harvard Business Review* 42 (1964): 60–74.

Ashton-Warner, Sylvia, *Teacher*. New York: Simon and Schuster, Inc., 1963.

---

[1] Credit is due to Alfred Alschuler, Terry Borton and Norman Newberg for their earlier efforts in compiling extensive "humanistic bibliographies which served as important sources for the development of this one.

Assagioli, Roberto, *Psychosynthesis*. New York: Hobbs, Dorman, & Co., Inc., 1965.

Avorn, Jerry L. *Up Against the Ivy Wall*: New York, Atheneum Publishers, 1968.

Bennis, W. G. "Goals and Metagoals of Laboratory Training" in Bennis *et al.* (eds.), *Interpersonal Dynamics*, revised ed. Homewood, Ill.: Dorsey Press, 1968, pp. 680–687.

Berzon, B., L. N. Solomon, and D. P. Davis, "The Self-Directed Therapeutic Group: Three Studies." *Journal of Counseling Psychology*, Winter (1968).

Bessell, Harold, "The Content is the Medium: The Confidence is the Message," *Psychology Today* 1 (8), January 1968: 32–35.

Bettelheim, Bruno, *Love is Not Enough*. Glencoe, Ill., The Free Press, 1950.

"Bionics." *Journal of Creative Behavior* 2 (1) (Winter, 1967): 52–57.

Birnbaum, Max, "Sense About Sensitivity Training." *Saturday Review*, Nov. 15, 1969: 82–83, 96–98.

Black, Algernon, *The Young Citizen, The Story of the Encampment for Citizenship*. New York: Frederick Ungar Publishing Co., Inc., 1962.

Bloom, Benjamin S. (ed.), *Taxonomy of Educational Objectives; Handbook I: Cognitive Domain*. New York: David McKay Co., 1965.

Boocock, S. S., and E. O. Schild, *Simulation Games in Learning*. Beverly Hills, Calif: Sage Publications, Inc., 1968.

Borton, Terry, "Reach, Touch, and Teach." *Saturday Review*, Jan. 18, 1969: 56–70.

————, *Reach, Touch, and Teach*. New York: McGraw-Hill Book Company, 1970.

————, "Reaching the Culturally Deprived." *Saturday Review*, Feb. 19, 1966.

————, "What Turns Kids On?" *Saturday Review*, April 15, 1967.

Bradford, L., J. Gibb, and K. Benne (eds.), *T–group Theory and Laboratory Method: Innovation in Re-education*. New York: John Wiley & Sons, Inc., 1964.

Brown, George I. *Human Teaching for Human Learning*. New York: McGraw Hill Book Company, 1970.

Buber, M. *I and thou*. New York: Charles Scribner's Sons, 1968.

Bugental, J. F. T. *The Search for Authenticity*. New York: Holt, Rinehart, and Winston, Inc., 1965.

———— (ed.), *Challenge of Humanistic Psychology*. New York: McGraw-Hill Book Company, 1967. (Paperback)

Campbell, J. P. and M. D. Dunnette, "Effectiveness of T–Group Experience in Managerial Training and Development." *Psychological Bulletin* 70 (2), August 1968: 73–104.

Corson, John J. *Goverance of Colleges and Universities.* New York: Mc-Graw-Hill Book Company, 1960.

Cox, Archibald, *Crisis at Columbia.* New York: Vintage Books, 1968.

Fantini, Mario, and Gerald Weinstein, *The Disadvantaged.* New York: Harper and Row, Publishers, 1968.

————, *Making the Urban School Work.* New York: Holt, Rinehart, & Winston, Inc., 1968.

Featherstone, Joseph, "How Children Learn." *The New Republic* 157, Sept, 2, 1967: 17–21. (About the Leicester Schools.)

————, "Teaching Children to Think." *The New Republic,* 157, Sept. 9, 1967: 15–19.

Flanagan, J. "Functional Education for the Seventies." *Phi Delta Kappan,* September 1967: 27–33.

Goodman, Paul, *Compulsory Mis-Education and the Community of Scholars.* New York: Vintage Books, 1964.

————, *Growing Up Absurd.* New York: Random House, Inc., 1960.

Gordon, William J. J. *Synectics: The Development of Creative Capacity.* New York, Harper and Row, Publishers, 1961.

Gowan, John C., George D. Demosk, and E. Paul Torrance (eds.), *Creativity: Its Educational Implications.* New York: John Wiley and Sons, 1967.

Gunther, B. *Sense Relaxation: below your mind.* New York: Collier Books, The Macmillan Company, 1968.

Handbook of Staff Development and Human Relations Training: Materials Developed for Use in Africa. National Training Laboratories, Institute for Applied Behavioral Science, associated with NEA, 1201 16th St., N.W., Washington, D.C., 20036.

Hentoff, Nat, *Our Children Are Dying.* New York; The Viking Press, Inc., 1966.

Hobbs, N. "Helping Disturbed Children's Psychological and Ecological Strategies." *American Psychologist* 21 (1) 1966.

Holt, John, *How Children Fail.* New York: Pitman Publishing Corp., 1964 (Paperback by Dell Publishing Co.).

————, *How Children Learn.* New York: Pitman, 1967

Howard, J. "Inhibitions Thrown to the Gentle Winds." *Life,* July 12, 1968: 48–65.

Huxley, A. "Education on the Non-Verbal Level." *Daedalus,* Spring 1962.

Jacob, Phillip E. *Changing Values in College.* New York, Harper & Row, Publishers, 1957.

Jahoda, M., *Current Concepts of Positive Mental Health.* New York: Basic Books, Inc., Publishers, 1958.

Kelly, George, *The Psychology of Personal Constructs,* Vols. I and II. New York: W. W. Norton & Company, Inc., 1955.

Kepner, C. H. and B. B. Tregoe, *The Rational Manager.* New York: Mc-Graw-Hill Book Company, 1965.

Klein, Allan, *Role Playing in Leadership Training and Group Problem Solving.* New York: Association Press, 1956.

Kohl, Herbert, *36 Children.* New York: The New American Library, Inc., 1967

Kohlberg, Lawrence, "Development of Moral Character and Moral Ideology," in Martin L. Hoffman and Lois W. Hoffman (eds.), *Review of Child Development,* Vol. 1. New York: Russell Sage Foundation, 1964, pp. 383–431.

————, "Moral Education in the Schools: A Developmental View." *The School Review* 74 (1) Spring 1966: 1–30.

Kolb, David A. "Achievement Motivation Training for Under-Achieving High School Boys." *Journal of Personality and Social Psychology* 2 (6) December 1965: 783–92.

Kozol, J. *Death at an Early Age.* Boston: Houghton Mifflin Company, 1967.

Krathwohl, David R., Benjamin S. Bloom and Bertram B. Masia, *Taxonomy of Educational Objectives,* Handbook II: Affective Domain. New York: David McKay Co., Inc., 1964.

Leonard, G. *Education and Ecstasy.* New York: Delacorte Press, 1968.

Likert, Rensis, *New Patterns of Management.* New York: McGraw-Hill Book Company, 1961.

Lincoln, C. Eric, *The Black Muslims in America.* Boston, Beacon Press, 1961.

Lowen, A. *Physical dynamics of character structure.* New York: Grune & Stratton, Inc., 1958.

————. *Love and Orgasm.* New York: The Macmillan Company, 1965.

————. *The Betrayal of the Body.* New York: The Macmillan Company, 1967.

Lynd, Helen Merrill, *On Shame and the Search for Identity.* New York: Science Editions, Inc., John Wiley & Sons, Inc., 1966.

Makarenko, Anton S. *Road to Life* (Stephen Garry, trans.). London: S. Nott, 1936.

Malamud, Daniel I. *A Participant-Observer Approach to the Teaching of Human Relations.* Chicago: Center for the Study of Liberal Education for Adults, 1955.

————, "A Workshop in Self-Understanding Designed to Prepare Patients for Psychotherapy." *American Journal of Psychotherapy* 12 (1958): 771–786.

————, "Educating Adults in Self-Understanding." *Mental Hygiene* 44 (1960): 115–124.

————, and S. Machover, *Toward Self-Understanding: Group Techniques in Self-Confrontation.* Springfield, Ill.: Charles C. Thomas, Publisher, 1965.

Maltz, Maxwell, *Psycho-Cybernetics.* Englewood Cliffs, N.J.: Prentice-Hall, Inc., 1960.

Mann, John, *Changing Human Behavior.* New York: John Scribner's Sons, 1965.

Maslow, Abraham H., *Eupsychian Management.* Homewood, Ill.: Dorsey Press, 1965.

————, "Synanon and Eupsychia." *Journal of Humanistic Psychology,* Spring 1967.

————, *Toward a Psychology of Being* (second ed.). Princeton, N.J.: D. Van Nostrand Co., Inc., 1968.

————, "Farther Reaches of Human Nature." *Journal of Transhumanistic Psychology* I (1968).

————, *Motivation and personality.* New York: Harper & Brothers, 1954.

————, "Music Education and Peak Experiences." *Music Educators Journal* 54 (1968): 72–75, 163–171.

————, "Some Educational Implications of the Humanistic Psychologies." *Harvard Educational Review,* Fall 1968.

May, Rollo, *Existence: A new dimension in psychiatry and psychology.* New York: Basic Books Inc., Publishers, 1962.

————, *Love and Will.* New York: W. W. Norton & Company, Inc., 1969.

McClelland, David C. "Achievement Motivation Can be Developed." *Harvard Business Review* 43, Nov., 1965: 6–8.

————, "Changing Values for Progress," in H. W. Burns (ed.), *Education and Development of Nations.* Syracuse, N.Y.: Syracuse University Press, 1963, pp. 60–78.

————, *The Achieving Society.* New York: D. Van Nostrand Co., Inc., 1961.

————, "Toward a Theory of Motive Acquisition." *American Psychologist* 20 (5), May, 1965: 321:333.

McGregor, D. *The Human Side of Enterprise.* New York: McGraw-Hill Book Company, 1960.

McLuhan, M. *Understanding Media: The Extension of Man.* New York: McGraw-Hill Book Company, 1964.

"Methods and Educational Programs for Stimulating Creativity: A Representative List," from Sidney J. Parnes, *Creative Behavior Guidebook.* New York: Charles Scribner's Sons, 1967; also *Journal of Creative Behavior* 2 (1) Winter 1968: 71–75.

Miles, L. D. *Techniques of Value Analysis and Engineering.* New York: McGraw-Hill Book Company, 1961.

Miles, Matthew, *Learning to Work in Groups.* New York: Bureau of Publications, Teachers College, Columbia University, 1959.

Miller, George A., E. Galanter, and K. H. Pribram, *Plans and Structure of Behavior.* New York, Holt, Rinehart & Winston, Inc., 1960.

Mooney, Ross, and Eaher Razik (eds.), *Explorations in Creativity.* New York, Harper & Row, Publishers, 1967.

Moore, Sonia, *The Stanislavski Method.* New York: The Viking Press, Inc., 1960.

Moreno, J. L. *Who Shall Survive?* New York: Beacon House, 1953.

Murphy, G. *Human Potentialities.* New York: Basic Books, Inc., Publishers, 1958.

Murphy, Michael, "Esalen, Where It's At." *Psychology Today,* December 1967.

Myers, R. E. and E. P. Torrance, *Ideabooks.* Boston: Ginn and Company, 1965–66. Also Cunningham, B. F. and E. P. Torrance, *Immagi-Craft Series in Creative Development*: Boston: Ginn and Company, 1965–66.

Neill, Alexander S. *Summerhill.* New York: Hart Publishing Co., Inc., 1960.

Newberg, Norman, "Meditative Process." (Multilithed paper available at Office of Affective Development, Philadelphia Public School Building, 21st and Parkway, Philadelphia, Pa.) Newberg also has Cooperative Schools Program lesson sequences in communications, drama, and urban affairs.

Nowlis, David, "Research Report on the Cooperative Schools Program." Philadelphia Public Schools, 1966. (Available through the Office of Affective Development, Philadelphia Public School Building, 21st and Parkway, Philadelphia, Pa.)

Olton, R. M. "A Self-Instructional Program for the Development of Productive Thinking in Fifth and Sixth Grade Children," in F. E. Williams (ed.), *First Seminar on Productive Thinking in Education.* St. Paul, Minnesota: Creativity and National Schools Project, Macalester College, 1966.

Orme, Michael E. J., and Richard F. Purnell, "Behavior Modification and Transfer in an Out-of-Control Classroom." Harvard Research and Development Center, 1968. (Available through the Office of Publications,

Harvard Graduate School of Education, Longfellow Hall, Appian Way, Cambridge, Mass.)

Osborn, A. F. *Applied Imagination.* New York: Charles Scribner's Sons, 1967.

Otto, H. A. *A Guide To Developing Your Potential.* New York: Charles Scribner's Sons, 1967.

————. (ed.) *Explorations in human potentialities.* Springfield, Ill.: Charles C. Thomas, 1966.

————. *Group Methods Designed to Actualize Human Potential: A Handbook.* Chicago: Achievement Motivation Systems, 1439 Michigan Avenue, 1967.

Parnes, Sidney J. and Eugene A. Brunelle, "The Literature of Creativity: Part I." *Journal of Creative Behavior* 1 (1) Winter 1967: 52–109. (Includes abstracts, references, bibliographies, etc.)

————. "The Literature of Creativity: Part II." *Journal of Creative Behavior* 1 (2) Spring 1967: 191–240. (Bibliography of creativity research, including summaries from *Psychological Abstracts and Dissertation Abstracts.*)

————. "Programming Creative Behavior." Research Project No. 5–0716, Contractual No. OE–7–42–1630–213, Educational Research Information Center, Room 3–0–083, 400 Maryland Ave., S.W., Washington, D.C. 20202. (Self-instructional course in applied imagination.)

————, and Harold F. Harding (eds.), *A Source Book for Creative Thinking.* New York: Charles Scribner's Sons, 1962.

Payne, Buryl, "Extra-Verbal Techniques and Korzybskian Formulations." *ETC* 15 (1) March 1968: 7–15.

Perls, Frederick, Ralph F. Hefferline, and Paul Goodman, *Gestalt Therapy: Excitement and Growth in the Human Personality.* New York: Julian Press, 1951. (Paperback by Delta Books, Dell Publishing Co., New York, 1965.)

Perls, Frederick, *Gestalt Therapy Verbatim.* Lafayette, California: Real People Press, 1969.

Peterson, Severin, "Affective Techniques." Short description of techniques being used at Esalen. Reach author through Esalen, Big Sur Hot Springs, Big Sur, California, or at 1254 Taylor, San Francisco, California.)

Pigors, P. W., and F. C. Pigors, *Case Method in Human Relations: The Incident Method.* New York, McGraw-Hill Book Company, 1961.

Polanyi, Michael, *The Tacit Dimension.* Garden City, N.Y.: Doubleday & Company, Inc., 1966. (Paperback by Anchor Books, Doubleday & Company, Inc., 1967.)

Prince, George M. "The Operational Mechanism of Synectics." *Journal of Creative Behavior* 2 (2) Winter 1968: 1–13.

"Productive Thinking Program," available from Educational Innovation, Box 9248, Berkeley, California, 94719.

Randolph, Norma, and W. A. Howe, *Self-Enhancing Education, A Program to Motivate Learners*: Stanford, Calif.: Sanford University Press, 1967.

Raths, Louis, Merrill Harmin, and Sidney Simon, *Values and Teaching*. Columbus, Ohio: Charles Merrill Publishing Co., 1966. (A concrete lesson plan approach to the teaching of value clarification.)

Reich, W. *Character Analysis*. New York: Orgone Institute Press, 1949.

Rogers, Carl R. *Freedom to Learn*, Columbus, Ohio, Charles E. Merrill Publishing Co., 1969.

Rogers, Carl R. *On Becoming a Person*. Boston: Houghton Mifflin Company, 1961.

Rosenthal, Robert, and Lenore F. Jacobson, "Teacher Expectations for the Disadvantaged." *Scientific American* 218 (No. 4) April, 1968: pp. 19–23.

Ruesch, Jurgen, and Weldon Kees, *Non-Verbal Communication*. Berkeley: University of California Press, 1956.

Sarason, Seymour B. *Psychology in Community Settings*. New York: John Wiley & Sons, Inc., 1966.

Schein, E. and W. Bennis, *Personal and Organizational Change Through Group Methods*. New York: John Wiley & Sons, Inc., 1965.

Schultz, W. C. *FIRO: A three-dimensional theory of interpersonal behavior*. New York: Holt, Rinehart, & Winston, Inc., 1958.

Schultz, William, *Joy*. New York: Grove Press, Inc., 1968.

Seashore, C. "What is Sensitivity Training?" *NTL Institute News and Reports* 2 (2), April, 1968.

Seidman, Jerome M. (ed.), *Educating for Mental Health: A Book of Readings*. New York: Thomas Y. Crowell Company, 1963.

Severin, F. T. (ed.), *Humanistic Viewpoints in Psychology*. New York: McGraw-Hill Book Company, 1965.

Skinner, B. F. *Walden Two*. New York: The Macmillan Company (paperback), 1962. (First published in 1948.)

Slade, Peter, *Child Drama*. London: University of London Press, 1954.

Smiley, Marjorie, B. *Gateway English*. New York: The Macmillan Company, 1966.

Sohl, J. *The Lemon Eaters*. New York: Dell Publishing Co., 1968.

Spolin, Viola, *Improvisation for the Theater*. Evanston, Ill.: Northwestern University Press, 1963.

Taylor, Raymond, "Research Report of the Cooperative Schools Program." Philadelphia Public Schools, 1967. Copies available through Office of Affective Development, Philadelphia Public School Building, 21st and Parkway, Philadelphia, Pa.

Thelen, Herbert A. *Dynamics of Groups at Work.* Chicago: University of Chicago Press, 1954.

"The New School of Education, University of Massachusetts." *Trend Magazine* V (3) Spring 1969. (Entire issue devoted to the University of Massachusetts, School of Education.)

Torrance, E. P. and R. Gupta, "Development and Evaluation of Recorded Programmed Experiences in Creative Thinking in the Fourth Grade." A research project performed under provision of Title VII of the National Defense Act of 1958 (P.L. 85–864) with the New Educational Media Branch, U.S. Office of Education, Department of Health, Education and Welfare, 1964.

True, S. R. "A Study of the Relation of General Semantics and Creativity." *Dissertation Abstracts* 25 (4) (1964): 2390.

Upton, A. and R. Samson, *Creative Analysis.* New York, E. R. Dutton & Company, Inc., 1964.

Uris, Auren, "Work Simplification." *Factory*, September 1965.

U.S. Office of Strategic Services Assessment Staff, *Assessment of Men.* New York: Rinehart and Company, 1948.

Watson, Goodwin (ed.), *Change in School Systems.* NEA, 1967. Available through National Training Laboratories, 1201 16th St., Washington, D.C., 20036.

Watson, Goodwin (ed.), *Concepts for Social Change.* NEA, 1967. Available through National Training Laboratories, 1201 16th St., Washington, D.C., 20036.

Weinstein, Gerald, and Mario Fantini, *A Model for Developing Relevant Content for Disadvantaged Children.* New York: Fund for the Advancement of Education, Ford Foundation, 1968.

Weschler, I. R. and J. Reisel, *Inside a Sensitivity Training Group.* Los Angeles: Institute of Industrial Relations, University of California at Los Angeles, 1958 (paperback).

Whiting, C. S. *Creative Thinking.* New York: Reinhold Publishing Corp., 1958.

Williams, George, *Some of My Best Friends are Professors.* New York: Abelard-Schuman Ltd., 1958.

Winter, Sara K., J. C. Griffith, and D. A. Kolb, "Capacity for Self-Direction." *Journal of Consulting and Clinical Psychology* 32 (1) (1968): 35–41.

Yablonsky, Lewis, *The Tunnel Back: Synanon.* New York: The Macmillan Company, 1965. (Paperback by Penguin Books, Inc., Baltimore, Md., 1967.)

Yeomans, Edward, "Education for Initiative and Responsibility." National Association of Independent Schools, 4 Liberty Square, Boston, Mass., 1967. (Article on Leichester Schools. See also Featherston's articles.)

II. *Journals, Films, and Tapes*

Borton, Terry (with Oliver Nuse and Jim Morrow), "Prelude" (1966) and "A Lot of Undoing to Do" (1968). Two films about the Philadelphia Cooperative Schools. Films are available through the Audio-Visual Department, Philadelphia Public School Building, Room 327, 21st and Parkway, Philadelphia, Pa.

Human Potential, Institute for the Achievement of Human Potential, 1800 Stenton Avenue, Philadelphia, Pa.

Journal of Applied Behavioral Science, National Training Laboratories, National Education Association, 1201 16th St., Washington, D.C., 20036.

Journal of Conflict Resolution, Center for Research on Conflict Resolution, University of Michigan, Ann Arbor, Michigan, 48104.

Journal of Creative Behavior, Creative Education Foundation, 1614 Rand Building, Buffalo, New York, 14203.

Journal of Humanistic Psychology, 1314 Westwood Blvd., Los Angeles, California, 90024. Published by the Association of Humanistic Psychology, 584 Page St., San Francisco, California, 94117.

Lewin, Kurt, "Experimental Studies in the Social Climates of Groups," (1940). Film available through the Krasker Memorial Film Library, Boston University, 765 Commonwealth Ave., Boston, Mass., 02215.

Litwin, George, "Organizational Climate" (1966). Film available through the Audio-Visual Department, Harvard Business School, Soldiers Field Road, Boston, Mass., 02163.

Main Currents in Modern Thought, Foundation for Integrative Education, 777 United Nations Plaza, New York, N.Y., 10017.

Manas, Manas Publishing Co., P.O. Box 32112, El Sereno Station, Los Angeles, California, 90032. (weekly)

Newberg, Norman, "Build Yourself a City" (1968), film on an urban affairs course; "It's Between the Lines" (1968), on a drama course; "Making Sense" (1968), on a communications course. All films are available through the Office of Affective Development, Room 329, Philadelphia Public School Building, 21st and Parkway, Philadelphia, Pa.

"The Quiet One" (1948). Film about the Wiltwick School. Distributed by Contemporary Films, c/o McGraw-Hill, Text-Film Department, Heightstown, New Jersey.

Skinner, B. F., Esalen tapes on Affective Education which include interviews with Maslow, Skinner, Rogers, etc. Available through Esalen, Big Sur Hot Springs, Big Sur, California.

"Where is Prejudice?" (1967). Film available through the NET Film Library, Audio-Visual Department, University of Indiana, Bloomington, Indiana, 47401.

III. *Organizations*

American Association for Curriculum Development, National Education Association, 1201 16th St., N.W., Washington, D.C., 20036.

American Conservatory Theater, San Francisco, California. William Ball, Director. Reverses "method acting" to make the motion produce the expression.

Association for Humanistic Psychology, 584 Page St., San Francisco, California, 94117. John Levy, Executive Director. Focuses on experience as the primary phenomenon in the study of man; emphasis on choice, creativity, valuation, and self-realization.

Auron Institute, 71 Park Ave., New York, N.Y. 10016. Harold Streitfeld, Director. Interested in non-verbal activity and body movement.

Center for Humanistic Education, University of Massachusetts, School of Education, Amherst, Massachusetts 01002. Gerald Weinstein, Director.

Center for Research on Conflict Resolution, University of Michigan, Ann Arbor, Michigan. Ken Bolding, Daniel Katz, and Herbert Kellman, Directors. Publishes the *Journal of Conflict Resolution.*

Center for Studies of the Person, 1125 Torrey Pines Road, La Jolla, California 92037. Inaugurated a cooperative program of self directed change in a whole school system—elementary through college—which brought about innovative and humanizing approaches. Conducts summer training programs for individuals wishing to become group facilitators.

Community Makers, 13 W. 98th St., New York, New York. Uses theater games etc., to build community involvement and organizational knowledge.

Cooperative Program of Educational Development (COPED), National Training Laboratories, National Education Association, 1201 16th St., N.W., Washington D.C., 20036. National cooperative research project on the uses of social sciences in education.

Daytop Lodge, 450 Bayview Avenue, Prince's Bay, Staten Island, New York, 10309. Lawrence Sacharow, Director. Renewal center for drug addicts run by former drug addicts using confrontation groups.

Development Research Associates, Inc., 1218 Mass. Ave., Cambridge, Mass., 02138. Alfred Alschuler, David Kolb, and James McIntyre (President). Runs programs in self-assessment, motive arousal, and "the helping relationship" for Peace Corps, schools, and government agencies.

Esalen Institute, Big Sur Hot Springs, Big Sur, California, 93920. Mike Murphy, Director. Acts as a broker to bring together all types of psychological educators with groups of people who wish to go through the courses offered.

Education for the Future Project, Stanford Research Institute, Palo Alto, California. Willis Harman, Director.

Fayerweather Street School, P.O. Box 287, Cambridge, Mass., 02138. Matt Judson, Headmaster. U.S. counterpart of Leicester Schools in England.

Foundation for Integrative Education, 777 United Nations Plaza, New York, N.Y., 10017. Publishes *Main Currents in Modern Thought*.

Fresh Air Camp, University of Michigan, Ann Arbor, Michigan. Elton McNeil, Director. Here and now approach to juvenile delinquency.

Human Development Institute, Inc., Atlanta, Georgia. Produces programmed materials for affective development.

Institute for the Achievement of Human Potential, 1800 Stenton Ave., Philadelphia, Pa. Publishes *Human Potential*. Works with brain damaged children. Now setting up an experimental school to extend the teaching techniques used with brain damaged children to normal children.

Institute for Bioenergetic Analysis, 71 Park Avenue, New York, N.Y., 10016. Adele Lewis, Executive Secretary. Interested in body movement and its relation to psychological well-being. Lowen type therapy center.

International Foundation for Psychosynthesis, Suite 901, Linde Medical Plaza, 10921 Wilshire Blvd., Los Angeles, California, 90024. Robert Gerard, President. Center for research and dissemination of information on psychosynthesis.

Julian Primary School, 226 Leigham Court Rd., Streatham, London S.W. 16, England. Headmaster, E. A. Orsborn. School visited in London by the author where "discovery technique" is used.

Kairos, Wishing Well Hotel, P.O. Box 350, Rancho Sante Fe, Calif., 92067. Bob Driver, President.

Midwest Center for Human Potential, Stone-Brandel Center, 1439 S. Michigan Ave., Chicago, Ill., 60605.

National Center for Exploration of Human Potential, 8080 El Paseo Grande, La Jolla, California, 92037. Herbert Otto and John Mann, Directors.

NTL Institute for Applied Behavioral Science, 1201 16th St., N.W., Washington, D.C., 20036. Vladimir Dupre, Director. Runs training centers and schools for T–groups, basic-encounter groups, personal-growth groups, etc. (Publishes *Journal for Applied Behavioral Science*.)

Outward Bound, Inc., Andover, Mass., 01810. Joshua Minor, Director. Attempts to build self-confidence and self-reliance through a variety of physical tests of endurance.

Psychosynthesis Research Foundation, Room 314, 527 Lexington Avenue, New York, N.Y., 10017. Frank Hilton, Director.

Quest, 3000 Connecticut Ave., N.W. Suite 237, Washington, D.C., 20008. Bob Caldwell, Director.

Seminar House, Upper Black Eddy, Bucks County, Pa. Grenville Moat, Director. Runs Esalen-like program.

Simulmatics Corporation, 16 E. 41st St., New York, N.Y., 10017. Makes game simulations of life situations, e.g. life-career game, community disaster game, etc.

Social Dynamics Inc., 335 Newbury St., Boston, Mass. Paul R. Mico, President; Donald C. Klein, Director. Human relations training and social action programming.

Society of American Value Engineers, Windy Hill, Suite E–9, 1741 Roswell St., Smyrna, Ga., 30080. Distributes current information, conference reports, bibliographies, etc. on value engineering.

Summer in the City, 32 E. 51st St., New York, N.Y. Monseigneur Robert J. Fox, Director. Social action program using mass confrontations.

The Summer Program, Berkeley High School, Berkeley, Calif. Anne Hornbacker, Jay Manley, and Peter Kleinbard. West Coast extension of the Philadelphia Cooperative Schools.

Synanon, 1351 Pacific Coast Highway, Santa Monica, Calif., 90401. Chuck Dederich, Director. Total environmental approach to promoting self-actualization and, in the process, curing drug addiction.

Teen Challenge, Program run by the Pentecostal Church in San Francisco and other major cities as a re-training center for drug addicts.

Topanga Human Development Center, 2247 N. Topanga Canyon Blvd., Topanga, California, 90290. Thomas Greening, Chairman.

Western Behavioral Sciences Institute, 1121 Torrey Pines Road, La Jolla, Calif. Richard Farson, Director.

Wiltwick School, 260 Park Ave., South, New York, N.Y. Dr. Hagop Mashikian, Director. Total environment therapy.

IV. *People*

Allen, Dwight, Dean, University of Massachusetts, School of Education, Amherst, Mass., 01002.

Alschuler, Alfred, Assistant Professor, Harvard Graduate School of Education, Peabody House, 13 Kirkland St., Cambridge, Mass., 02138; Director, Achievement Motivation Development Project; Board of Directors, Development Research Associates.

Boulding, Kenneth, Center for Research on Conflict Resolution, University of Michigan, Ann Arbor, Michigan.

Borton, Terry, Chairman of the Affective Education Group, 59 Pemberton St., Cambridge, Mass.; Co-Director, Affective Education Research Project, Philadelphia Public Schools.

Bradford, Leland, Director, National Training Laboratories Institute for Applied Behavioral Science, 1201 16th St., N.W., Washington, D.C., 20036 (See sections I and III.)

Brooks, Charles, c/o New School for Social Research, New York, N.Y. Developer of sensory awareness movement in the U.S. (with Charlotte Selver).

Brown, George I., Director, Ford Project in Teacher Education, Esalen, Big Sur Hot Springs, Big Sur, California. Professor of Education, University of California, Santa Barbara.

Bugental, James, Association of Humanistic Psychology; Esalen; Psychological Services Association, Los Angeles, Calif. (See section I.)

Cooper, Jack, Psychosynthesis Research Foundation, 527 Lexington Ave., New York, N.Y., 10017.

Dederich, Chuck, Director, Synanon, 1351 Pacific Coast Highway, Santa Monica, Calif., 90401. (See section III.)

Driver, Bob, President, Kairos, Wishing Well Hotel, P.O. Box 350, Rancho Santa Fe, Calif., 92067 (See section III.)

Farson, Richard, Director, Western Behavioral Sciences Institute, 1121 Torrey Pines Rd., La Jolla, Calif. (See section III.)

Fox, Monseigneur Robert J., 32 E. 51st St., New York, N.Y. Runs Summer in the City Program. (See section III.)

Gerard, Robert, President, International Foundation for Psychosynthesis, Suite 901, Linde Medical Plaza, 10921 Wilshire Blvd., Los Angeles, Calif., 90024. (See section III.)

Harman, Willis, Education for the Future Project, Stanford Research Institute, Palo Alto, Calif.

Hilton, Frank, Director, Psychosynthesis Research Foundation, Room 314, 527 Lexington Ave., New York, N.Y., 10017. (See Section III.)

Hornbacker, Anne, The Summer Program, Berkeley High School, Berkeley, Calif. (See section III.)

Judson, Matt, Headmaster, Fayerweather Street School, P.O. Box 287, Cambridge, Mass., 02138. (See section III.)

Katz, Daniel, Center for Research on Conflict Resolution, University of Michigan, Ann Arbor, Mich. (See section III.)

Katz, Richard, Assistant Professor, Department of Psychology, Brandeis University, Waltham, Mass. Conducts programs in non-verbal communication and self-assessment. (See section I.)

Kellam, Sheppard G. (M.D.), Woodlawn Mental Health Center, 841 E. 63rd St., Chicago, Ill., 60637.

Kelman, Herbert, Center for Research on Conflict Resolution, University of Michigan, Ann Arbor, Mich.

Kleinbard, Peter, The Summer Program, Berkeley High School, Berkeley, Calif. (See section III.)

Levy, John, Executive Director, American Association for Humanistic Psychology, 584 Page St., San Francisco, Calif., 94117 (See section III.)

Lyon, Harold C., Jr., 2700 Upton St., N.W., Washington, D.C., 20008. Leads humanistic education groups.

Mashikian, Hagop (M.D.), Director, Wiltwick School, 260 Park Avenue, S., New York, N.Y. (See section III.)

McNeil, Elton, Fresh Air Camp, University of Michigan, Ann Arbor, Mich. (See section III.)

Minor, Joshua, Director, Outward Bound, Inc., Andover, Mass., 01810.

Moat, Grenville, Seminar House, Upper Black Eddy, Bucks County, Pa. (See section III.)

Moffet, James, Harvard Graduate School of Education, Longfellow Hall, Cambridge, Mass., 02138. Has designed a complete English curriculum based on drama.

Murphy, Mike, President, Esalen Institute, Big Sur Hot Springs, Big Sur, California, 93920 (See sections I and III.)

Newberg, Norman, Specialist in Affective Development, Philadelphia School System, Philadelphia Public School Building (Room 329), 21st and Parkway, Philadelphia, Pa. (See sections I and II.)

Orsborn, E. A., Headmaster of Julian Primary School, 226 Leigham Court Rd., Streatham, London S.W. 16, England. Discovery Techniques School visited by the author.

Otto, Herbert, Co-director, National Center for Exploration of Human Potential, Stone-Brandel Center, 1439 S. Michigan Avenue, Chicago, Ill., 60605. (See section I.)

Progoff, Ira, 45 W. 10th St., New York, N.Y., 10011. Runs dialogue center and works with depth imagery.

Ripley, Wilbur, Director, 15th St. School, New York, N.Y. Reported in *Look.* Connected with Creative Playthings.

Rogers, Carl R., Resident Fellow, Center for Studies of the Person, 1125 Torrey Pines Rd., La Jolla, Calif., 92051. Former President of the American Psychological Association.

Rudman, Masha, Director, The Learning Theater, University of Massachusetts, School of Education, Amherst, Mass., 01002.

Satir, Virginia, Director, Training for the Family Project, Palo Alto, Calif. Founder of Conjoint family therapy which used entire family in role-playing group situation.

Schiff, Sheldon K. (M.D.), Woodlawn Mental Health Center, 841 E. 63rd St., Chicago, Ill., 60637.

Selver, Charlotte, New School for Social Research, New York, N.Y. Developer of sensory awareness movement in U.S. (with Charles Brooks).

Shapiro, Stewart, School of Education, University of California, Santa Barbara, California.

Streitfeld, Harold, Director, Aureon Institute, 71 Park Ave., New York, N.Y., 10016. (See section III.)

Weinstein, Gerald, Director, Center for Humanistic Education, University of Massachusetts, School of Education, Amherst, Mass., 01002.

INDEX